Sabine Lichtenfels

GRACE

Pilgrimage for a Future without War

VERLAG MEIGA

About the book:
Shaken by the threat of a possible war against Iran, with the question what one single person can do to stop future wars, Sabine Lichtenfels decides to undertake a pilgrimage in June 2005. She gives away everything she owns, covers long stretches on foot and is without any money. Her driving force is the decision to uncover and change those internal structures which externally lead to war and violence. Doing this, she discovers a strength which begins to shine for ever clearer and brighter: "GRACE", the connectedness with Creation which empowers her to follow her inner voice more precisely and trustfully than ever before.
Her pilgrimage takes her from Germany via Switzerland, Italy and Greece to Israel/Palestine. There for a period of 3 weeks she leads a group of 40 pilgrims, Israelis, Palestinians and Internationals, through Israel and the West Bank. In the name of GRACE support actions and unusual encounters take place, walls of fear and rage which for a long time have seemed insurmountable are now crumbling. GRACE is a force "stronger than any government or any army, because it is at home in the hearts of all human beings."

About the author:
Sabine Lichtenfels, born 1954, author, free-lance theologian and peace activist, one of the "1000 Women for the Nobel Peace Prize 2005", co-founder of the Healing Biotope I Tamera in Portugal. For years she has been engaged in international peace work especially in Israel and Palestine. She has a profound knowledge of community development, conflict resolution, spiritual life practice and the reconciliation of the genders. With her political compassion and her feminine insight she is a leading ambassador for a global peace perspective.

Impressum:
ISBN 978-3-927266-25-4
© 2007 Verlag Meiga
Translated from the German by Frieda Julie Radford
Original Title: GRACE. Pilgerschaft für eine Zukunft ohne Krieg.
Layout and Cover Design: Jana Mohaupt
Coverphoto: Sabine Lichtenfels in Israel 2005, © Tamera Pictures
Print: Books on Demand (BoD) GmbH, Norderstedt, Germany

Table of Content

Foreword   5
What is the Meaning of "Grace"?   7

Part I
Pilgrimage to Israel

Prelude to a New Path   14
First Letter of a Pilgrim   29
The Pilgrimage to Santiago de Compostela   34
The Movement for a Free Earth   47
The Dream of the Returning Templars   56
Departure for the Promised Land   68
Through Europe, always in the Direction of Israel   77

Part II
In the Holy Land

Acknowledgements to the Leading Team   98
Arrival in Israel   101
Pilgrimage to the Sea of Galilee   110
On the Way to another Life   119
Historic Significance of November 9th   129
Night Vigil at the Wall   134
Entry into the West Bank   144
Encounter with a Palestinian and an Israeli Soldier 149
We Shall not Remain the Same   156
The Miracle of Anata   165
The War Game in Bethlehem   177
Visit to the Settlers   190
Entry into Jerusalem   201

Part III
Ending the War

The Issue of Guilt   214
The Dangerous Fight against Evil   225
Do Victims and Perpetrators Exist?   231
The Battle of the Genders, the Ego Trap
and the Ending of War   238
First Analysis: Thirty People can Change the World   250

Addendum   257
Recommended Literature   260
Further Information   262

Foreword

Sabine Lichtenfels belongs to those people on this Earth whom I would describe as "the will to peace incarnate". These people are here to build up a global peace force through a worldwide cooperative movement which is stronger than war. The pilgrimage GRACE as described in this book is one of various examples of how new force fields for hope and reconciliation can be created through well executed action. We are looking for a change both in the internal and external world. The correlation of creating peace in the external world and correcting the path of the internal world may never before have been described in such a vivid and near-to-life manner as has been done in this book.

For some time now Sabine Lichtenfels has been on a cosmic journey. Her special perceptive and spiritual capacities as a medium help her to research information and forces which have been manifested at many sacred sites on Earth. In this context she visited stone circles, the temples of Malta and Gozo, the Cheops Pyramid, the oracle sites of Delphi and Dodona, the Qumran caves and other places in the "Holy Land". She received a peace message of such intensity that she decided to dedicate her entire life to the dissemination of this message. Not only to talk or write about it, but above all, to live according to it and to build centres throughout the world where human beings learn to live together in the spirit of this message.

The attentive reader will find this message in every chapter of this book, also in seemingly trivial and unimportant incidents. Always the focus is on opening up the inner space to the divine flow. This is the way guidance ensues, helping us to realise our goals all the more by for example learning better to leave behind hasty conclusions and emotional habits. The more we learn to determine the right moment for energies to be guided in a new direction and to replace reflexes of fear, the more we become aware of this guidance. Always the result is salvation, healing and gratitude.

All this is written from a feminine source and point of view. It is an ancient, a primordially new and a supra-feminine force that is speaking. Without frills of any kind, female mystic knowledge is translated into simple, everyday scenarios. The dimension of an all-encompassing peace becomes visible by shedding light on small incidents, such as, a walk through the Abuzzi, an encounter with soldiers or the words of a young woman mutilated by a suicide assassin. Despite the terrible things the author has witnessed she is able to write:

It is a large all-encompassing peace which is waiting for human consciousness to penetrate its complexity. Those who know no inner separation will be the ones to help initiate a new future and nothing hostile will cross their path.

The chapters describing the legs of a long pilgrimage – from the Southern part of the Black Forest all the way to Jerusalem – transmit something that one might call "pilgrim's vibes". They are loaded with the power to spread the message. May these vibes be transmitted to all the readers of this book. And may the readers let themselves be touched by the thoughts and ideas which continually play in the background of the texts, namely: a functioning community generates the power of realization – truth in love relationships – the ego trap – the inter-changeability of victims and perpetrators – the "no self" (Anattà) and its interception in cases of emergency – the irrefutable connection between politics and committed and non-hesitant spiritual practice.

I wish this book the success it deserves and a wide distribution.

Dieter Duhm

What is the Meaning of "Grace"?

The pilgrimage is to lead us to Israel/Palestine to the so called Holy Land, a region which has been dominated by war, conflict, struggle and division for a long time.

If this pilgrimage is to be a success in terms of inner and outer peace work, then a spiritual source will be needed. This will make us as pilgrims act in both a correct and healing way despite any difficult situations. In search of a name for the pilgrimage we came across the term GRACE. Grace has many connotations and in English comprises more than the word "Gnade" does in German.

GRACE is mercy, favour, charm, sweetness, readiness, charity, consideration, congeniality and also stands for the act of Grace itself.

GRACE reminds me of walking in the service of the higher mission, in the service of life and its inherent justice.

Those who are walking in the name of GRACE do not come to accuse. They do not come to impart a new ideology on a country or on a land and its people – they come in the service of openness, of perception and of support.

GRACE pledges not to worsen a war but rather to end it wherever it happens to be. In the name of GRACE I am always on the look out for a non-violent solution, a solution which creates justice and healing amongst all concerned. Often clear judgement is necessary to do this, but never condemnation.

GRACE says: I am willing to end the war and to understand the means by which it can be ended and I place myself in the service of a solution.

You can easily examine just how far you have committed yourself to act in this way by the way you react, especially when you feel that someone has tried to hurt you or treated you unjustly. In such situations we are quick to forget our determination to live in peace

7

and readily enter into disputes and wars, large or small.

Here is a small example, perhaps a little humorous but it makes the point: If you hear that the car of a distant acquaintance has been stolen, you will probably take the news very calmly. If you hear that your best friend's car has been stolen, you will probably get a bit agitated but still stay cool enough just to pass on a few words of commiseration. When, however, your own beloved car has been stolen, inner peace is shattered and perhaps for some time. The setting of the course is far reaching and profound and takes place at a totally different level of consciousness. We can, however, understand more about the correlations on a large scale, when we have learnt to become witnesses to ourselves on the smaller scale.

GRACE is not man made.

GRACE catapults us to a higher level of order in life itself.

It is not me that will judge, but life itself.

No matter where I happen to be and where I am coming from, I put aside all prejudice and judgement.

I do not arrive with preconceived ideas of who the other one might be or might not be and I do not make my opinion the yardstick for my actions.

I practised and learnt to see the Christ in every human being wherever I was and during all of the pilgrimage.

At first I turn to the human being who happens to be my counterpart and let myself be touched by his or her history. To do this, I anchor myself as far as possible in the present moment. Again and again I imagine that the person sitting in front of me could just as well be me. I could be a woman settler, a Palestinian woman or a young Israeli woman about to enter the military. I could be the soldier that is about to shoot at Palestinian kids with tear gas.

I look for the core of the human being in all its roles and behind all the masks of alienation. It is often difficult to be in this kind of presence. How often have I been outraged about the views of the world which I had to endure listening to from, for instance, an extreme rabbi or a fanatical Muslim? And how often did I feel an inner defensiveness or a reaction of disgust when listening to the never ending accusations and stories of suffering from the Palestinians in the West Bank or to the fanatical speeches of the settlers?

GRACE demands self-knowledge. And self-knowledge is not always easy. To discover flaws in others is much more pleasant and easy, than to unmask oneself. Everything within me wants to cry out in anger and outrage when I sit opposite a young officer listening to his excited explanations about the ideological values of his country.

All of a sudden it occurs to me that he could just as well be my son and immediately I begin to see in him not only the soldier but the human being behind his role. This is a first step which creates an opening. Now everything depends on whether I will be able to tell him the truth of what I see without any fear.

Then GRACE happens.

I let myself be touched and I try to touch others. Whenever possible, I enter places with my heart open. This was the case when I met with soldiers and officers, Palestinian peasants or farmers, or Israeli settlers.

GRACE comes from the strength and the connectedness with the source of life.

This must not be confused with a timid attitude where I dare not speak up against injustice when I see it.

I do not condemn anyone or anything when I am in the state of GRACE, rather, I gather up the courage to speak the truth. I want to speak the truth in such a way as to reach out to others and to change them. It is not done in a way that I am the only one who has the point, as this would only further worsen the war situation. In our everyday reality we shut out both sides. We shut out the truth of the victim as well as the truth of the perpetrator. We then are quick to impose our view of the world on either one of them. And most important of all is that our view of the world is the right one! We do this to protect ourselves from being touched. We can only bear to watch the constant and terrible news because we are so closed up. And we are relieved when we are able to distinguish the good guys from the bad guys. We carry on living our comfortable every-day lives and believe that we are good people when we manage to show some little charity in our lives. This is the way the insidious fascism of our times is bred through indifference.

People shut their good middle-class front doors in the face of reality. They do it until suddenly they themselves are caught by a wave of real life which up till then they have been successfully suppressing. Suppression now hits back and shows its most cruel and violent side. It is not life itself that is cruel. It is through suppression that it appears to be cruel and violent. We see this in marriage crisis, in illness, in growing suicide rates, in mental illness, alcoholism and other similar problems. That is until we wake up!

GRACE reminds us of another truth and reality at work behind the terrible dimensions of a culture which will soon have exhausted its last resources. The truth is simple and the same everywhere.

When forming an opinion, we tend to forget that we do this mainly from a level of interpretation. The truth lies beyond all opinions. The truth is distinct from ideology in as much as truth is both simple and true.

I was shocked to realise that conflicts more often than not are kindled and rekindled by the ideologies and the convictions which people continually fire at each other. Because of our fear of the truth of life we consider our opinions and views to be true and defend them right up to the bitter end. This is psychological warfare that finally results in real war. We hold true what has nothing to do with truth. This is the story of our socialisation with which we identify. All of a sudden you look into the distorted mirror of mankind which has separated itself from its roots. You look at the same patterns of fear, anger, powerlessness and trauma which are everywhere and at the resulting war with its destructive acts of revenge. It is the suppressed life itself that chooses revenge in order to survive.

At this point appeals to morality are useless. Just imagine, your child is killed in front of your own eyes. Is it not revenge that is your foremost and strongest impulse?

You see it everywhere sometimes in lesser sometimes in worse forms, but the basic pattern remains identical everywhere. It can be found behind every ideology, behind all religions, behind all views of the world. We have, in equal measure, all become victims of an imperialistic culture. Behind this avalanche that rolls across the regions of war on this planet writing its painful history of victims and perpetrators, behind all this, you come across the same hunger everywhere – a hunger for life, a hunger for love, a hunger for trust and belonging, a hunger for acknowledgement and a hunger for wanting to be seen and understood. This hunger is independent of race and creed. It simply exists, in every human being for as long as he or she still deserves this name.

When I am out there in the name of GRACE, I try to meet the human being and let myself be touched by them rather than by the world views they represent. All would be lost whenever our meetings started with a debate about world views. Nobody remained listening and as a result the meetings ended in emotional upheaval. The meetings unfolded in a completely different way whenever people were touched by each other in a deep and humane way. GRACE always reminds you of this.

GRACE is like a consciously chosen naivety that helps you find your way through the welter of world views so that you recognize and protect the elementary and simple truth behind all things. You create an opening for the cry for life.

You see the collective body of pain in front of you, this body that has presented the Jews with their terrible fate. You equally recognise the collective delusion of the German people who have still not been able to truly look at and heal their past. You see the effects of a patriarchal religion and culture which has taken a wrong turn for thousands of years, and you see how war is an inseparable part of it, just as much as thunder and lightning are part of a stormy night. The history of victims and perpetrators and our identification with either one of them has to come to an end. At this point world history awaits a big transformation, the final awakening!

GRACE REMINDS YOU ALWAYS THAT THIS CHANGE DOES NOT COME TO PASS BY WAY OF ONES OWN FORCES.
GRACE reminds you of the sacredness of life itself at every moment.
GRACE reminds you that the only way back out of the dead end street is for mankind to successfully return to the very basis of life and love, of trust and truth.

GRACE is the power of a long breath that is going to last because it can see a new dawn at the horizon of history, a paradise of love and charity, a culture honouring variety while at the same time acknowledging common values.
GRACE is the umbilical cord that connects us to this vision and guides us, as of this moment, to act and behave out of its "Geist"*, its freshness, abundance and beauty.

* The noun "Geist" (adj. "geistig") is used throughout this book to better reflect the notion of "intellect, spirit and soul" as expressed in this German term.

Part I:
Pilgrimage to Israel

Prelude to a New Path

This first part of the book describes my decision and preparation for the pilgrimage to Santiago de Compostela as well as the pilgrimage through Europe which I undertook without any money. Only now, looking back, do I see how during all this time I had received wise guidance. Some events and decisions which at the time seemed fairly chaotic did only later reveal their deeper good sense. It was a time which prepared me at all levels for the pilgrimage to Israel and Palestine.

It began in February 2004 when Charly Rainer Ehrenpreis and I set off on a journey together with the aim of attracting sponsors to invest in the future Monte Cerro Experiment. Charly, a physicist and musician is a long-time friend and companion, and he together with Dieter Duhm and myself founded the Peace Research Project of Tamera in 1995. We were committed to developing Tamera as a centre for peace education. We intended to start a 3-year educational experiment with 200 people from May 2006. The education was to focus on the development of living forms which would serve as models for a future without war. It was planned that Monte Cerro would offer a new range of studies especially for young people who wanted to cooperate in the areas of world conflict, in helping people and in developing peace research villages.

Research experiments in ecology, technology, architecture and community-development would be built up and tested at a location in a peaceful country in such a way that they could be later copied in areas of conflict and in areas where little or no money was available.

Now as I write this book the Monte Cerro Experiment is underway.

But in order for Monte Cerro to be fully realised additional funding is now required to construct the necessary infrastructure, above all for a large assembly hall.

Launching this project was an enormous task as at the time there were no public funds available for this type of work. In order to realise our projects we had for years lived as simply as monks in monasteries begging for alms! All money received was invested into the growing projects. Our income was just enough to feed ourselves and the many young people who came and wanted to stay. But there was no money available to realise the urgently needed construction work.

The time came when we decided it was necessary for us to go out into the world and to travel in order to encourage people from industry to invest in this project. It was not the first time that Charly and I had undertaken such trips. We knew what was involved and that we would have to reckon with many ups and downs. There is hardly any other subject that is so charged with taboos, fears, self-revelation and so bogged down in all sorts of beliefs, as is that of money.

At first our path took us to Switzerland. It was the beginning of a lengthy process which for me was to have many consequences. We were, however, committed to this experiment, and trusted ourselves to follow our inner voices. At that time I was reading Peace Pilgrim's book: "A pilgrim of love". She was an exemplary peace pioneer, who, in an unusual way brought together political action with a radical personal life. She had been born on a little farm in the East of the US in 1900 and grew up in modest circumstances. Slowly she made some money and gained material wealth. But later she came to recognize how meaningless was her egocentric life and how material wealth was more of a burden than a joy. For an entire night she walked through the woods and asked to be guided until she felt "a full readiness to dedicate my life to God with no reservations and to put it in the service of my fellow human beings." A spiritual "education and preparation" began for her which was to last for fifteen years until, on January 1st, 1953 she started out on her pilgrimage for peace. She walked alone, with no money or any other means of support. The only worldly possessions she still had were a comb, a fold-up toothbrush and a ballpoint pen. In 1964, after having walked forty thousand miles she stopped counting the miles. She had discovered a life of inner peace, free of fear, in the service and in the belief of a possible fulfilment of worldwide peace on Earth. Her thoughts are captivatingly simple and clear when she describes in an elementary way her path of change.

"So I undertook a most interesting project which essentially consisted of living all the good things I believed in. I no longer confused myself by trying to manage them all at once, but instead, took to getting rid of those habits which I was aware of having, but really should not have. These were always easy to be discarded. This is the easy way. To change gradually takes a long time and is very difficult. If I missed out on something which I knew had to be done I set about doing it immediately. It took quite a while until life overtook belief, but of course it works, and if today I believe in something, then I live it. Otherwise, it would have been totally meaningless. The more I lived in unison with the highest light which I possessed, the more light was given to me and the more open I became, the more light I received."

The book touched me deeply, both in its simplicity and its truth. It bears witness to the life of a woman who had been successful in walking her path without any attachments and with a continuously active and sympathetic participation in life itself. She had a changing effect by changing herself. The world was her home. She earnestly took the path of trust. Without a sleeping bag and without a penny in her pocket she lived in the streets up the age of 86.

To me, to be on a journey to visit potential sponsors and to motivate them to invest in the project Monte Cerro and at the same time to investigate the life of a woman who had lived without any money at all and who had demonstrated her compassion for all the suppressed people of this world by leaving behind all her material belongings, was a most interesting and exciting challenge. Touchingly she describes situations where gifts were offered to her from all sides. She however walked always the path of simplicity and took only what she absolutely needed.

Reading this book a strong yearning unfolded inside of me, a yearning that I had already known as a 15 year old. At that age I had the vision of becoming a wandering preacher. In my imagination I carried a rucksack on my back with all my belongings and I walked from place to place staying only as long as it nurtured my heart. It was a wonderful, free picture flooded with romantic and adventurous notions of love. When I now come across certain clearings or pass through certain small villages, through fields and alongside brooks their atmosphere immediately triggers this image that still vibrates in my soul. This vision of wisdom involves both the wish and the realisation of living free of any attachment.

One year later, at the age of 16, the vision grew into a desire to establish, together with my friends, a village where we would prove to ourselves and to others that another life is possible, a life in freedom, community and love.

Now, 34 years later, I am out there as the co-founder of a Peace Research Project which we had been preparing since 1978 and finally started to develop in the Alentejo in Southern Portugal in 1995. The young people who carry forward this project today are now at the same age as I was when I began to dream my big dream of a better future. Was it coincidence that I am now on this journey together with Charly whom I got to know when I was 16? Filled with enthusiasm, I had talked to him about my youthful dreams of "our village" in which we would lead entirely different lives. Nowadays, we are the veterans of the project, still full of vigour and full of dreams for a better world. The incorrigible ones!

It was clear to us that we still needed to raise a lot of money for the realisation of our dream of an international education centre for peace villages. Within me the pressing yearning persisted to lead a simple life, an open and elementary life without too many material constraints, without an engagement diary, without seemingly endless "to do" lists. During my travels I remained fully connected to my goal but at the same time I was looking for a new way of life. I wanted to reach my goal in such a way as to make its aim visible in everyday life.

I wrote in my diary:

The path is the goal. I have big hopes and intentions but because of this the goal must reflect itself in my own life.

The inner arguments regarding this subject repeatedly led to enormous tensions in my soul. On the one hand I saw, how for years I had been on the move and engaged with big plans, but how on the other hand, I was called upon to totally let go and live without any attachments. How could both of these aspects become compatible? Was it possible to follow a plan without planning? Would it be possible to move millions and, nevertheless, live without being attached to them?

Especially, when being on tour to ask for money, the thoughts of scarcity and sorrow soon creep in. Even if one does not ask anything for oneself, one is connected to the overall idea and one soon has the feeling of asking for oneself. To be a beggar is possibly the lowest status our culture has to offer.

However, my inner guide saw things in completely different categories. This guidance saw no contradiction to living at one and the same time in utmost poverty and abundance.

"Ask and you will be given. Knock at the door and it will be opened." Or: "See the birds under the sky, they do not sow, they do not harvest yet our heavenly father feeds them nevertheless." These were some of the guidelines given to me for orientation.

Again and again I received the same instruction: *Behave as if you already have it.* Or: *You have to see what you want clearly and concretely in front of you. Materialise it mentally, only then it can and will be realised.*

We had many interesting contacts on this journey, but so far financially we had hardly been successful. We spoke a lot about a possible "Plan B". Maybe we are asked to realise our Monte Cerro project without money? In the real world too there is often no funding for people who want to develop something new. Maybe the cosmic world wants us to set an example of how to realise something out of nothing. We needed a new motivation to look calmly at the subject again.

Inside of me a decision was forming.

On March 2nd, while still travelling through Switzerland I went together with Charly up to the top of a mountain so as to be nearer my heavenly source. We stayed the night at a small mountain hotel. Alone, in a flurry of snow and with an icy wind blowing, I took a chair lift to go up even further. At the top a little mountain hut was open and I drank a hot cup of tea. Right there the first deep decisions were made.

I decided to make a new contract with God.

I decided to live for one year in such a way as to better understand my own inner guidance and to follow it explicitly. This decision was accompanied by the desire to see better through the push and shove of everyday life that so continuously preoccupies us and to get to the deeper ground of all-consciousness and above all, to do this not only during my retreats and spiritual courses, but also in normal daily life. I wished to come into a state of being where even the smallest everyday action is filled with divine consciousness.

I wrote in my diary:

It is a strange feeling to reach for non-attachment while at the same time seeking to move millions. It is at this point that I deeply want to understand something and then let go of it. The following decisions shall further my radical inner nature and my commitment. They might at first seem quite ascetic but they release joy inside of me. These are my basic rules for power and strength: I walk the path of connection. I walk the path of simplicity. I walk the path of trust. I walk the path of truth, solidarity and surrender to divine life. I dedicate my life to service. I give myself an outer set of rules for orientation: Tonight I shall clink glasses with Charly and afterwards will not drink another glass of wine until I have received the sum of 300.000 Euros in donations. From my clothes I shall select two outfits and give away the rest. Later on in this year I will undertake a pilgrimage. This is one easy way to help me to be connected closely to the Goddess. I can do this either on my own or in a group. I live as healthy, as ethically correct and as simply as possible. I shall nourish myself mainly from raw foods and the things I am able to find. I want to learn to be aware of divine guid-

ance at any moment. The simple life is intended to enhance the perme-
ability needed for this to happen.

Till this day I am touched by the guidance of my inner voice. I wrote in my diary:

Go into the light on a higher plain.

Conflicts are resolved on a higher level of order. Connect to the power of meditation, your highest inner source. Go to this source because it is there where you are needed. Recognise how much fear and turbulence is released in human beings when they approach the point of transformation where they have to let go of everything. You too, leave fear behind and watch out for the gates of life and those of joy. They will open up if you do this whole-heartedly. If your contacts with human beings are difficult, show compassion, but do not identi-fy with either their fears or their anger. What they project onto you, is not you. Go into the light and stay physically connected and ground-ed. At this point you are a forerunner. From here on you can hold out your hand to anyone who wants to take it.

Go to those places where joy, trust and certainty can stay with you, even in the difficult times. See, I am eternal and always with you, until the end of the world.

Filled with new strength I went down into the valley again. Completely wet through and freezing cold I reached our lodgings, clinked glasses with Charly and spoke to him about my plans. It was the beginning of something new to come into my life. I still did not grasp the full meaning of the guidance. It took me almost a year to get to the bottom of it and from there to go on to make my next decision.

One struggles, fights, one wants to leave everything behind one-self, one falls, gets up and starts all over again. Nevertheless such sentences imprint themselves deeply into the memory of the unconscious, rather like a spiral entry into the inner centre of truth which leads us all into a new dimension of consciousness, into pri-mordial trust and life itself. To my question of how we shall obtain the money needed for the realisation of our project, I received some downright sobering answers:

Speak about your life in the most intimate and true manner. Describe your plans and talk about your way of thinking about money. Remain truthful.

Do not let the question of whether you will be given money or not become an inner fixation. The money will come to you at the right time. Go deep, as deeply as you can, into trust and inside of you, you will discover and understand the higher wisdom, go deeper like you have never been able to go before and you will see the correlations which hitherto have been hidden from you. It is all about unravelling the last knots of fear. Due to the prevailing situation many of you will undergo radical inner changes as never before. This will entail many consequences with regard to the shaping of Monte Cerro and, in part, have it look very different from what you now expect.

Those who are earnestly looking for the Sacred Matrix will find it and will free themselves of attachments that distract them. This alone you have to believe. It is enough to believe in it, as long as you maintain your consequent search, the rest will happen all by itself.
This will invest you with new power. Above all with a new joy and inner certainty.

Walk this path of belief and do not worry too much about the turbulence it causes. Walk the path solidly and clearly, since it will take a while before life will catch up with belief itself. The light is in you, it wants to expand to become larger and wider and shine brightly through to the outside.

These statements were the essential harvest of our "money trip" of February/March 2004. Little did I know at the time, that these statements would call for ever deeper reaching decisions. In the autumn of the same year, after walking the pilgrim's way to Santiago de Compostela, which I did most of the way alone, I was at last able to drink a glass of wine to toast the 300.000 Euros which had been received at Tamera through gifts and donations. Finally we were able to begin the construction of the urgently needed infrastructure, to develop a waste-water-system, to buy a digger and many other tools which were necessary for the realisation of

Monte Cerro. Now we were able to concentrate on the centre-piece of it all: the long desired assembly hall, without which Monte Cerro would have been unthinkable.

Nevertheless, the cosmos held more trials in store for me.

Labour pains and awakening

The next profound decision was due in February 2005. An immense natural disaster had dealt an enormous blow to the world. On December 26, 2004 a Tsunami killed 300,000 people in South-East Asia. It seemed as if the whole world had entered on the apocalypse. On the political plane, rumours were spreading that the US was considering the idea of going to war with Iran. The news from all parts of the world shook me so much that it made it impossible for me to carry on with the "normal" daily routine.

With the distribution of a flyer, the peace journalist, Leila Dregger, appealed to the world population to intervene. Here an excerpt from the text:

Did you see the pictures about the war against Iraq? And, did you see the images which depict Iraq today, still the daily pictures of chaos, of assaults at wedding celebrations, blood in the streets? The terror that prevailed under Saddam has been replaced by the daily terror of the occupation of this war-torn country. In Afghanistan a similar situation persists. What do you think is going on in the minds of the people of Iran right now, fearing that the same might happen to them?

Bush and his gang are consciously planning the death of thousands of human beings; they utilise horrible dictatorships as a subterfuge for war and terror in order to satisfy their immense hunger for power and oil. The opposition movements of these countries need support, not bombs! We let it happen once –never again!

Are we really unable to do anything about this? What a mass hypnosis! Think, everyone! The truth is that this time we can do it. This time we can prevent war!

No one is to remain sitting quietly on his backside! We can stop this war if only we will act together in good time, intelligently, and decisively! We can be successful if only enough committed people worldwide will do nothing else for the next six months but work to prevent this war.

Many intelligent considerations for a strategy on how to prevent the war followed, amongst them: mass street rallies, appeals for boycotts and action by artists and many other ideas intended to motivate the young at heart and awaken revolutionary spirits.

The appeal kept bothering me.

I am no longer able to believe that the world will be changed by mass movements, by resistance and revolt against those who hold power, however beautiful and vital the image of power might appear. A strong, non-violent revolution in the street may be part of something bigger. The changes that have to take place in order to prevent wars on a long term basis are infinitely more precise, more subtle and profound. The revolution in the external world has to go hand in hand with a conscious revolution of the inner world. Without it true change will never be achieved.

Too often we are witnesses of a repetitious process where those who once went into the streets to stand up against the oppressors, when they get in power themselves start to utilise the same strategies and means of power as those they once fought against.

Who knows about how corruptible human beings really are once new enticements are dangled in front of them? Who can imagine the intricacies of fear and rage, of comparison and competition? Who can see through the powerful hypnosis of a system of power which exerts its play of intrigue? Who knows about the latent attractions that money, fame and recognition have? Who can see ahead the well thought-out structure which awaits him, a structure that has solidified over the centuries in such a way that an individual can hardly escape its traps? We are dealing with a rigid system, with socially fixed roles that will swallow the young revolutionaries just as easily as it did those who are now the targets of the revolt.

Despite my misgivings, Leila's appeal no longer let me sleep. I knew something exceptional had to happen. Restlessly my mind wandered to and fro during the next few days. I tossed and turned in bed, unable to sleep. Sometimes one does not want to talk anymore. Seldom had I felt physically such unrest and frailness as I did during those days of reflection. The idea bothered me day and night of another war where I would just watch without taking any action. Everything within me was in upheaval. It probably was the body's healthy energy looking for a new way out. Feverishly my mind was looking for peace and quiet, for protection, for perspectives. I studied books of art: Klee, Kandinsky, Käthe Kollwitz. All of them had been witnesses to wars, to insoluble political situations and had consoled themselves through art and in joining communities too. Alas, I did not come across any such consolation. I decided on a self-imposed news embargo for a few days to protect my wounded soul. I looked for sources of strength, which might let me believe in the success of a peace movement without having the feeling of being some sort of human mutant who does not have any idea of the bone hard facts of reality.

What are your reasons for hope? The history that those in the West are proud of is nothing but a never ending tale of war. I hear the words of a typical patriarch who said smilingly: war is a law of nature and will always exist. My father spoke like this, although he was a convinced pacifist; Teilhard de Chardin, a Jesuit priest, wrote like this, although he sincerely followed the path of God; our pastors preached like this and so did most of our textbooks. And the matriarchies to which our female souls turn for comfort and appeasement have no evidence to offer that there ever existed a more peaceful Earth. There is no evidence for a non-violent culture. All that exists is the yearning, the untamed hunger for a better world, and this only, as long as we still admit to it.

How I can understand those people who prefer to go numb, become indifferent rather than be aware! To grow up means to adapt oneself to a given reality. It takes much strength to not "grow up" in this sense.

I cannot grow up. I have friends in Israel and Palestine, in Africa, in India and in Colombia. The nearer the world of the oppressed comes, the more indignant becomes my outcry against the world of the rich, the protected, against the world of my own roots. But alas I do not find any consolation in this outcry against it all!

I search for empowering literature in the peace movement in order to be able to quote it in the *Ring of Power*, a spiritual and political peace network that I founded. With the texts I send out I want to remind the peace movement that the world contains things of beauty and gentleness, of happiness and music. If it is not to create beauty, what is it then that we are fighting for?

A revolution which wants to find a way out of the dead end street has to be accompanied by the development of a positive alternative. The revolution has to go to the trouble of including the inner psychological processes of us human beings in order that we can offer real answers to inner questions. One of the causes of war is to be found in human longing and in human life energy that are wrongly channelled. Or, do we seriously believe that young soldiers really stand ready to go to war, or really would follow orders, if they had another perspective for their strength, their courage, their longings for adventure and community? How would it be if they were to be guided by different archetypical soul images instead of those of heroism which prevail in our patriarchal culture? Could there be a military world at all based on order and obedience if human beings learned to follow their longing for love and thereby find and return to their own true source?

The unquenched thirst for community, love and religion has driven us into this present collective madness. If we only knew how to integrate rather than suppress the longing for love, the hope for trust and community, the surplus of vitality and life energy and the immense power of sexuality in our lives, then war would long have ceased to exist.

I have been to Israel/Palestine often enough to study this phenomenon closely. Many Palestinians who have witnessed Israeli attacks want revenge. This is only too human a reaction if one really knows the means with which the State of Israel acts against Palestine. The Israelis act the same way when a close friend, a child, a husband or wife is killed in a suicide attack. They feel continually threatened by the radical Hamas and by the suicide-bombers and their insatiable raging need for revenge. One needs to have been in the country in order to get an impression of the feelings an Israeli has when he steps on a bus, goes through a department store or sits in a restaurant. The whole of Israel is under the effect of a subconscious ghetto of habitual fear. Where fear has become daily life, the call for violence is easily followed. Our peace messages will be of no avail as long as we do not know how men and women feel when their child is shot by hostile neighbours, when their land is stolen from them or when their wives are violated and their husbands killed. One single voice cries out of all those hurt: I want revenge! At such times no one bothers to ask: How do we stand by a commitment to love? Hardly anyone is interested or has the strength to find the background political reasons or finds the necessary peace and quiet to be able to look for real solutions.

We, however, who participate on an international level and watch with dismay from afar, we ought to be asking ourselves what could it be that would give power to the peace movement? How can the spreading powerlessness be turned into a source of belief and power? Everyone who is seriously concerned must set themselves to finding a solution to the question "Is it possible that the Earth can still be saved?"

Much of the population, when asked whether they want war or peace, will answer: "We want peace, but what can we do about it all alone?" But if all these people could only be brought together in an initiative that offers peace knowledge and a peace vision, one that is more powerful than the globalisation of violence, then this could lead to a turning point in peace work. To express it somewhat paradoxically: powerlessness is one of the biggest latent potentials for power! If the worldwide feeling of powerlessness could be transformed into a force for peace, if it could be changed into knowledge that pursues a defined goal, then the peace movement could easily succeed.

It is obvious that the international power systems rely on the weakness of their people in order to make them more governable and to keep them quiet. They do this so that ever more atrocities will be tolerated across a world where no one dares to stand up against them.

A turning point must be found. The immense reality of war needs to be countered with an immense dream. Our source of strength lies in the courage to remain true to this dream and to feed it with power and knowledge so that it can be realised. We dream the dream of a large and strong movement: the Movement for a Free Earth.

The purpose of this movement is the dissemination of a credible alternative; its task is to initiate a strong, joyous and non-violent revolution, one that is full of the zest for life and one that has the ability to provide everyone with the perspectives that will show how we can leave behind the global system of violence. Let us get out of being an accomplice to the system and get into the system of peace! This calls for a change of all our daily habits, it calls for a profound personal decision, a social revolution and a global alternative.

My decision began to take shape. I wanted to take a step, one which would surpass everything I had ever done so far. I strongly believed, and still do now believe, that we could have an effect with but a few people, if only we were to search seriously enough for new solutions.

After a few days of inner reflection everything became clear. In a small bungalow not far from Tamera we met in a group and looked at all aspects of our project. Sitting in a bathtub of hot water, I suddenly knew what I had to do. I would go on a pilgrimage. I will go on a long pilgrimage! I will walk with a group of peace pilgrims through Israel and Palestine. It is there that the central issue of conflict exists and its resolution would send a new impulse through the entire region. In order to thoroughly prepare for this large pilgrimage I would first take a small group on the pilgrim's path to Santiago de Compostela. There we shall connect to the larger vision.

I will listen deeply to my inner voice, connect with nature, with the universal sources of life and love in order to receive an image that will accompany me on my pilgrimage. If we want something profoundly enough, its image will concentrate enough power and strength, so as to create a change and build up a corresponding field which will have its effect on the whole of our planet Earth.

At the end of February 2005 I sent out into the net of the Ring of Power a first appeal: "My Steps against War – Creating Perspectives for Peace." At the beginning of March we set off from Tamera to Spain and there we went on the pilgrim's path to Santiago de Compostela.

First Letter of a Pilgrim

My Steps against War – Creating Perspective for Peace

Before leaving for the pilgrimage I sent the following appeal out to our network:

If we want to survive the ecological and social crisis which we have brought about, we would be well advised to embark on entirely new and dramatic community ventures. (Lynn Margulis)

The Earth is in upheaval. The Tsunami carried off more than 300.000 lives. The US is now planning a new war. Even if at present they appear to show appeasement we know their system needs wars so as not to collapse economically. Besides that the construction of so called "Free Trade Zones" is part of the globalisation of politics. The entire Middle East is to be turned into a Free Trade Zone in order to secure new production sites and opportunities for the big international corporations on the world market thereby extinguishing small and middle-sized local industries. Now they plan a war against Iran, just as before they planned the war against Iraq regardless of whether weapons of mass destruction are found there or not. The streets in which children are still playing today could soon look like those of Fallujah, the town in Iraq that has been totally destroyed. In the face of such news I am unable to continue the same as before.

Never before have there been so many wars on Earth. Very bravely we Germans still speak of the post-war period as one of peace for over 60 years. What do we have to do with the suffering on the other side of the world? How closely is my own well-being in my part of the world connected to the suffering in other parts? Very close! Is it my duty to think about this? Yes. Yet are we aware that human beings are the cause of the trouble and that we have to also develop the intelligence to put an end to it? Before I describe the action I want to take, I want to write down some ideas. Yes, millions should take to the streets – but this time with a positive perspective for the sound development of a better world. Give indignation a positive direction! If we do want to change the world, then we shall have to change ourselves. External peace can only come about if we are capable of creating peace within. Those who are against the war need a workable vision for peace. The globalisation of violence will only be overcome by a realistic globalisation of peace. What the well known biologist, Lynn Margulis, formulated, (namely, that we would be forced to undertake entirely new, dramatic community ventures) has now become an imperative for us.

From my longstanding community experience I know that at first we have to create social structures that allow peace and trust to become possible. Create systems for living together and for trusting each other in which war does not exist anymore! Another life is possible! Already now! In Tamera we are preparing the education project Monte Cerro which is to start on May 1st, 2006. Amongst other things, a peace village ("Solarvillage") is planned that is to serve as a model for non-violent cooperation between human beings on planet Earth. This is our primary contribution which we can and will make.

From my spiritual research I know, that if we want to be successful, we have to listen to the voice of life and the voice of nature. I am thinking of the Tsunami. I see before me the village elder Salaman of the indigenous tribe Morgan, who lives on an island off Thailand. Before the Tsunami tidal wave hit their island he instinctively followed his inner voice, took his people up a mountain and saved them all. What was it that had warned him? Or, the animals which survived? Why were they able to save themselves? For a long time non-violent communication and cooperation with animals has been part of our peace concept. Animals are animated frequency and information carriers and form part of the worldwide peace syndicate, if only they are integrated in a good way.

All of my work of this year will be done according to the maxim of making every endeavour to find the frequency of peace and to disseminate it. I shall do all I can to end internal and external war on Earth. I will therefore take concrete and positive steps to invite others to participate in order to visibly work for peace in the face of the renewed threat of war.

At the beginning of March 2005 I, together with a small group, shall go on a pilgrimage lasting several weeks to Santiago de Compostela.

We shall walk the well known pilgrim path to Santiago de Compostela starting in the North of Spain. Anyone is welcome to join us on Tuesday, the 15th of March. We shall meet at 12.00 o'clock at the main entrance of the Cathedral in Leon. There, as a first act, we shall hold a meditation for peace. The group of pilgrims will reach Santiago de Compostela on March 25th. Everyone is invited to a rally at a peace meditation. Subsequently, all those people who wish to involve themselves further and think together with us - including those who hitherto had not been walking with us - are invited to take part in a consultative meeting. We shall meet at 12.00 o'clock on Good Friday in front of the main entrance of the Cathedral of Santiago de Compostela.

On this pilgrimage we shall develop further ideas and agree on the next steps, part of which will be the preparation of a larger initiative in Israel/Palestine. I envisage that this pilgrimage will be a good opportunity to meet new people, to create new cooperations and develop new friendships.

As a next step a peace meeting will be held at Tamera from May 15th to June 11th with co-workers of the Healing Biotope under the heading: Preventing war through the development of independent peace projects.

Presently a "Solar Power Village" (developed by Jürgen Kleinwächter and his team) will be built up at Tamera as a pilot installation. Basic models of social, technological and ecological life forms will be demonstrated. These will show how people living in poverty stricken areas and conflict burdened countries, can be released from their fight to survive and be helped to be independent. Also taking part in the meeting will be an active peace group from Israel/Palestine with whom Tamera has been cooperating for a long time. They will take the opportunity to further develop the plan of a peace village (Peace Research Village) to be set up in the Middle East. Everyone who is interested in this type of future work and might want to take part will be very welcome.

Every year we organise a Summer University in Tamera to the issue of the "Movement for a Free Earth."
The main focus is on networking, which under the present threat of war has to be taken to a new level. Foremost on our agenda we will be inviting young speakers and thinkers, all of them visionary forces for peace to make this a meeting for engaged people from all over the world!

The last public peace action which I am planning for this year will probably take place in Israel/Palestine in October or November. We intend to undertake another, larger pilgrimage during which the play "We refuse to be enemies" will be staged at various locations. Perhaps we shall be able to celebrate that the planned war against Iran has not yet taken place?
We chose the Middle East for this next pilgrimage as it is the place where one of the biggest acupuncture point lies which will decide whether or not there is to be peace or war in the world. Here too, according to our plan, an international peace research village shall be set up as soon as possible. The peace pilgrimage will end in Jerusalem with a large peace rally. I wish, that all those who have decided to give their best to end the system of war, will participate in this important event. I am also thinking of setting up an international board of trustees, which would bring together people who are, or have been, engaged in peace in an especially convincing and effective way.

Let the soldiers become human beings again. They have fought enough. Let us together with them organise large peace camps where peace rather than war will be taught. I appeal to well known musicians and other artists: Lend us your voice! Help, so that a new perspective can arise in the Middle East and help, so that the voice of peace is heard world-wide!

For a non-violent planet Earth, for a future without war.
In the service of warmth for all that has skin and fur
and in the name of all creatures.
Sabine Lichtenfels

The Pilgrimage to Santiago de Compostela

It is early in the morning on March 7th, 2005. The weather report predicted large snow falls for the North of Spain. This does not hinder our start for the long awaited journey on the pilgrim's path to Santiago de Compostela. We want to walk from Burgos to Santiago, about 500 kilometres. The rucksacks are packed. The small Ring of Power buttons blink on our winter anoraks. We are surrounded by many friends who want to bid us farewell with last minute best wishes for our pilgrimage.

My first pilgrim companions are Benjamin von Mendelssohn, my younger daughter Vera Kleinhammes and Rico Portilho. This is the core group from Tamera, which for some years, has been engaged in the peace work in the Middle East.

After the morning attunement at sunrise we go the first few steps and leave House Akron in Tamera. To me this is a historical moment.

Walking is a tried method of meditation. I become the witness of all my thoughts. It is a path that leads inside.

With the first steps perception begins to shift already. It is as if the barometer of perception changes everywhere in the body. We drink from the valuable elixir of time. Everything slows down. The steps are carefully chosen. The thoughts too take on a different speed. Carefully we put one foot in front of the other as if each step had a meaning in the world's structure. Each step is a thought, and each thought is accompanied by the valuable feeling of: "I have time". I let the world come inside me. I throw my anchor into the present and at the same time I move towards the birth of a larger vision. One is under the impression that the walking holds the vision in the cells and lets it grow into an inner certainty.

We do not yet walk without money. As a guideline, each person has been allocated a daily allowance of 10 Euros. This includes all expenditures such as train, bus, board and lodging. We planned to reach our starting point either by train or bus and included in our calculation overnights at hostels. As we would walk during the coldest season of the year sleeping outside was not an option. At the same time we wanted to live as simply as possible in order to be reminded that we walk this path in solidarity with those parts of humanity who live in poverty.

The first night at the Stone Circle

The first night we spend outside in the Stone Circle of Evora. The first trial awaits us. The temperature falls some degrees below zero. At 3 o'clock at night an icy wind starts to blow across our heads. Although the small fire looks comforting in the wind it gives little warmth. I am more than thankful for my warm sleeping bag and have to think of all those who live in the streets during such conditions, left alone, without any blanket, without shelter, without friends. How many human beings die right now of hunger and cold? Although we live simply, we still live very much on the comfortable side of life.

Mentally I wrap myself in light which immediately creates a feeling of added warmth and comfort. At six in the morning I go into the Stone Circle and watch the sunrise. The experience of meditation is a divine gift also in the face of adverse outer circumstances. I am experiencing bliss despite the icy cold. Meditation is a high power of protection from cold, from fear, from anger and rage. How do animals manage when they settle in their sleeping places and do not feel the cold? They seem to be true masters at meditation - in the manner of their movement, the manner of their quietness, the manner of alertness even during their sleep.

True meditation immediately opens up a space in which it is possible to anchor ourselves firmly in the present. In such moments we notice that it is not reality itself that creates our emotions but mostly the interpretation of it. Alone and identifying with the idea that it is too cold is enough to make us immediately cold. Only beyond this process true reality exits, shining and crystal clear.

After the morning meditation in the Stone Circle the next stretch of our journey begins. In twos we tramp in the direction of Spain. One time a truck driver stops and takes us with him on the back of his open vehicle. There we sit in the whistling wind, at zero degrees, while he races down the motorway at 120 kilometres per hour. Getting in touch with people whom we do not know makes us very aware. The smallest gesture decides whether a contact would be established or not. On our way we meet some Roma. They ask us for something to eat but unfortunately we did not have anything with us. At the end a young man offers to take us with him. He talks about his atheistic way of believing. I am astonished how all of a sudden we are able to understand quite a lot of Spanish. Benjamin and the driver speak about profound things in life in a language which is relatively foreign to us. The mere fact that we try to speak it creates an atmosphere of joy in the car. I sit at the back in semi-darkness with no windows and listen to the smatterings of Spanish which are exchanged between the driver and Ben.

Shortly behind Salamanca we take the train to Burgos. We see from the train the first traces of snow in the distance and all along the route the typical Spanish prairie-like countryside. Everyone has warned us about going on a pilgrimage at this time of the year. We were even told of pilgrims who froze to death on their way through the mountains.

I completely trust my guidance. If we walk the path in high awareness we will receive protection and that guidance which we shall need later to stand up to the challenges of our task when we will walk in a region of conflict. Rather than nourish thoughts of anxiety I nourish thoughts of power.

Burgos is no place to look for quietness. In the church we see a depiction of purgatory where a woman is to be executed, probably the image of a Saint who is about to be burned at the stake. Vera wants to leave again immediately.

"Why do they always depict scenes of violence?" she asks. I can understand her question. On the roof-top of the church another

Saint stands with a sword held high conquering the forces of darkness. How will the images and icons of a peace culture look? Will the sword finally disappear completely from our memories?

Church history has never endowed my soul with a lot of peace. There has been too much spilling of blood and too much inquisition for a childlike soul to want to find trust and reassurance in it. When will it be, that children may learn about a history which will make them truly proud of their ancestors?

We quickly leave Burgos where the world is so full of scenery and frantic activities that it is difficult to get through to the reality behind things. Now the real pilgrimage begins. As soon as I begin to walk I experience deep happiness. "Make someone happy and you will be happy." This simple sentence remembered from early youth enters my mind again.

We become familiar with the first pilgrim hostels. Right at the outset Rico develops a high fever. Immediately I start to worry, but my inner Shechina corrects me immediately. On a pilgrimage it is my duty to think differently. I have to learn to put things into the hands of inner guidance. I am on my way. The kingdom of heaven is always now. No other time exists. I take as a gift whatever I receive. I am here to help and serve wherever it is needed. Things will unfold for everyone in their own way. What beforehand was reason enough to worry, i.e. Rico's illness, is now seen from this point of view, a possible gift to him and us. Benjamin stays behind with Rico. After two days they join us again, their friendship having been strengthened.

Becoming a witness of inner war

I am in a state of being quiet. The subject of our pilgrimage "to end war and live peace" is with me at every step. There is a difference between watching the world with a basic feeling of being a powerless spectator and letting myself be touched consciously by observing my thoughts and what I do in the "here and now." This can be the "small difference", deciding whether there will be war or peace. Often while walking I am conscious that at this very moment I assemble the whole world inside of me. I am the microcosm in the macrocosm. The small reflects the large. The I Ching says that those who have started to see and understand themselves "can move the world as if it turned in the palm of their hand." Whoever is able to change himself is also able to change the world. To walk with this consciously in mind, every step becomes an adventure.

While I walk I collect certain characteristics with the help of which we are able to recognize whether we are at war at any given moment. I discover typical criteria of war. War always starts when you believe that you stand on the right side of something. You reinforce the thought within you to justify your right to attack. To witness what we are doing at any given moment while walking provokes much merriment. We walk through the most beautiful countryside, but instead of perceiving what surrounds us, we defend an inner dialogue against some person who is not even present at the time. Sometimes, weeks ago, somebody might have said something that hurt you and now weeks later, with that person nowhere in sight, something in you begins to defend itself. Almost continually we dwell either on the past or the future, very seldom are we in the present with full consciousness.

At the core of all of these manoeuvres, in some hidden niche within, we finally come across the deeper reason for this hick-hack: *At a very profound level we do not believe that we are lovable!*

This is the reason why we need to defend ourselves. We are fixed on certain ideas and the notion that things have to be exactly the way we imagine them to be.

An essential scene of our war manoeuvres is to be found in the realm which we call love! Wherever we believe that something belongs to us, we begin to fight. What we call love is usually soaked with thoughts of ownership. The notion of someone being my friend is enough to give me the right to defend him or her against any danger coming from the outside. Against this background any other beautiful woman whom he might desire immediately turns into an enemy. Everywhere there are the same patterns. It can be our country, our friend, our religion, our view of the world, our ideology.

Even our best friend, the person we believed we loved most turns into our greatest enemy. Have you ever witnessed how often you entertain an inner dialogue with your beloved? Mostly we are not willing to look into this open book of our inner processes. Frightened by this scenario within ourselves, we close this chapter again, cover it up with everyday fake harmony and the war takes over and directs things from the subconscious, until such time, when it breaks out in all openness.

We fight as soon as we define something as belonging to us and are fraught with the thought that someone else might want to take it away from us.

Our fight starts at a point where we are not willing or open enough for something new, for the change of life, but instead, we cling to anything that in some way seems to belong to us. Our deepest fear of abandonment originates at this point. Inside we know that everything we cling to cannot last, though we basically know life is different! When will it be that we start to own this truth of life? Life does not belong to us, God does not belong to us, the lover does not belong to us. We ourselves do not belong to us. There is only one truth, albeit showing itself in many different shapes. At the very moment I am willing to confront the fact of this continual change, I will stop fighting. The fear disappears. I am no longer a victim of the circumstances. I take responsibility for the circumstances that life has dealt me in order to learn from them. I accept the gift of God, for him to be able to act, think and further develop through me.

Unconsciously, we all partake in the war as long as we do not take the time to understand what exactly happens. Our culture is set up in such a way that no one has the time to understand what happens. War relies on this large battleground of the unconscious.

Where there is consciousness, war no longer exists. Where consciousness exists, there is God. And God is hardly going to fight against himself.

I walk the "Path with God"

All these things come immediately into our consciousness when we stop being at war with time. We will not run after things anymore but become aware of what is with us at any given moment. We experience the depths of the moment. God can only be experienced NOW. Life can only be experienced NOW.

Happiness sets in when we are firmly anchored in cosmic trust. The largest thought is the one of walking the path with God. Whether I speak of God, the Goddess, of the universal source of love, of the Sacred Matrix or of the world spirit, the names are of little importance to me. After all the searches, after all the atheistic processes and after repeated attempts at an explanation, things become simpler, more elementary and true. At the centre of life shines one truth and it is unimportant which name we give to it. The truth is neither male nor female. These are later manifestations of a reality which create the play and tension of life. You will come across this truth in art, in science and in religion. Most importantly, you will find it in life. The path of connectedness leading towards this truth does exist. I had to part from the church and all other religions in order to advance to this core insight, nevertheless I still speak of God or the Goddess within. It is the personal spiritual aspect of universal love, the "one" spirit of Creation, which may be discovered in all its glory in even the smallest of life's details. High forces are released when I am there, where God wants me to be. I could also say: I am connected to the force when I am there, where life wants to have me. When I am in this place the world is in order. This God is no outer authority. It is from the connectedness to life that the true force flows. It is the force of an "I" in the Universe which shines towards us everywhere in a personal way. The same force of the "I" lets me experience myself as "I", as it does the beggar in the street, the whore in a brothel, or the Buddhist monk. We are all nourished by the same source, we live this source and we are this source. The more we open up to this phenomenon in a conscious way, the more the world is able to enter into us, the more life, the more truth, the more God.

This simple truth is expressed in the Bible through the words: "Therefore, you shall be like God." It is not important to God what name you give to him or what you think of him: HE IS. At the moment we step into this state of being we are at home with God.

Every morning we hold a simple morning attunement in the group to remember this truth beyond all religions. We each choose our empowerment sentences that are to accompany us throughout the day. Whenever our thoughts slip into inner dialogue we choose a thought and repeat it for as long as the mind takes to come to rest again.

O come, spirit of truth, take hold of me.
O come, spirit of love, take hold of me.
O come, spirit of power, take hold of me.
O come, spirit of speech, take hold of me.
O come, spirit of joy, take hold of me.

I walk the path with God.
I walk the path with strength.
I walk the path of peace.
I walk the path of truth.
I walk the path of beauty.
I walk the path of connectedness and joy.

It is astonishing how fast physical exhaustion and tiredness vanish and turn into new joy and vitality by repeating just one of these empowering sentences. At such points we experience the correlation of spirit and body most elementarily. Thoughts create our physical reality. It is the unconsciousness within ourselves that creates unrest, bad humour, exhaustion, etc. As soon as we become aware and witness these processes we are able to change them. At times, I can even successfully ward off an oncoming influenza by merely working with empowerment sentences.

Being able to recognise this game, in all of its diversity, is the great gift a pilgrimage offers. We walk through magic light. Snow drives lightly. Sometimes the snow flurries become heavier and are played on by friendly rays of sunshine. Many birds of prey circle above us. It is this primordial feeling of being on the way which makes me very happy. The world is my home. Being on my way enhances my ability to be unattached to things. This is part of the basic education of a peace worker, to become clear about what it means to live without attachment.

Ending war, living peace

While walking, I often think of my father who is now almost 92 years of age. He was a prisoner of war in Russia. What a feeling it must have been for him to march for miles through the Siberian cold of Russia? Marching and being surrounded by supposed enemies. He successfully escaped. Almost everyone of his company was killed soon after he left. How does one feel after something like that? It has always been difficult for him to talk calmly about his war experiences. Many of the things of his life I shall never know. Today, much of it no longer exists in his conscious memory. Our whole generation is overshadowed by the unresolved trauma of the war. And consciously or subconsciously we are all occupied with the trauma and its suppression.

I carry two little books with me. One is entitled: "The Decision" by Dieter Duhm. The other one: "Ending War, Living Peace" by Claude AnShin Thomas which is a very touching book. I can only read a little at a time as it describes the history of a soldier in the Vietnam War in such a deep and true way. It has to do with all of us. Benjamin reads "The Odessa File", another book that should be required reading for every peace worker and above all for German peace workers. Although it is a thriller, it seems to me, that every word of it speaks the truth. It offers deep and comprehensive background information about World War II with special reference to the post-war-period.

We walk between 22 and 26 kilometres a day, overnighting in hostels, meditating in the mornings and walking the first few kilometres in silence, while reflecting on certain questions or visions. It is coldest winter. The small brooks flow beneath a thick layer of ice. We walk through barren countryside, across bare fields and meadows. The way the winter light touches the earth, the hoar frost on the few trees, the prairie-like width of the landscape, enchant our hearts. The plain landscape offers a good backdrop for our rich inner life.

Isolated megaliths and many Roman and early Gothic churches bear witness to times long gone by. Our own search and our questions merge into a long line of millions of people who have walked this path before us and will walk it after us. The narrow preoccupation with one's own questions and one's own person is opened up and corrected by this historical background.

You feel to be called by something higher. There is no longing more powerful than to arrive at this inner place where God wants to be. It is as if a pulsating power line across the Earth is accompanying us on our search.

In the small Spanish village of Carrion de los Condes we overnight in a convent. I am asked to play the flute during mass in one of the oldest Roman churches. I give a small improvised concert. To the priest who preaches like Don Camillo and would probably have liked to become an actor, it is absolutely new that one can believe in God without belonging to the Catholic Church. Full of fervour and with much reverence he talks about "Nuestra Senora."

The inward path

During the first phase of the pilgrimage we mainly walk the inward path. The same way as physical cleansing exists there exists inner mental cleansing too. Age old fears and old deposits of mental sludge wash up. It feels rather like entering a dark cave. Carefully one shines a light into the darkness and all of a sudden, startled by the ray of light, bats flutter through the narrow corridors. One takes a look at all the areas that have remained untouched for a long time and where old wounds have been stored away unnoticed. I welcome this inner view although often it is not easy. Rather than looking for romanticism I look for the insight to help me to see through and end my small undercover warfare so that I can gain strength for difficult political activities. In difficult situations it is not ideology that helps but compassion and insight. This is the case both internally an externally.

During quiet hours I am occupied with the subject of love and the battle of the genders. I am aware that this is the predominant worldwide scenario in the background of all physical fighting. In my memory and above all in my dreams unresolved situations crop up which time and again are accompanied by fear, rage and pain. Those who walk the path of awareness will no longer want to push aside their personal history of suffering. We learn to acknowledge our own pain and embark upon this path although it may be cumbersome and slow to walk. Living in full awareness we shall some day refrain from following desperation even in the most difficult of situations.

During the climb up a mountain I draw the strength needed to negotiate the obstacles of this inner walk. I experience the symbiosis between the inner work and the outer experience. Often resistance makes us grow and lets us experience will power. Resistance is not only something that one wants to get rid of. We should learn to see through it clearly and to use it intelligently. The material world exists due to resistance. We grow when confronted with our internal and external resistances and by and by we learn to connect to its strength in a healing way.

I experience this at the steepest part of our ascent. Every step wants to be conquered. Again and again the body is about to cave in but an untamed will connects me to my goal, the mountain top. Bathed in sweat we reach the middle station at Faba. There we find a little oriental bar where a man offers us tea. A fire is burning in the room and the smoke is taken away by a large chimney. Many oriental things are lying about – it is a special place and for us a festive arrival point. It rains. Inside of us exhausted gratitude and a full inner "yes." The body is thankful for having been able to wear itself out and now even more thankful for the rest. Everything is flooded with the soft glow of plain physical simplicity. In the hereafter it may well be possible to move through all of resistance with the velocity of light, but in the here and now, I am but physical and elementary and there is a deeper meaning to physical existence. To be physically present, to be in a body, is the gift of our earthly existence. I experience this space in an elementary way and in all its materiality, as I find it in some of the paintings of van Gogh where all things shine in their materiality. I know of no one else who was better able to express this elementary and divine glow of things than did van Gogh. Things do not become divine by transfiguring or mystifying them but by their elementary being that shines towards us. Exhausted I sink into a chair and let myself be refreshed by the simplicity of the room.

We have still not yet reached our goal. We climb up the mountain for another two hours. Now the last inner struggle comes up. I reach my limits. Every now and again resistance screams inside of me becoming fiercer each time: "I can't any more, it is too much, I can't manage it!" Quietly I witness this inner process. It seems as if the one who is screaming inside of me and wanting to rear up is not me at all. The play with the sentences of empowerment has already become stable enough to quietly take over the direction.

It does not matter if you cannot go on, is the simple reply. *Let the force do it since the force is capable of doing it at all times.*

Indeed, even when totally exhausted, something within me is still able to carry on if only the inner dialogue comes to a halt - some authority lets me go on silently. It feels as if it pushes me from behind. So I stumble the last 900 metres of the path up the mountain - in the true sense of the word, not out of my own strength!

Meeting with the inner sun

At some point the inner view was concluded for the time being. I had ascended the inner mountain. The message was explicit like an inner command. During one of the nights I was suddenly woken up. It seemed to me as if a voice called out loud: *Let go! Turn to the power which you are! Affirm fully your own inner source that seeks the truth! Touch the Christ nature within yourself and in others!*

I fell asleep again. In the dream that followed an image appeared. I saw a pyramid which apart from reaching upwards also went down into the Earth. At the line where the upper and the lower pyramid met there was a luminescent and reflecting expanse. I looked down and saw a brightly shining sun in the centre of the depth. This sun went directly to my heart and seemed to flood my whole being with light. I was woken up again by this picture. My heart was beating rapidly and I still felt as if my whole body has been gripped by something wonderful, everything felt clean and flooded by light. I was very grateful and happy. I had the feeling as if I had just encountered God. I felt a large responsibility to listen now to my inner voice with awareness and in relatedness.

After I had noted down my dreams I was full of zest for action. A feeling overcame me as if I had left all old stuff behind: "Now I am free for the world, knowing full well that I have to keep my inner spaces clean."

Since this morning we had talks about the plans we have for all our projects, above all about our vision for a planned peace rally and about the wide-ranging ideas for a large peace movement. I call it the "Movement for a Free Earth."

The Movement for a Free Earth

The family of pilgrims

Being on the path of a pilgrimage, dreams which have been dormant for a long time come alive again helped along by the steady rhythm of walking, the sound of footsteps and the simplicity of life. It is the Earth itself which, inside of us, awakens an age old dream to new life. I often have vivid dreams about a large peace movement. The walking itself and the connection to the fellow pilgrim open up a special quality in communication. One experiences a feeling of belonging to something one loves. Maybe it is only through walking that the system of the cells recalls a long forgotten past when as nomads we were connected to Mother Earth and all of Creation.

One has the feeling that all pilgrims belong to one large family. The most beautiful vision is one where we are all one family seeking peace. No matter what religion or what world view we adhere to, we help one another and we are curious about one another. The mere fact of being on pilgrimage tells others that: "I am a seeker. I am looking for a deeper sense in life. You may talk to me and you may put deeper questions to me than is normally the case when meeting people." Pilgrims meet with a true interest in each other:

"Who are you? Where are you coming from? What do you bring to us in terms of wisdom and experience?"

Each listens to the other. It is an ideal environment in which to dream about a new peace movement. I imagine the kind of rules such a movement would give to itself. They would be simple ethical guidelines which everyone could easily adhere to. By living according to such very simple rules those concerned signal that they are part of a new family of peace seekers. I am ready to change my personal life.

The movement will have a simple badge to be worn as a sort of signal to the world and as a way to recognize each other. Those who wear the badge demonstrate that they are on a pilgrimage for worldwide peace. Along the pilgrimage paths there will be hostels offering lodging to the pilgrims and giving them the opportunity to think together about renewal. The peace research villages that are to be developed worldwide will be oases of silence and strength for all those on pilgrimage. In these places peace in the community can be tried out and understood.

Pregnant with an idea

The cloth of a new reality is always woven from visions. If we are touched by a large idea the first step towards its realization consists in taking care that others are able to see what we see.

The word "idea" stems from the Greek *idein* and means *to see*. With the act of seeing creation begins. Presently the Earth is pregnant with a new idea. Those who tend it carefully will be able to bring it to birth. At first, consciousness dances playfully and creatively in the not yet manifested space, moves to and thru amongst the millions of particles and their hitherto not yet manifested possibilities. At some point, out of the variety of possibilities, a creative will attracts a vision closer to the reality of manifest space. The "Geist" checks it out, moves here and there and wants that something manifests itself. It examines possibilities, dismisses them, until finally, it focuses on one idea in a crystal clear way and then breaks through the boundary between the world beyond and the existing world in order to bring alive a new dream in the light of manifestation.

We ourselves are pregnant with the idea of a large movement, a Movement for a Free Earth. We walk the path to Leon. It is one of the stretches of lesser beauty. For almost 20 kilometres it follows a regular road. Walking on the asphalt is normally much more tiring than walking through the varied countryside and along romantic footpaths. This time, however, it is astonishingly easy. We reached a peak of inspiration and vision building. The world may seem ugly on the outside but for us it is beautiful. Beauty too creates itself in the play between objective world and contemplative consciousness. The very thought of Rico's empowerment sentence today: "I see the beauty of the world", affects me deeply. I see everything, whether industrial areas, pylons for electricity cables, graveyards, construction sites or road crossings through the eyes of a painter. I am enthusiastic about the large house walls since they strongly remind me of Paul Klee, the painter.

The expansive no-man's-land gives me the freedom to think of a new world. There, where almost everything has been destroyed, creation can start anew.

An easy path leads up the hill to a graveyard and inspires my transformative power of vision. I walk the path of eternal return. The feeling is as if for ever more "world" would want to flow through me and grasp my spirit, as if the past, the present and the future want to come together and in unison take in as much of the world as possible.

Not a shadow of doubt is able to enter into our souls at such moments. We see the whole and are part of it. We are receiving and being creative all at once. I am able to see excerpts of the building plan of Creation right in front of me and God's eye sees through me in this inspired hour. I feel, I am where the Goddess wants me to be. I am one of her transformative organs. Who is the subject in such special situations? Is it me, who thinks, designs and dismisses? Is it the Goddess inside of me? The "I" feels rather like a base station of the divine force and leads to boundless homecoming and universal happiness all at the same time.

Mentally we forge a world cartel for peace whose members are in constant and direct communication with each other. This world cartel issues common statements expressing their views on important world events and injustices. This circle distinguishes itself by ethical maturity rather than officialdom. Precision, truth and trust are the basis of their communication. The circle jointly administers all the donations that are received. The conditions for membership in this circle are for each member to have made the decision to lead a simple life and not to hoard any private property. The richest person in this cosmic peace family is not the one who owns the most, but the one who gives the most.

The communist idea which was doomed to fail in all imperialist states is now revived and enlarged by the idea of communities which are built on trust and therefore remain transparent. The participating communities are building a net of communication amongst themselves and complement each other's qualities.

Could it be possible to develop, already now and with the experience of Tamera, the paradigms and basic guide lines for organisational structures which no longer depend on individual, charismatic leadership, but ensure continuity and make a community function?

Walking through the countryside, we receive much joy from thinking in these larger terms. The many methods and forms of co-operation and research which have already been developed in Tamera could be put to the test and prove themselves. One would try to develop an organisational principle of such magnitude as to correspond to the functioning principles of nature rather than those of bureaucracy and appointment calendars.

During a rest, while spinning our visions further, I observe the vivid life of a tribe of ants. Is it not amazing how life organises itself among these smallest of animals? Without any bureaucratic rules, without any coordinating meetings and accords, nevertheless, their entire tribal life is organised in a highly precise manner. Who or what organises this social life? We ourselves can only dream of such self-organisation which takes place on a higher level of consciousness. We are challenged to again discover the conditions necessary for this. Inspired by these and similar questions we spend the whole day in avid dialogue.

"Greenhouses of Trust" and the development of educational centres

At this moment it becomes completely clear to us that Creation itself is in favour of the plan for new peace models to be realised anywhere on Earth. What these installations will be called and who invented them are of lesser importance. All that is important is that the future peace villages will be developed in a global sense. It is as if Creation was to design through us a new most complex plant. When the plant is fully mature it will be able to grow anywhere adapting to local climates and all cultural diversity. To begin with, it is paramount that the first model is fully functional. God's eye looks and feels through us. A Healing Biotope is an experiential laboratory of Creation. Here, the transformation of existing conventional social systems occurs and adapts to the new universal conditions of growth in order to guarantee a chance for survival. It is more than obvious that the old systems are not able to survive. The new developing models stand in close relationship to the universal forces of nature. Basic ethical rules and biological realities are no longer opposites. Just as dolphins are not able to lie, the human being living in the future peace villages will no longer be subjected to bear the continual separation between its biological constitutions and an artificial role it has to play. The human being will return to the bottom of truth. To develop the greenhouses of trust is the strength of survival within the models of the future.

Mentally, we deepen the thoughts we have been working on for many years and let them dance playfully. In our vision we establish various educational centres all over the world one of them is already developed and built up as a first prototype in Portugal. These are places which lend themselves to study the conditions for the development of peaceful cultures at all levels. We consider in which countries we would begin the building up of peace villages. We then

51

direct our attention to the first curricula of the educational programme.

Where should the first "Healing Biotopes" be developed? Where would their field building forces unfold in the best way? Who are the persons to be prepared to become moving forces? How do we find most effectively additional new specialists for the educational programme? Meanwhile, enough know-how exists in the different specialist fields. Still missing though is their proper combination and a general view of them. The idea of self-change too, has meanwhile taken root. More or less neglected up till now has been the necessary structural change which is to give the human being the space to grow in a healing way. Self-change and structural change must go hand in hand. At times, the key to things appears so banal and self-evident that it is overlooked by everyone. We need new technologies, new living systems, new information flows and networks for the realization of non-violent life models. And, above all, we need a new social knowledge about love. This idea must go out to the world now! It is in this realm where the Holy Grail of our times lays hidden. The wisdom of the Goddess is calling out to us: for too long have you been looking for hidden treasures, for gold and gems, for the holy chalice and holy geometry. Over all these enticing things you have missed out on the essential code, the code of love between the genders. This is where the biggest enticement and the biggest promise is to be found. At last, retrieve what you have been thirsting for all this time! When the solid development of non-violent cultural models will include the questions of love and sexuality and as such find broad public support and acknowledgment, then the peace movement will have achieved its first essential step. We must not be allowed to remain Neanderthals in all that concerns love and the knowledge about functioning communities.

Besides, we have to learn about cooperation with the forces of the Earth, about new types of technology and ecology which cooperate with nature rather than exploit her energies. The knowledge about sun energy serves the development of Solarvillages with ecological

systems for energy storage. The development of new social structures, schools of love, teaching group facilitation, new art and theatre, new forms of communication are no longer the resort of esoteric pastimes, but central components of a sound course of studies. These are the central research subjects.

After completing 3-years of study the graduates will be equipped
to facilitate developments in areas of conflict worldwide. In addition, courses in peace journalism will be offered. It is evident that
the mood in a country might be largely influenced by the media
and the information they disseminate. It is therefore vital to distinguish between information that provokes and furthers war and the
information that serves to foster peace.

Courage for a new awakening

The Movement for a Free Earth, I call it GRACE, shall strength-
en the courage for a new awakening worldwide. GRACE shall make
it possible for more and more people to participate in the development of new visions for the future and in the invention of new professions in which they are able to serve the Earth.

In the name of GRACE, the Movement for a Free Earth shall raise
its voice to overcome violence all over the globe and participate in
the development of peace villages wherever credible initiatives may
surface. The future model villages will become oases of rest where
all peace workers who serve in areas of conflict can renew themselves. The movement will help to disseminate the peace news
quickly around the globe by way of word, art, and music. It will
participate in peace marches, aid initiatives and support the development of peace paths in areas of conflict. The movement shall
further develop professional perspectives for young people to
become peace workers. With the aid of peace concerts, plays, multi-
media-shows and short lectures the movement will inform the
world with the intention of encouraging people to leave behind
fear and powerlessness. This is the central task of the movement.

The comrades will find out and learn how to defend themselves against a system of power that serves to extinguish countless species of plants, animals and human beings, because they have recaptured their belief, their vision and their way to heal the Earth. The Movement for a Free Earth cooperates and networks a course with peace initiatives that exist already. We think of worldwide peace initiatives, of conscientious objectors, liberation movements, active animal protection societies, we also think of communities in many countries in this world. We think of dedicated medical doctors and other professional groups and compassionate representatives of different religions. Religions and world views shall no longer be separating elements; the *Holy Grail* of every culture is elementary and equally true. Gradually the peace movement adopts the global idea of peace models and of community building; it will recognize the necessity of a global community movement and support it by all means.

The movement's rules

In our vision we see how a veritable pilgrimage route leads from peace project to peace project. The projects are happy to put up pilgrims who participate in the Movement for a Free Earth and wish to further develop themselves. Each place and project contributes in the bounds of its capacity and strength to add to the success of the whole. Every participating project develops to its appropriate size and professionalism. Their members recognize the necessity and the planetary importance of global peace models and stand behind them. With joy more and more people take responsibility for the whole and its parts. More and more people know and accept their professions and fulfil their purpose in this worldwide net of a forceful growing peace force. The vision includes simple rules for everyone in the movement. They are binding orientations which give testimony of the willingness to undergo a change in consciousness; guidelines to orientate the participants in their personal everyday life.

Here are some of them:

- GRACE is independent of the world views, religious and political affiliations. GRACE serves life and its peaceful unfolding. We face each other with respect, solidarity and the readiness to help.
- The participants of the peace movement lead a simple life and are careful to pass on any surplus resources to places where it is desperately needed. Monthly we donate part of our income to the development of the peace movement. Those responsible for the movement commit to owning no private property.
- We begin each day with powerful thoughts for peace.
- In the name of GRACE we refuse to be enemies.
- We leave each place we entered a little richer and more beautiful.
- We behave in such a way that we do not harm any other being. Every creature has a right to life.
- We behave in such a way as to free ourselves more and more from being accomplices, this with regard to our contact with human beings, animals and plants. Our clothing and nourishment is orientated by these guidelines.
- The wellbeing of mankind has priority over the wellbeing of any group. We do not stand up against existing systems, but use our forces for the development of a perspective in life. Another life is possible!
- If we come across injustice in our surroundings be it close to or far off, we name it but do not accuse. You increase happiness by being helpful as you move on your way.
- With the aid of art, music and inventive creativity you help to make the peace movement known to others.
- Every day we dedicate part of our time to study further steps towards peace in both theory and practise.

These or similar ones could be the simples rules. With the observation of these rules the initiators of this movement demonstrate their willingness and readiness to put all their forces into the service of peace.

The Dream of the Returning Templars

In front of the small chapel

It happened in front of a small Roman chapel. I see ourselves in front of my inner eye time and again meditating in the icy cold at sunrise, in the light of the first sunrays. It was one second during the meditation, when I was suddenly touched by the image of the nine Templars and their departure to Jerusalem. I think of the famous pilgrims who, at the beginning of the 12th century, set out on their journey. Was not this too the beginning of a wider movement with a changing power? Who had prompted them to venture out? With what kind of mission were they underway? Who was it of the nine that had the idea to go to Israel and why? Their pilgrimage was a marked break in the history of the church. Never before had this group of persons and this historic event come so close to me as it did during that moment of meditation.

Countless books exist about the movement of the Templars. A great mystic secret revolves around them. It was the legend more than the historic facts that made history. I have never given much attention to the subject of the Templars, too much mysticism, too much occultism and too much spilling of blood stick to it. Now though, I am almost being pushed after them. It is not the aim of this book to look into the history of the Templars and Cathars. Nevertheless, I include this chapter quite expressly, since I have repeatedly come in touch with the subject of the Templars throughout my pilgrimage. This was the reason that I began to read thoroughly the history and the background of the Templars. I read about the many assumptions woven around them and the stories of the Grail. Time and again I came across theories of where the Holy Grail might still be hidden to this day. One story about the Grail, a criminal story at that, entwines like a legend around the essence of the Templars traces of which can be found right up to modern day fascism. Repeatedly I found confirmation that the

Templars and the Cathars guarded a secret pertaining to the truth of Jesus and Mary Magdalena. I came across those early Gnostic quotations again which had fascinated me during my studies of theology and which featured Mary Magdalena as the preferred disciple of Jesus. I found versions of the Holy Grail which referred to it as "Manna-machine", as the giver of eternal life, culminating in the statement "The Holy Grail is a woman." Encrypted feminine Goddess knowledge, esoteric-erotic vestiges of romantic minstrels and seekers of the Grail led me via the Templars, the times of the Gothic and the Celts back to primordial history and the primordial knowledge of peace. It was therefore no miracle to me that I came across old dolmens and megaliths whenever I was in the vicinity of Gothic cathedrals. The path leads us back to primordial peace tracks.

Until this day the truth remains hidden and maybe it lets some people grasp it more or less intuitively. How true is the sentence which Napoleon is supposed to have coined: "History is but a lie on which we all agree." History books have always been controlled by the prevailing culture. Those who thought anything different were pronounced heretics. I just want to note how deeply the image of these nine departing brothers from the 12th century has made me come into touch with our past – whether it be true or merely a legend. All this has profoundly shaped our view of the history of Christianity at its high points as well as its low ones. In the legends of the Templars I found mirrored a profound search for truth and community, a search for the essence of the Goddess who has left her traces in all cultures. She never has nor ever will let herself be ousted.

Some day a simple and elementary truth of life will behold the light of the world and reveal a loving humanity and a connectedness between all creatures which goes beyond any religion, world view and all history. This will be seen by all those who seek with their eyes open.

In the meditation I clearly saw with great intensity the nine brothers in front of me. For nine years these nine Templars had kept to themselves and had not accepted any new members into their community. It seems they had lived in complete poverty. To live in complete poverty was one of the rules of the later Templars who were closely connected to Bernard von Clairvaux and the order of the Cistercians.

At the same time they moved large sums of money about and to this day no one can say where the money came from which they used to finance the large cathedrals, the grand estates and much more. They seemed to have had more money at their disposal than many kings or sovereigns and in the political situations of the time they were often the ones to tip the scales.

Historic view of history and presence – a play of thoughts

During meditation I let myself be playfully guided by the image that we might be these pilgrims ourselves, having returned to Earth, after all this time. What would happen to them if having returned after all these centuries, they were able to see the line of their original search for purpose, leading them through incarnation after incarnation? I allowed myself to dwell on this image for a while and observed our little group with the eyes of an alien who consciously reincarnated herself on this day.

Meanwhile centuries have gone by. The participants of this group look back at their former incarnations.

Today, they are able to recognize, how their decisions of hundreds of years ago, have shaped history for many generations. They look at their idealism, their hopes and dreams and they see how major wars have been ignited around their Order. Apart from their impulse for humanisation they also see power and corruption spreading in their environment. They are able to recognize how over the years their original idea of the foundation of a humane culture became more and more perverted and finally they turn away with a shudder. Too bleak is the awful downfall of the

Templars during the 14th century which they have to witness. Now, after a long time of contemplation they have returned to their starting point in order to understand and correct the committed errors. This time they consciously chose to come back as men and women. Already at that time they had a premonition of the secret of the Goddess and the woman. At that time the woman stood in the transfigured light of their search for the Grail. Today they know more about how much the Holy Grail is connected to the woman.

They know that the adoration of the "Saintly Madonna" alone, as it was expressed in the building of churches and cathedrals, would not serve a humane culture in the long run. They know that in this way the battle of the man against the woman had not come to an end, even though the history of suppression spurred on masculine insights with the refinement of mathematics, the arts and architecture. The Gothic era was made to bloom through their cultural impulse and contributed to the uplifting of man.

At that time people were enlivened by the realization of being a partner with God and as co-creators were carrying their own responsibility for the cultural development of what might happen on Earth. No longer did they want to submit to an old God, the God of romanticism. God wanted man to be upright, perceptive, enlightened and creative. The Earth was to become the home of the divine Shechina. Finance was made more sophisticated, exchange and trade blossomed. A new cultural idea shaped the arts, social welfare, philosophy and history. Hospitals were founded and research was on the rise in the Christian occident. Islam, Judaism and Christianity could draw closer to each other and bloom into a triplex to complement each other.

At the centre they had guarded the mystic knowledge about the Goddess, about the essence of the Eros and its central power. The historic situation however was not yet ripe for this knowledge to be divulged to the world. Thus, they kept on furtively guarding what has been the great secret of the Goddess since primordial times.

The devastating crusades were connected to the departure of the Templars too. In those days one went off to war in the name of peace even though it led to immense human suffering and ideological battles between the religions. Occultism, perverted sexual practices, spiritual conventions and finally the terrible persecution of the Cathars and later on of the Templars threw a shadow on a great idea which was also a great fallacy. Was this all due to nine brothers having once decided to found a new order with revolutionary cultural ideas? Was it because they had decided to go to Jerusalem to the Temple of Solomon?

They still shudder today when they see how their original, maybe once pure, idea has been capable of provoking mankind. For a long time they refused to return. The reality in whose face they would have to look would be too horrible, too painful. What had they left behind for their children and their grandchildren? How many more bleak chapters of war must follow until humanity wakes up to a new, more human dream? More enlightened, detached from the all too romantic mysticism of old heroic sagas, of men who had never grown up, they kept going out to look for the Holy Grail, the chalice which promised eternal life. They had been looking for it in transfiguration instead of in holy life itself.

Now after almost one thousand years they return again to reconcile themselves with history. Then they came as peace seekers. Now they come again to hold up the torch of peace, more alertly, more knowingly and more profoundly and with newly gained peace knowledge. To end wars is what they have come for - this is their new adventure. Now it is peace and no longer war that is their adventure, and above all peace between the genders. This time they do not come to proselytise but to realise directly the foundations for a new life. Today's experiment consists of bringing the holy marriage between God and Goddess down to Earth in full. Humanity itself, and together with it the Earth, have become the adventure of divine self-actualization.

If we have today a quarrel with any of the prophets, saints, commanders or other personalities from history, you might as well let yourself be touched by the thought that it could have also been us. How would we act today having returned with all the experiences, the knowledge and the mistakes and misunderstandings of past times? I am reminded of the lines in the Parcival poem of Ernst Stadler: "You are being washed clean by your mistake and only the one crowned by pain is greeted by the Holy Grail."

This pretty legend that we ourselves might be the returned pilgrims quickens my "Geist". When we do not take these pictures too seriously they might help to open the "Geist" in such a way as to enable us to look upon our present life with more inspiration and with a better historical perspective of our own persons. Our present life too takes place against a grand backdrop of history and evolution and it needs to be seen and understood against this. Should the history of the nine Templars be true, then it is an example of the force of field building. It would then have taken only nine people who were capable of transforming an entire culture, a religion and a historic point of view.

Ever since this meditation at the small chapel the thought stays with us of making pilgrimage all the way to Jerusalem. I keep pushing it aside since I know that it is not realistic. Too many tasks and projects are waiting for me. Persistently though it reappears to suggest that it might be my task to take leave and not only to do a pilgrimage through Israel but to do one all the way to Jerusalem. I talk about the idea. Benjamin is enthused with it. He would love to take off at once. I immediately receive many creative images. I see us in a little group, a theologian, a rabbi, a sufi master, a descendent of a concentration camp survivor, a person from a noble family who has been dispossessed and as such we would take off and on the way visit the Pope in Rome.

High spirited we let our child-like imaginations run freely without exposing them too soon to reality. Yes, we would even ask the Pope to make reparations by investing some money in our ideas. The one who studies the history of the Templars is only looking at a small part of the dark chapters of church history. It was the church which in cooperation with King Philip le Beau had the entire Templar movement brutally crushed. Consciously I allow myself the naïve thought that today's Pope might let himself be moved by a peace pilgrimage in such a way that he would invest reparation monies into such a peace movement. Today few would ever invest money into the construction of monasteries and cathedrals. Today the sacral corpus would consist of a lively community with a profound knowledge about the interaction of male and female forces.

The power of money

Thinking about the Templars has also quickened our thinking about the essence of money and its function. It was characteristic of inventors, artists, visionaries who set sail for entirely new shores that they had often very little money. It would appear that the realization of their ideas failed due to a lack of money. But what seemed to be a lack at first ultimately disclosed itself as a kind of self-built-in resistance from which a budding will would grow. This resistance is the yardstick by which realization of an idea may be tested. It is at this point that it has to be decided whether an idea can already withstand the rules of manifestation; whether it is round and conclusive; whether it can be realised despite all resistance; or whether the visions are but ephemeral and will soon disappear again.

At the moment we entertain no doubts and commence with a long-term view, knowing that sponsors will turn up, as soon as the vision has reached the state where it can be realised. "Behave in such a way as if you already have it" is often the wise advice offered by the inner guide when faced with the danger of giving in to scarcity.

At this moment we are still swimming in the floating lightness of the vision. We have not yet been dragged down by the weight of a worrying mind full of all sorts of arguments about the impracticality of it all. Our thoughts are entirely connected with the joy and the amorousness and the wonder of Creation. At the moment we walk as if the divine eye was looking through us, creating anew;

inventing and trying out its countless colours on the rich palette of its Creation workshop; correcting and sketching anew until the picture fits.

Yes, dare to dream, take MY dreams for your strength, the great mistress, Creation herself, whispers to me. *The more "world" your dreams encompass, the more your dreams are connected with the whole of Creation, the more certain it becomes that you are acting in the placenta of the whole of the Universe. The strength needed to realise your dreams will be available to you.*

The bigger the task which we accept, the more the world streams to us in order to realise it. All that is compatible with the whole of Creation will connect to the force of an immense will to be realised. The economy of the divine world is indeed inexhaustible.

Benjamin walks next to me. He is the descendant of a long line of ancestors of the German-Jewish family of the von Mendelssohns, who became known for their art and money. Great musicians, great humane philosophers and bankers have incarnated themselves into this family. Their bank like all banks was involved in the financing for wars. Under the sway of the Nazis their bank was "coerced to be aryanised." At present huge sums of money are at stake in various court cases for reparations to which the Mendelssohn family may be entitled.

The wide view which quickens our sight today also changes our sight regarding the subject of money. It is understood that the money that is put at our disposal shall be used to finance the "Plan for the Peace Villages" since it is obvious that if these models are to be built they must of course be also financed. It is also understood that part of the money shall be invested in regions of conflict. From this point of view it is obvious that the necessary resources will be available as soon as the idea is fully developed since it complies with the will of a greater force for survival.

It is also clear that the supporters of this idea need much power of perseverance. The more comprehensive the coming change is, the larger the inner and outer resistances will be. By dealing with these correctly, the power for realisation grows.

Suddenly, in this large context we also see the personal history of Benjamin. Nomen est Omen, Benjamin, son of the right hand, the right, the lucky side, the second son of the biblical Rachel who before she died during childbirth gave him the name of "Son of Pain." Maybe he was incarnated on this Earth to humanise finance. Maybe he has come to pass on wealth and healing to those places where it is needed, and to get it from where hitherto it has been wrongly hoarded and used for destructive purposes. And maybe it is my task to accompany him doing this.

We speak and think from the abundance of taking and giving and not from scarcity, which keeps on wanting to show us that much of what we really need is not available. We speak of our overall situation as if 20 million Euros or more are already at our disposal. With an almost childlike joy we enter into vision building with great abundance.

We shall develop a form of pilgrimage for the humanisation of monies and ask all those who have money: "Invest into the development of a global peace force!" Help with the reallocation of the monies so that a future worth living can also be secured economically. And we ask all those who may have other resources at their disposal: "Invest your intelligence and your power of love for the exploration of peace!" We have learnt and experienced that to all intents and purposes we can *be* the change for which we all yearn so much. The realisation of the idea for a world-wide peace movement with the peace villages at its centre needs contact with the public at large. It needs contacts with financial experts and economic specialists who have for long recognized the necessity of a comprehensive rethink and want to support it. Our contribution lies in the preparation of the appropriate technological, ecological and social pilot models. At the same time we are glad to pass on our spiritual knowledge and our experience in the field of love.

I am thinking of what Pia Gyger and Pater Brantschen of the Lassalle Institute of Switzerland had to say: "Peace has to be learned and practiced by humanity with the same engagement as it learns and practices war. Let us not be deceived! Until we leverage the same amount of money into peace research and peace education as we have done for war, peace will remain an illusion. As soon as we utilize our psychic-"geistig" and material forces for the learning of peace then the spinning wheel of the war machine will start to turn in the opposite direction."

We shall devote ourselves fully everywhere on Earth to the development of universal cells and communities where peace can be learnt and practiced at all levels. In the name of Mother Earth!

About the fate of the dropouts

One evening we were invited to a finca, a small farm, where a couple put their kitchen at our disposal. Two of our newly joined pilgrims cooked rice and paprika for us. One of them, Annette, is a member of a community of dropouts in the Pyrenees by the name of Matavenero. While we pilgrimaged she told us a lot about the fate of this community. The daughter of our host is a 15 year old girl and very beautiful. Her father is an attractive Mexican. Everywhere we meet young dropouts from the modern culture. All of them are longing for community living but they do not know how community works. They followed their longing for a different life but did not know what they were getting into.

Through our inspired talks, the dream of the movement of the "Bauhütte" historic mason's lodges comes alive. In the Middle Ages new knowledge was disseminated through mason's lodges and the construction of cathedrals. The new way of building was one of the elements that helped the movement to spread. Today it could be the knowledge of community living that initiates a new movement.

Right now I look into the world through the eyes of history. It is as if I am in touch with Cathars, Templars and people from the old mason's orders who settled in the foothills of the Pyrenees. They built up networks to help each other. However in most cases their attempts to live together in communities failed. They did not find a new "geistig" orientation. Quite the opposite, they were taught

65

that "Geist" is a relic of middle class society and as such, one had to fight against it. Believing that it would be enough to follow ones longings and feelings they all walked single-mindedly into a dead end street. They followed the "belly" of spontaneity and were not aware that by doing this they followed unconscious thoughts since all emotions result from thoughts. Many of them had gone off with plenty of idealism. They demonstrated against nuclear power plants, against mistreatment of animals, against the Vietnam War and against all sorts of other grievances of society. They wanted to do it all differently.

In addition there was the dream of living in nature. It was their belief that the humans, if only they would live with nature, would automatically become good. Finally an awakening takes place after many painful experiences in love relationships, disappointment, anger, separation, drug and alcohol abuse and finally resignation. They have no knowledge about what leads and holds a community together. The figures of Hermann Hesse`s "Glass Bead Players" also were on the go without anyone having showed them the rules of the Glass Bead Game. Idealism alone has misled many seekers of the Grail before.

Symbols like the chalice and the sword were of no use, neither was the transfiguration of the Goddess or that of the minstrels. The only thing that would help would be concrete knowledge about love. What is creating truth, faithfulness, solidarity and vitality in relationships? What is it that keeps two people in love from isolating themselves as a pair? May there be a knowledge that spreads truth and trust so that community can develop to provide protection for those concerned and which they so badly need!

In my vision I see Tamera in front of me, a place of power, where those who seek it can acquire knowledge about the development of communities. How many detours could have been spared them!

Behind all of it, a power can be felt to which one ought to give absolute support. It seems that beyond all these developments the "Geist" of the world is on the lookout for a new state of being on this planet Earth. A world encompassing process of transformation has taken hold of us. We are all part of it and fulfil our tasks in it. God searches through us. He casts his seed here and there. The alchemies of a newly developing matter fill our "Geist" and our bodies.

The same way as in evolution fishes had to form entirely new breathing organs when they moved from water to land, so the human species is preparing itself for a completely new form of existence. The faster we are ready to prepare together for this process of change, then the less painful and the lighter this new birth will be. What is needed of us all is the collective awakening to a new consciousness.

From dream to reality

After the days of visions I lie awake at night and reflect in silence. With this abundance of vision power we had the idea to choose November 9th, a historic date, for a day of action. The "Reichspogromnacht" of 1938 under Hitler and the day of the fall of the German wall in 1989 both occured on a 9th of November. Now the walls will be able to open themselves worldwide. By learning to overcome inner walls we shall also be capable of opening the outer walls.

Quietly we want to prepare an action at a good point at the wall in Israel and project images of peace onto the wall, perhaps for instance, a picture of a young woman handing a rose to a soldier through a crack in the wall. Visions open walls! Visions are free! All committed peace workers we know from everywhere are invited to participate.

The seed of a new idea has been planted. Now may it fully mature and see the light of the world.

Departure for the Promised Land

The will of realisation

After returning from the pilgrimage to Santiago de Compostela, the picturesque scenery of our generously sketched visions faded again into the background of reality. The idea of setting off to Israel already seemed far too unrealistic.

The planned Monte Cerro project drew closer but the money for our building projects was nowhere in sight. Many unsettled community matters led to too much down-to-earth thinking. These changes of the inner dimensions occur almost unnoticed in our consciousness. Small everyday patterns want to lead us back to thinking in terms of separation. In our minds a wall barricades our consciousness and what we take to be our daily duty and equally our daily burden, is incommensurate with what our higher self expects from us.

At such moments we deeply believe that we have to painstakingly earn the fulfilment of our dreams. These transitions unfold stealthily. These are thinking habits which we follow being quite unaware. Even if in our "every day life" we maintain a relatively conscious life practice, we are seldom successful in remaining alert for these unnoticed thinking habits. All of a sudden the "Geist" is occupied with the subjects of the day, here a phone call, there some worry about money, or an important date and already the bold lines of purpose of the free "Geist" retreat into the background completely unnoticed.

Nevertheless, from our pilgrimage to Santiago de Compostela, we did bring back some clear conclusions. Chief among them was the will to realise the pilgrimage through Israel/Palestine in autumn and a firm decision to hold a solemn vigil at the wall in Israel on November 9th. A small group had already embarked fully on the preparations. They decided to travel ahead to Israel in

September to plan the route and make the necessary contacts.

The second unconditional will was to go ahead with the construction of the 'Aula', the much needed assembly hall for the students and participants of the Monte Cerro Experiment. This, to me, seemed the most important component. I was firmly decided to make the vision a reality with the lever of my will. Unfortunately there were still no monies in sight for the construction.

In order to get things moving, I set off once more on a journey to Germany, Switzerland and Austria to set up contacts, this time together with Paul Gisler, a long-time friend and co-worker at Tamera, and at a later stage with Benjamin von Mendelssohn who had accompanied me on similar trips before.

Inspiration

While on the motorway in the South of France the inner voice reported again with a forcefulness that could not be ignored.

Leave for the pilgrimage now and only return when the money for the Aula has been collected. Maybe you will visit Tamera as part of your journey to be able there also to ask for donations. It is important that you take on the status of a pilgrim.

In my mind I began to calculate: the costs for the Aula came to 400.000 Euros. I therefore would need 1 person to give me 400.000 Euros, or 10 persons to give me 40.000 Euros each, or 100 Persons to give me 4.000 Euros each, or 10.000 persons to give me 40 Euros each, or 100.000 to give me 4 Euros. This ought to be possible. To set off with this information and then be guided by God is a powerful image and requires a powerful imagination! So compelling was the thought that it held me fixed.

Something still hesitated inside of me and I was not sure whether it was my higher guidance which came up so insistently or my own childlike fantasies which wanted to escape the known form of networking trips with the usual full agenda of meetings.

I entered into a dialogue with the divine authority within me in order to find out what was her will. I went into meditation, putting all personal preferences aside and opened myself to something new. I then formulated a prayer about my concerns. I only do this when I am ready to accept the new proposals that come to me.

Mostly the answers come quickly and clearly to me. It is important for me to note them down or tape them so that I can check back later. Memory so often veils things in one way or another. Personal interpretations also tend to slightly change what was originally said and own notions are added to it. At this point it is important for the spiritual research to be very aware and precise.

Dialogue with the Goddess

I entered into the dialogue with an authority within me, an inner voice that I perceive to be the Goddess. After describing my vision of the pilgrimage I noted down the following dialogue in my diary:

Sabine: Goddess, I ask for inspiration and guidance. Shall I set off on this pilgrimage? And if yes, how do I best do it? Is it your will that we receive the money for the Aula and that I pilgrimage for it?

Goddess: *Primarily I wish that you find your path of connectedness and of trust in God completely. If this path strengthens you, then it is a good path.*

Sabine: Inwardly I feel ready for everything only if I know that it is your will inside of me. But sometimes I wonder whether this is again already far too fixed, fixed to thoughts of money, and fixed to the construction of the Aula and that this preordains a path of separation and its subsequent strenuousness. I know full well that it is all about not acting from my own strength but rather to let you be effective through me. But how do I get to this?

Goddess: *Play with the idea of the pilgrimage for the humanisation of monies. Play for as long until it makes you really light and until it gives you joy. When this is the case, I shall be able to go with you. If the reality of the task provokes a feeling of heaviness and helplessness then something is still missing. Go to the place in your "Geist" where you can perceive my abundance.*

Sabine: Is it your will that the Aula will be built and more money flows to Tamera?

Goddess: *Your will is my will. When within you no more thoughts of separation exist, then it will happen.*

Sabine: Why do thoughts of scarcity and disbelief come up inside of me so easily, as soon as I come close to the idea of asking for money? I even think that it is not wanted by you and it might just be a pigheaded idea of mine.

Goddess: *Always, when you have the wish to completely connect with me, thoughts of separation pop up at the same time. They are very powerful since the entire world of the old matrix feeds on them. Money originally came into being from the thoughts of separation and of scarcity. It is for this that whenever you turn to the subject of money you come in touch with the thoughts of separation in an extraordinarily strong way. Certainly and unerringly you have to find the point of a different abundance inside of you, the abundance of life. If you have this fully then you will no longer be susceptible. You create a fulfilled life. To procure the money for the Aula is a by-product since it complies with your wish. This path is workable.*

Sabine: Can you make this visible to me in my mind?

Goddess: *Yes. You begin with it right now. You live a simple life and you renounce all private property. You live this life in the conscious- ness of abundance. You write a text and you send it to your network and you get some clothes which will strengthen the idea of being a pil-*

grim. And then you let yourself be guided. Wherever you go you ask to be supported so that the money for the Aula is procured. It does not matter if this thought still causes a little stress in you. At the same time you do not have to think that you have to make large sacrifices for it to succeed. Stay with the alert joy and see to it that you are well. This is the will of the Goddess within you.

Coming from the old world, and as a woman at that, you tend to repeatedly entertain the thought that God will only listen to you if you make sacrifices. God does not ask for sacrifice. All he asks is for quiet connectedness and as little complicity as possible so that no feelings of bad conscience come up. Now, write the text.

Upcoming doubts

The same day I began drafting the text. I composed an appeal in order to be able to mail it out via the internet. While I was writing again all the fears and doubts promptly resurfaced. I became aware that the planned construction of the Aula was not yet visible to my inner eye. Too many discussions and differing opinions floated around the vision. Should it be a temporary building due to the shortness of money or could we afford to go for a model type assembly hall which is constructed with environmentally compatible building materials? Do we have enough human resources at our disposal that are needed to complete such a building despite the many other tasks that stand in line? After all we are dealing with quite a large project, an Aula to seat 400 people. Looking the facts in the face it seemed totally absurd. Could it be that I have to return to Tamera first in order to clear up all these matters? I asked about the Aula which is to be built.

Sabine: Again and again I have the feeling that in Tamera a true field does not yet exist for the development of a university. Many still associate such an idea with very old notions of studies and of thinking. Apart from this, very differing perceptions exist about the construction of the university hall, the Aula, and these are still competing with each other. Do you have any suggestions of what has to be done?

Goddess: *Yes. Write a letter. Take a stand and see to it that these subjects are now taken up and that a field for it is being prepared.*

Sabine: Are we at all able to build the Aula with our own resources?

Goddess: *Yes, it is much more in harmony with your scheme. The right people have to be brought together to think about it.*

Sabine: Is it part of my pilgrimage to take the time to build up a field from afar?

Goddess: *Yes, and to be able to do this so as to fully hear my voice you have to abandon any wrong thoughts of a sense of duty.*

Sabine: Thank you. I ask you that you accompany me today so that joy and light and inner readiness are with me entirely.

After this processes I caught a heavy influenza. It was no surprise to me, in all the turmoil of inner conflict. In the meantime we arrived in Switzerland. An acquaintance gave me a gift of a massage. While having this I had the feeling of thousands of angels being around me and helping to cleanse my body and to give me healing thoughts to strengthen me. It was a true spectacle of light that went on inside of me. Again I got in touch with my inner "board-computer."

Throwing the switch

Goddess: *During the next few days you should find your affirmations. Be silent and all of a sudden you will know them.*

Sabine: Will you help me to find my strength again?

Goddess: *The force of confidence is with you. Let confidence enter into your heart. Let certainty enter into your heart.*

Sabine: Will you soon help me to find, see, understand, and to accept my mission? Storms may break out around me but I shall not be taken aback if only inner certainty is with me.

Goddess: *Yes, arrange your setting in such a way as to be open for inputs. And please – accept ever more that the way you are is perfect! Today you need time and peace for the inner clearance of your strategy. You have to find the inner switch so that at any time you can turn to silence, quiet and strength. This switch exists and it functions easily once you have found the mechanism. Let God do it. This is meant in a very deep way. Already when putting your question you have to leave behind all thoughts of wrong conscientiousness. Please do never ask out of a sense of duty. Ask in such a way that you let God be inside your question. God always wants the most beautiful, the most powerful and the most effective for you. Let yourself enter into the flow, again and again, and connect to the knowledge that God presides within you.*

All of the messages that flow to us from the world of light sound so easy and promising. You simply have to maintain your inner attitude of letting the Goddess act within you. Can there be a more beautiful promise than that of letting yourself have a good time? Can there be a more beautiful promise than that of having ones wishes fulfilled all by themselves? It sounds rather like the land of milk and honey. The only thing we have to do is to leave behind old thinking habits and to train our vigilance for our own inner voice. Does this not collide with our Spartan ideas that the good in us can only be fulfilled by the hardest of work and frugality! If I look upon the impending pilgrimage anxiously then all I can see ahead of me is a cumbersome path in solitude and austerity. Being cold, looking for sleeping places, straying in dark streets of a foreign city, asking for alms to at least secure the food for the day. Sometimes even to go hungry!

Being in the state of trust however, a completely different and free world opens up in front of me, a world without inherent necessity, a world of presence with many new contacts, an infinite cosmic abundance full of adventure and discovery. The Earth with her firmament is my playground and my living room.

Slowly the channel of joy opened up and a clear decision became visible. Once more, I stepped in front of my inner oracle with the last remaining questions to be cleared.

Imagine your pilgrimage starts right now at this very moment. You will no longer run after things, rather they come to you. This is the special secret of throwing the inner lever. You listen to the world differently. You do not have to prove anything to anyone. But you go connected to God. It does not make any difference where you happen to be. You walk your path.

For this, affirmations will arise in you. It is a deep all encompassing new force. Do not ask now whether you ought to go back to Tamera or not. At first perceive this swell, this large swell which carries and guides you. This is what is special not whether your life will pass slowly or rapidly, that is not important. Important is the inner shift. By turning the lever, peace and silence is coming to you which you need. You need affirmations which continuously remind you of this.

The decision

Now I had come far enough to be able to make a final decision. I would not return to Tamera.

We drove to the Southern Black Forest in Germany. There I would make the last preparations for my journey into the unknown, and from there, send the appeal to the network. I bid farewell to Paul and Benjamin who would set off on their long journey back to Tamera on their own. We had a last picnic and then I let myself be dropped off at the house of my parents. I now had only the most necessary things with me. Money and all superfluous utensils went back to Tamera.

My baggage included: a flashlight, a little pocket knife, a notebook, a small drawing block with aquarelle colours, my transverse flute, a peace flag, an aluminium sheet as a sleeping pad, a change of underwear, a little fleece hand towel and a light skirt. After much thinking, I decided to take a sleeping bag with me. This gave me a feeling of real luxury. My little high-tech apparatus, a handy minicomputer reminded me that I was not a begging nun from the middle ages. Tamera had financed this luxury so that I had the possibility of writing my diary and sending it off straight away. My homepage, the Ring of Power was to inform all those interested about the course of the pilgrimage. In a way, I was to be a high-tech pilgrim!

Through Europe, always in the Direction of Israel

I wrote and sent off an appeal for the "Humanisation of the Money." In this I wrote: *I myself have no longer any private belongings, instead I have put everything I own and all my effort into community service of all beings. If you wish me to talk about the project in public I will come and give a presentation. I will travel by any means if invited and given the money necessary for the fares.*

My path was roughly in a south-eastern direction towards Israel/Palestine with numerous detours to respond to the many invitations I received to speak in public. I used opportunities to speak to the press and on television to draw attention to my main concern: "We can only end the war if we create perspective for peace." In this context I introduced the idea of models of peace and talked about the humanization of money. At events I would either pass out our bank account number or I would accept gifts of money right there no matter whether they were small or large. I regularly transferred these gifts to Tamera. Again and again people would give me money for my personal use but I usually put this into the fund of the Aula. I wanted to prove to myself and to others that it is easy to live without personal money. It was much easier than expected.

The sum total of my pilgrimage-appeal grew and with it the financing needed to construct the Aula. Since my main challenge consisted in putting all personal needs last and to trust to my inner guidance, I put up with many unplanned detours. Getting up in the morning I rarely knew where the day would take me. It was during my regular morning meditation that my inner voice gave me instructions which I then followed. They led me through Southern Germany, Switzerland, Austria, Slovenia, Italy and from there, via a short excursion to Tamera, to Greece and finally to Israel. If at all possible I went by foot and did not spend any money. The diary entries of this time alone - of adventures, encounters, realisations and talks - could fill a book. I received blessings from the different religions – Christian, Sufi, Jewish, Hindi, Indian – and during various rituals the Star of David alone appeared three times. In hindsight I can say that these travels with all its experiences and realisations were the best preparation for the tasks that awaited me in Israel and Palestine.

The voice of the Goddess

The adventure begins in Hänner in the Southern part of the Black Forest. I tune in, walk past cool streams and across many clearings. I ask myself whether there might have been a person before me setting out from the "Hotzen Forest" with the aim of reaching Jerusalem and not knowing where he or she would sleep for the following nights. I take a lot of time to experience my new state of being. I walk for about three hours until I reach Laufenburg where I arrive at the shores of the river Rhine. It is wonderful and very hot walking along the shore. I take my first bath and cool down my hot body in the strong currents. In the small towns along the way I look into the windows of bakeries, ice cream parlours and many little restaurants – alas, with a somewhat changed view, knowing that I would not buy anything. "What beautiful things there are to be had here which I do not need." Humorously, this famous saying from Socrates crossed my mind.

Behind Bad Säckingen I start to look out for a place to spend the night. I steal a glance at some of the many allotment gardens and look for a person I could ask. Then I remember that an acquaintance of mine lives in Mumpf, on the other side of the Rhine, where she has a house right on the shore. Sure enough, she offers a place to me on her terrace. From my encampment I can see the mirroring of the water. Gratefully I roll myself into my sleeping bag full of expectations of what the next week will bring.

The next day I stroll through Basle. Slowly and cautiously I expand the boundaries of my soul. In one of the street cafés I dare ask for a glass of water. No lunch today! Obeying the Goddess I had gone to this town. She is my mistress for the day. I go to the "Münster" (the cathedral) where I meditate. I have lived in the streets before. Two years ago, without money and without sleeping bags, I led a group of men and women in a street retreat in Berlin. This is the first time though that I am alone in such a situation. Being alone, the hurdles of asking people for something are higher. At this point I would prefer to fast rather than sit down somewhere to beg. But my inner Shechina is persistent. I know that I cannot get around this and that I have to make the step today. Again and again I stroll through the small streets of the old part of the city in order to find a suitable place.

"What are you doing here? You are 50 years old and no teenager! If you meet acquaintances! What will they think of you?" With these and similar comments the timid ego tries to keep me from my decision. Whenever I see a place that would suit I find an excuse to go on. All the time I know there is no way past this. I get a piece of cardboard. I have a peace flag with me and my flute. On the cardboard I write in bold letters: "Pilgrimage for Peace."

Finally I am ready. Fine energy bubbles through my body, the inner boundary wants to be crossed now. It is a similar feeling to that which I had when I made my first header from the swimming pool three meter board. I sat myself down, unpacked my flute and began to play. Hardly a minute had passed before I hear my name spoken: "Sabine Lichtenfels!"

An acquaintance, herself engaged in peace work for Israel and Palestine, approaches me. Immediately she hands me a 100 franc note. More than grateful I accept this gift. A good omen! While I play I begin to feel more joyous, more secure and lighter in the heart. Occasionally a coin is thrown with a jingle into my flute box. Afterwards I have the feeling that I have passed a test.

My way takes me to Bern. The visit coincides with the public announcement of the nominations for the "1000 Women for the Nobel Peace Prize 2005." I am one of the women nominated. It is a Swiss initiative which has traced women from all countries of the world, who are working untiringly for peace. Most of them are not known to the public. In order to honour their work some Swiss women had the marvellous idea to nominate 1000 of such women for a joint Nobel Peace Prize. Even if in the end we do not receive the prize, the action will have helped to create a greater public interest in the work of the 1000 nominees.

On June 29th, at 10 a.m., I set foot into the hall where the press is assembled and our work is presented to a large crowd. About 90 reporters, men and women, are present and I give various interviews.

Afterwards I leave this scene and continue on my way. Days afterwards I sit in front of an old peoples' home. An old man comes towards me and utters some unintelligible words. Crows are croaking. The elderflowers are in full bloom. At the wayside lovely, red strawberries wait to be discovered, strawberries recalling childhood happiness. Below me are the "Beatenhöhlen", a series of caves, where in old times pilgrims rested their weary heads. I draw a tree and think of my friends in Tamera. How good, to know these loving companions so near to me!

Grandmother Sara

During a visit to the "Schweibenalp – Zentrum der Einheit" (Centre of Unity) in the Bernese Oberland, I listen, amongst others, to the American-Indian wisdom of Grandmother Sara of the Mohawk Turtle Clan from Canada. I am impressed by her simple clarity and wisdom. I feel empowered by my own elementary source of belief and everything that I describe in my book "Dream Stones" comes alive, is touched and revived again. The book is the narration of a pre-patriarchal age, where human beings, animals, stones and plants are able to communicate with each other in an animated way.

I quote from memory from the teachings of Grandmother Sara:
I am the living knowledge of the medicinal plants. They convey their

wisdom to me. A global search for the original primordial knowledge exists. At their core, all traditions share the same vibrant source and in all cultures primordial knowledge is the same. It is given to us by the stones, also by plants, animals and all that is alive. Spirit is imbued in all that exists. We are one single homogeneous human race. The planet Earth, the galaxies and the cosmos: this is our home. Nobody owns a piece of Earth, or a country or a human being. It is about remembering our divine origin. The here and now is the most important moment from which to create a positive future. You have forgotten, but you are your ancestors, here and now. They are always present.

Many of us have forgotten to speak to the animals, the plants and the stones, to give thanks and to keep the contact with them alive. However, we preserve our songs and our wisdom given to us by our ancestors. Become as simple and plain as the heart of a child! This way you will be able to feel what the plants, the animals and the stones want to tell you. We have allowed our gifts and talents to fall asleep, but we have the thinking and the intuition at our disposal to wake them up again. If we suppress our relatedness to all things then we lose our true qualities. The spirit in each and every thing is alive. This truth is very simple and elementary and we all carry it in our hearts. All we have to do is to remember. When we are ready to truly live from the heart, then a new dimension opens up. This is the only certainty there is in our existence, there is no other. Each human being carries within it self the responsibility to accept his or her higher self. It is possible to change reality only by thought. When some danger comes up we all of a sudden forget our personal importance and we wake up to our real humanity and sympathetic compassion. Therefore, the big spirit enters us only in situations of danger, since it is only at such times that we remember.

She keeps emphasising self-responsibility:
Live your own self. You must find your own, very special way and it is you who is responsible for it. Friends can give you hints but it is alone your responsibility. Everyone carries the wisdom in his heart - all we have to do is to be willing to listen. Most important, we follow

our own true path. You have to rely on yourself. You can neither rely on your partner, your children nor on your community. Automatically we form a unity when we take on this kind of responsibility.

It is therefore your duty to ask the deepest of questions, to find answers to them and then act upon them.

Open the heart, live in gratitude, in respect and love for each other - this is what the Earth needs from us. Only when we come together again, we can truly change the situation on Earth.

Unusual encounters

I am singing inside a wonderful chapel the Ave Verum from Mozart. Raindrops are my only listeners. As the rain did not stop I started to think about where I would find a bed for the night. I'm told from within: *Do not worry, soon you will find a wonderful place to sleep in.* Two minutes later I see a barn and on it in bold letters "Overnight in Straw." I look for the farmer and he allocates a space to me in a huge stable situated above the lake. All alone, a kingdom all to myself, with shower and toilet!

Funnily enough I keep landing on the path that people took on their pilgrimages to Santiago de Compostela. One of its branches leads through Germany via Switzerland to France and finally on to Spain where it ends near Santiago de Compostela at Capo Finisterre. From the beginning of my pilgrimage I come across signposts pointing in this direction. I follow in the footsteps of Niklaus von der Flüe. This Swiss Saint left his usual life at the age of 48 and upon his death bequeathed a spiritual legacy. He was married and held political posts. A deep crisis about the purpose of his life took possession of him and as a result of it he left house and family. The later years of his life he lived quietly in a remote hermitage without food or drink. Many well-known Swiss contemporaries came to seek his advice, the advice of "Bruder Klaus." At this place of force I immerse myself in quiet prayer and afterwards go on walking through the heavy rain.

While still in the pouring rain and in the middle of the forest I come across another pilgrim. A curious scene unfolds:

"Where are you going to?"

"To Israel", is my answer. "And you?"

"To Portugal to visit the place of pilgrimage of Fatima", he says. We stand there in the rain and laugh.

At the mainline station of Lucerne I want to fill up my water bottle. Two francs they want for this at the lavatories. Since I have a backache, I want to leave my backpack for a while in the baggage room. For this service they want six francs. I do without all of it and think of all the homeless people and how they might feel in such a town. Even the elementary sources of life such as water are under the control of the money elite. When do we have to pay for the oxygen we breathe?

One evening, shortly before leaving Switzerland, a dark sky urges me to be on the look out for a place to stay the night in with a roof that will protect me. Shortly afterwards, I come across a small barn which happens to be open. With bails of straw I build myself a comfortable bed. The place is alive. Cheerfully, many little mice and rats run around in the timberwork overhead. In the middle of the night I am woken up suddenly by heavy footsteps! A man with a torch on his forehead approaches the barn. He enters the space carrying a load of things on his shoulders. I cannot make out who is more startled, him or me.

"Who is there?", a masculine voice demands.

I explain that I had to look for a dry sleeping place for the night to protect me from the rain.

"Ah, that is o.k.", he mutters and leaves the room. For a short moment the situation had felt dangerous. It could have taken another turn. Something within me had deeply reminded me not to react with the usual misgivings. This allowed me to remain calm and composed. In the morning I discover that the mice have tried to pull my pullover into their nest. My hair band is not to be found either. So, whether I like it or not, I have to leave it to them as a gift.

After weeks of being on pilgrimage I am invited to speak at the

Summer University of Tamera. I am grateful that my inner guidance is in accordance with this call. The Swiss entrepreneur, Kurt Eicher, spontaneously decides to accompany me and invites me along on a flight to Tamera.

There I hear that a large donation has been received. A participant of the Ring of Power has pledged to donate one to two tenth of the construction costs of the Aula. It takes me some time to realise that we are talking about a substantial sum of money. Now my pilgrimage fund had reached the considerable sum of 140.000 Euros!

On top of this, I hear that the construction of the Aula is moving many hearts at Tamera. The question of which type of building shall be chosen becomes more and more pressing. Janosh Valder, a young co-worker, takes on the management of the construction and the overall responsibility for the realisation of this large building. After two weeks of turbulent life with much love, many planning sessions, spiritual vision quests, speeches and forums, I leave Tamera, this time for four months. After a few public appearances in Switzerland, I return to walking and to taking up my pilgrimage afresh.

Heavy rains have passed across the land. The rivers flowed over their shores, pulled down bridges, some people died and many were injured. The apocalyptic signs of our time come right up to our doorsteps to remind us that war and catastrophes do not only happen in faraway lands. Mother Earth is an entity. We are all part of her suffering and her joys and carry the responsibility for her changes.

I return again to the walking I was longing for where all the thoughts come to a rest and the many impressions assemble in one single picture. For many hours I walk through the valley of the river Inn. The good weather plunges everything into a wonderful light. Only the many tree trunks laying about and some lifeguard helicopters humming overhead remind me of the catastrophe which had taken place only a few days ago, where in many regions masses of water have torn with them houses, streets, bridges and people too. Now the sun is shining again as if nothing had happened. The next day I follow an invitation to go to Austria.

The concentration camp of Mauthausen

An important station of this trip is the concentration camp of Mauthausen. The people who have invited me live nearby. It is surely no accident that my path has led me here. I walk to the place along a beautiful forest path. Flowers are blooming, birds twittering, nothing on this path even slightly reminds one of the massacres that happened here. While on my way, deep mourning comes upon me. Since I cannot defend myself against it, I open myself up to the feelings that want to come through to me. On the forest path I come across a stone slab. I am now at the place where the ashes of the countless burnt corpses had been thrown down a slope. I meditate quietly. Early on a gust of wind rushes through the trees and thousands of leaves fall down on me.

It seems like a greeting from the many deceased who thankfully take in each tear or each minute of silence spent in their memory. Like a belated life elixir that is given to them in order to be able to deal with all the pain and the unutterable suffering that has been inflicted upon them during their lifetimes.

A leaf with a unique capsule falls right on my foot. At this moment something deeply moves me, something, I can hardly find words for. If today, we want to heal, we have to remember the suffering and pains of those who came before us. This sad past still lies upon Europe like a vast trauma of fear. Like a tight body of pain it holds entire countries caught in their collective trauma. Similar to the flame of a candle which, when it extinguishes, does not simply vanish, rather, its energy remains in the invisible, the immense suffering and agony does not simply vanish. Only in silent meditation and prayer can we start to comprehend the past and give space to the self-healing powers of the Universe.

122.766 interns were murdered in a bestial manner. The many pictures and tableaux of information cannot be taken in all at once. The first reaction within me still remains the same as when it used to pour out of me as a child. Neither intellectual analysis nor psychological explanations were ever able to resolve this, only the mute questions remain: How is something like this possible? Why are human beings capable of inflicting such suffering on fellow human beings? How is it possible that in this Creation, in this miracle of the Universe, human beings can be so cruel to each other? What would I have done had I been in their place? Oh Lord, why did you let this happen?

I take a long time to digest it all and do not want to talk to anyone. Speechless, I look at the photographs of bodies of prisoners reduced to mere skeletons and photographs of the commanders in their uniforms. They free a sea of tears within me. So this after all is humanity? Words fail me. The context is not new to me but still it touches a deep layer in my soul. I take a long time to digest all this. Deep down I know again what it is that I am walking for on my pilgrimage. This misery must disappear from Earth. War must come to an end!

Meeting with the soul of my father

From Linz I visit the newly developing community "Viverde" at their lovely estate in the midst of a marvellous landscape. For almost two hours I sit together with ten leaders of the project and let myself be asked about all community issues. An inner voice reminds me to be on my own. I sit down in a meadow in order to meditate. All of a sudden, I feel my father very close to me. It feels as if he is standing right next to me and directly I know that he is going to die this very day. I write a letter of farewell into my diary. Of course, afterwards I ask myself whether I just imagined all this, but something within me "knows." I want to dedicate the speech which I give later in the day to my father. I think of his experiences in the war, his escape and his days as a prisoner of war. An expansive silence takes hold of me.

In the evening I speak in a cinema in front of approximately 70 people. I speak in a firm and clear way, as if inspired. After the event I learn that my father has died. I lay awake for a long time. A gust of wind blowing through the window and a loudly croaking frog in front of it, seem to me like a greeting from his soul. Inge Seher, my host, lights many candles. "For the souls of our dead friends", she says.

Some days later during my morning meditation I playfully say: "Papa, let us open this book and see what message the page has in store for both of us." I take the little book with meditation texts into my hands and open it with my eyes shut. I read the following sentence: *It is given to me to see over death and see the life beyond it.* It is the only page in this booklet that refers in any way to the subject of death.

The gift of peace

After many visits and speeches at conferences and the events in Venice, Florence, Assisi, in the Toscana and Rome we take up the pilgrimage again – in the meantime two fellow pilgrims from Tamera joined me, Birger Bumb and Karola Koslowski. We walk through the mountainous landscape of the Abruzzi in the direction of the coast. The Goddess provides us with the riches of the land, there are nuts, almonds, tomatoes, figs, apples and wild herbs, everything we could wish for. One evening it starts to rain and we have to find a dry sleeping place. We find a stoneworker's room and are just about to arrange our edible gifts on a marble slab and even find a mattress, when a policeman drives up and asks to see our papers. We tell him that we are on a pilgrimage. After some initial scepticism he gradually becomes more and more friendly. He exchanges a few words with the owner of the place who in turn invites us to sleep in his office.

The following days we celebrate the pure bliss of existence. What a life! We walk through the Parco Nationale d'Abruzzo and enjoy the presence of life. In a small town I pay the flute in the church. For miles we walk through the solemn mountain landscape, the streets empty with no cars in sight. Once we find a sleeping place under a bridge. Trees and ferns offer a beautiful ambient. The expected rain does not fall. Birger who speaks some Italian is a real artist at begging. And pizzas, fruits, bread, nothing is lacking!

I receive the gift of peace - this deep happiness of landing - when all inner dialogue comes to a halt. May those who have been touched by it find the intelligence to pass it on, give it continuity so that this power of existence may find its place among all human beings. May Peace Prevail on Earth!

Finally, in Brindisi, we take the ferry to cross over to Greece. I am still engrossed in the blissful existence of a pilgrim. When the police wake you up at night and then tell you to carry on sleeping, you take it with joy and gratitude. When they wake you up and ask you to move on, you accept it without resistance, knowing, that the police too are part of God, who right there teaches me a lesson in the cosmic classroom which I gratefully accept. The key lesson consists of getting to know your vast inner emptiness. The inner Shechina does not spend much time with inner commentaries because she knows that this is a waste of energy and all it does is to deflect from the here and now. It is always the presence, where everything happens. In this presence hides the entire happiness of existence. How often do we let it pass us by and, instead, scurry on seeking for happiness in completely different places? The tucker-tucker of the ferry, the diary in front of me, two friends with me on board – "I need nothing and everything that I receive I accept with gratitude."

The silence of Dodona

The first night in Greece we spend on the concrete floor of a building site. I raise my gaze and watch the play of light of the

Greek sun. I see how some of the clouds throw their shadows onto a chain of freshly washed hills glittering after the rain. Warmly breathes Mother Earth and longingly she reaches out to us. She lets the sun rise within us as soon as we get in touch with her heart.

We visit the oracle site of Dodona, one of the oldest of the sacred places of Greece. Silently we climb up the hills and want to use the place for meditation in order to clarify some important questions we have. It is a special feeling, when one approaches an oracle site with the respect and the devotion of a pilgrim. The idea touches us that the place is full of a lively wisdom. Near the oracle I come across a praying mantis. I take it to be a sign telling me to carry on walking in silence and with great attention from this point on. Getting to know inner silence and becoming aware deeper and deeper of ones own thoughts is the most important lesson of a pilgrimage. Silence does not only mean the absence of talking. Everyone who has some practice in this is familiar with the many dialogues and inner chats that usually occupy us. True silence, devoid of any commentaries, creates majestic power and deep joy. At Dodona some of this wisdom of silence is alive and pulsating and those who become engrossed in it receive answers to essential inner questions. We spend a few hours at this almost deserted sacred site. Still today, the amphitheatre – one of the oldest of its kind – breathes the spirit of Greek theatre. Under an old oak tree, right next to the temple and in quiet contemplation, I find the answers I look for. Is it not a miracle that we are able to find the answers to our most important inner questions if only we learn to become quiet and to sincerely ask for the answers? Nothing spectacular happens just the calm and light. Inwardly strengthened I leave the site.

Birger and Karola bid farewell. Two new pilgrims take their place, Sonja Chaida and Chryssa Sotiraki, two young Greek women. We are also joined by Benjamin and Rico who had organised the pilgrimage in Israel/Palestine and now wanted to spend some time to prepare themselves mentally and spiritually for the weeks ahead.

Together we now have the time and the luxury to immerse ourselves in the soul of the Greek world. After speeches in and around Thessaloniki we walk below Mount Olympus. Majestically Zeus is enthroned above our heads. The first night we spend at the beach. I surrender to the sound of the waves and give thanks for the day which has led us through the wonderful coastal region at the foothills of Olympus. The continual roar of the surf washes away all unnecessary thoughts and cleanses the soul.

Chryssa and Sonja love to go to little taverns or shops to ask for some provisions. Our meals consist mostly of bread, tomatoes and goat cheese. We set out on a wonderful walk along the coast on easily passable paths. On the way it looks like rain. We have to look for shelter.

Meeting a Greek peasant

We enter a tavern to ask where we might find some quarters for the night. After keeping us waiting for some time a stout peasant appears who is the owner of the tavern. We explain to him that I am on a pilgrimage with no money and that the others have joined me out of solidarity. He is incredibly friendly. He offers that we spend the night in his garden, or, if it should rain, to come into his house in the tavern.

In the talks at many places I notice that a strong anti-American attitude prevails. In peoples heads the US is seen now as the perpetrator of evil. We get to hear the philosophy of a Greek peasant more intimately. Although he speaks quite good German he keeps changing languages. He had quickly copied out my information sheet on the pilgrimage.

"What you are doing right now is fabulous but you know, there are people who will not let this happen", he says in heavily broken German. "You know, they are only greedy for oil and money and power. And you want peace. Pang! They will destroy everything. If you say out loud that you want peace you have no chance. But God, up there", and he points to the sky, "God up there, he also sees this, he sees that while they pray for peace, they make war. And he punishes them all. You can see it, the natural disasters and all that. He will punish them even more. Not one of them will be left, if they do not get the message."

I throw in, that one could also refuse to follow those who engage in war, otherwise God will have to punish endlessly thus creating anew more fear and subsequent revenge. This chain has no end to it. If so many people do not want war, why then do they not simply disobey? "If we all stop participating, then God does not have to punish such a lot and they lose their power", and we both laugh about the simplicity of this logic.

Visit to the Oracle of Delphi

We take the bus for some of the way and then walk towards the oracle of Delphi. Surprised we find a 5000 year-old footpath which leads us up the hill. In my mind I connect with the many pilgrims who have walked this path before us for thousands of years. Today this path is seldom used, other than by a few mountain peasants. On the way we come across a sort of "Thing" place. Here we stop and look at the questions we wish to find answered at the place of the oracle.

Directly opposite the much-lauded oracle source, which normally is not open to visitors, we set up our camp for the night on the terrace of a little tavern. My inner voice gives me clear directions that we should hold a meditation there and so I ask to be woken up very early the next morning. At 4.30 a.m. I am woken up by the loud sounds of strange animals I do not recognise. Immediately I know that this is the sign for me to get up and meditate. What a magical place! I wake up Benjamin who also wants to experience dawn and to get in touch with his questions. In the darkness I step over a small fence. The high rock face with a high crevice fills the space with a dense frequency. Even the smallest stone falling can be heard. The source which must have run dry for some time now bubbles again. I have my recorder and my writing pad with me so that I can immediately note down all information I might receive. Sternly I am reprimanded by my inner voice and asked to leave these things aside. I have the impression that the soul of the guardian of this place is talking directly to me. I receive the clear instruction to remain quiet and to wait and see what will happen.

Remember the way the oracle was originally used. The information is meant to enter directly into your cell system. Connect to the living library of your cells. All knowledge is available there to be called forth. Writing or speaking only detracts from it and weakens the cellular memory.

With quiet respect and full of awe I sit surrounded by cosmic silence. Then, slowly, the words rise within me, powerful like a gushing source. I am still not allowed to write them down. For hours I sit and await the sunrise.

Meanwhile the others have also come and sat themselves down. It feels to me, as if the rock faces start to move, as if I can look through them and through the history of the stone and enter into the dimension of eternity. Everything is happening now. To me it all seems like a perfect, magical and mystical experience. In front of me the high-reaching rock soars up. Each falling stone, even the smallest, echoes loudly. The niches hewn into the walls and the old oracle font set in them make the past come alive. I can feel the energy of those who came to seek answers, who sat here fasting for days in order to prepare their souls and their spirit for the visit to the temple. I am in a space of absolute silence. I can almost touch the layer of existence in which all matter is pure consciousness. With the dissolution of all inner thoughts which create separation, it seems that the outer wall too is dissolving right there in front of me. It becomes transparent and pervious. The dimension of eternity becomes noticeable behind all of the assembled history of this place. It is the metaphysical aspect of life which looms straight into my perception and almost takes my breath away. From inside words are now coming out like a pulsating force, individual, very alive, very definite, very simple, very clear.

Now I am allowed to make notes. I record the following words:

The message of the oracle

Few words, clear words, simple words, true words.
The great gate of reunification opens up in a silence devoid of comments.
When knowledge is extended where it is not wanted, it creates resistance.
Therefore, enter through the gate of silence and listen from there.
Open up the chambers of your heart from where the power of eternal love flows to reconcile the past, the present and the future.
Enter into the great light of the eternal view.
From there history emerges.
Recognize the great "Tat twam asi": You are this.
Out of a pure heart a non-violent culture will grow.
It is waiting to be recognized and found.
Simple words, true words, clear words, loving words hold out a hand for reconciliation.
Exercise patience and wait until you are asked.
This is the secret of pure teaching.
It is the secret of many wise women and men. It opens the gate to understanding.
Find your way back to the bottom of the soul where you know: I am loved.
I am loved.
I have been made by love and I create love.
Open up the chambers of the heart to this eternal view.
Any type of teaching that uses too many words still originates from the high-spiritedness of youth.
In the big silence the door to the new dimension opens up.
Here, your great eternal and Marian nature begins to shine.
Anticipated mental disappointment, anticipated misgivings seduce and lead you into the world of legends, into the world of separation.
Keep your spirit clear, true and pure.
Recognize your thoughts of misgivings early and learn to use the switch in your hand, more and more.

Send out the living light.
Open up the great gate of the view of love.
Draw back all remaining bolts, so that you learn to let God in.
Trust that you will receive all the knowledge at the right time. This trust speeds up the process of healing.
Send the light to the experts of finance and industry.
Send to them the light of love for them to learn what it means not to hoard but to give and, therefore, to expand their inner richness.
May the flow of money find a humane path.
Open up the gate so that the spirit of humanisation may flow freely into humane projects. This helps to initiate the immanent shift in the present era.
Use spiritual might to send to the human beings ethical maturity, that those who receive the money will administer it with love and spend it in the name of healing.
Guard the gate of simplicity, of modesty and of the power of the heart.
Pay attention and hold the chambers of the heart open.
Accept the gift of self-love. This is the key to increase peace power wherever you are. Those, who have learnt to love themselves, will no longer exert violence against others.
Those who have learnt to love themselves are connected to the divine light. Love and recognize yourself, this is the beginning of all things.

The aftermath

I pause with quiet respect and with gratitude. The sacred aspect of the world, the Sacred Matrix, is within reach. I experience how reality is permanently created by the power of thought and how it writes the book of history. Throughout all of Creation the Sacred Matrix of a larger, eternal reality is shining through from beyond, a reality which has never been absent. It is an all encompassing peace which is waiting to enter the consciousness of mankind with all its complex dimensions.

Pioneers are active - as helping forces - to open the gates and make it easier for others to pass through them. Those who are not subjected to inner separation anymore can help to initiate the new future and nothing hostile will come across their path.

In between I dare ask a few critical questions, such as: How was it possible that Jesus was nailed to the cross? Very clearly and very intensely the following answer came: "Because thoughts of separation as a field building force still form your history and also your idea of history. In the next higher dimension this history will change itself and you will recognize the reality of resurrection."

Such statements originating from a spiritual dimension have often raised my anger and indignation. It seems that the reality of the crucifixion and with it the reality of human suffering on Earth is being totally ignored. Presently though, I am in a state of being, where I allow this statement to have an effect on me without any comments. Behind all the words I sense the larger power of universal love and compassion. It is not a time for discussion.

I experience these quiet hours as a highlight in my preparation for the pilgrimage through Israel. Will I be able to keep this experience with me when I sit in front of a wall that is eight meters high and separates two peoples?

The visit afterwards to the temples of Delphi I experience as in a dream. I sit on the top of the mountain and look down on the temples while I let the reminiscence of the experience dwell inside of me. Over all the mystic experience I completely forgot to eat. Mostly in silence and with thankfulness we walk back on the path towards the seaside.

Appearances on television and meetings in Athens follow organised by friends from our network. I am touched that the earnest search for new forms of living is spreading throughout Europe. We are even offered land for the foundation for a Peace Research Village in Greece - a possible base for GRACE, the Movement for a Free Earth?

From Athens our flight leaves for Tel Aviv. This distance is covered a little too fast for the soul of a pilgrim. I very much regret that no other means exist for me to get to Israel. The shipping traffic between Greece and Israel has completely shut down. Passengers off freighters are not accepted into Israel and are turned back.

Part II:
In the Holy Land

Acknowledgements to the Leading Team

In the following part of the book I hardly ever mention anything about the organisation that went into making this pilgrimage possible. This is entirely due to the high quality of our team. The team members could fill a book of their own of how in the background throughout the pilgrimage through Israel/Palestine they took care that the group was not bothered by any organisational questions. Benjamin von Mendelssohn, Vera Kleinhammes, Kate Bunney, Tamir Yaari, Klaus Wuttig, Rico Portilho, Juliane Eckmann, Janka Striffler, Amelie Weimar, it is incredible what these people were able to accomplish and undertake together. Big thanks go to them all. Special thanks go to the support team with Benjamin, Kate, Vera, Rico and Klaus. At times they were challenged to their limits. Generously they provided services all day and often at night too.

They were challenged to the utmost to adopt the spiritual rules of the pilgrimage with the abundance of daily organisational tasks. It was a very real challenge for them to be able to adapt the daily wide-ranging tasks organisation to the spiritual rules of the pilgrimage. Not react, not judge, flexibility in every moment. *I need nothing and all that I receive I accept gratefully.*

To keep this sentence of empowerment alive in everyday life amounts to a spiritual training course for advanced students. Without the full commitment of this team and their good team spirit the pilgrimage could not have become what it did. Everyone who participated has developed further his or her cosmic professional formation and receives the "Certificate of Creation" for having proven themselves in difficult situations.

In the background a team of journalists with Leila Dregger and others accompanied the pilgrimage. They rightly call themselves peace journalists. The group initiated action for the long-term effect. Almost every day Leila coordinated a meeting for the journalist group. The subject of the meetings was always focussed on the question of what the next steps could be.

Angelika Reicherter accompanied us as an independent film-maker. For her too it was a big challenge to be part of what happened and to nevertheless retain the impartial eye of a documentary filmmaker. Often this tested her to the limit. Her film "We refuse to be enemies" is now being shown publicly.

Every one of us is occupied in his own way with the harvest. All are now asking themselves what remains to be done so that healing and effective peace work can go forward. To all of us it is a concern that the public learns more about the real situation in this country and in such a way that the information reaches open hearts. Thanks are due to Kate and Klaus for the flexibility and effectiveness of their organisational abilities and as well to their good humour. Thanks are also owed to Tamir for his caring and nature-loving accompaniment. And thanks are due as well to Benjamin for his unstinting operational readiness and leadership which was always supported by the quieter but equally committed and helpful Vera. Because of them we were able to wander through a land in conflict as an effective communitarian body and were also able to invite more and more people to participate in this experience. It was the spirit of community which often brought about the miracles opening up to us doors which otherwise might have remained shut and in the most difficult situations gave us the humour and the perseverance to see the country through many eyes in a way that would have been impossible for an individual. The veterinarian, Irma Fäthke, a member of the eco-village "Sieben Linden" in Germany subsequently said: "We never had a real quarrel. I have never before experienced this in a group. This is a sign of true leadership quality." There were disagreements, but they never became emotional but rather led to understanding on a higher plain. I thank all those who have contributed to this miracle.

I also thank all the friends of Tamera around the world who have helped to sustain our energy with their meditations and those who have financially, or in any other way, supported the entire venture. May the light of a future worth living and a future of love warm their hearts, and make a new fulfilling tomorrow dawn for all of us and for the generations that will come after us.

In the Name of GRACE!

Arrival in Israel

Arrival on the day of Sukkot

Israel is expecting me! For me it is a feeling as if I were coming home. For long have I yearned for this day! Now it has become a reality. Tired, almost asleep, we let the many passport and arrival controls simply wash over us. There are some complications since I cannot prove that I have a return flight booked. After much of this examination and at four in the morning we are finally allowed to pass into Israel. Vera is there to collect us. Venturous, tall, blond, she stands in front of me. What joy to see each other again! A full moon is shining in the sky. Is it coincidence that of all days I arrive at Sukkot? It is the feast of booths, a Jewish day of celebration. Believers build little huts in the garden or on the terrace to remind themselves of the pilgrimage of their ancestors and of the divine guidance. For one week some of them sleep in these huts instead of in their houses.

It is also the day for GRACE, explains Emma Shamba Ayalon, one of our long-time Israeli friends, as she invites us into her little hut on the roof of her home for the evening meal. Utterly deprived of sleep, I feel like I am in an endless film. I am so moved and grateful for all I have experienced thus far and for all that is still to come. Tomorrow we are going to visit the place where we shall hold the Wall Meditation on November 9th. During the next few days we shall also begin rehearsals for the play.

The play: We refuse to be enemies

During our four weeks of pilgrimage through Israel and the West Bank we shall perform our play "We refuse to be enemies" in many places. The piece was created in 2002 after our first peace camp together with Israelis and Palestinians in Tamera. The many moving stories of struggles, conflicts and longing for peace from both Jewish and Palestinian history were translated into a theatre manuscript by the students of Tamera. From this manuscript, during a journey, I staged, rehearsed and finally put on a play with them which went on for almost an hour. Wherever we performed, the spectators were moved by its human and political depth and its healing power. In summer of 2003 we took the play on a peace tour together with Palestinian and Israeli musicians among them the well-known Israeli musician Yair Dalal which took us through Germany, Switzerland and Austria. Spectators kept asking us to stage the play also in the Middle East. The pilgrimage should now make it finally possible to fulfil this request.

The story: The piece tells of the conflict in the Middle East from the viewpoint of an alien. It opens with a young Palestinian suicide attacker, Jamal, who enters a crowded discotheque in Tel Aviv counting the seconds for the bomb to go off. Also in the disco are Stella, an alien, and the reporter Kim of Cosmic Radio together with many Israeli youth who are after a good time just like any other young people anywhere in the world. They do not know yet that this night something is going to happen. Kim interviews the young suicide attacker: "What led you to this decision?" Embittered Jamal answers. He talks about the other side of the country, about the suffering of his people, the Palestinians who have been deprived of everything: the villages, the trees, the land. "And at last Fatima, my Fatima. They shot her. Simply shot her."

Jamal wants revenge. Kim looks for his mother and wants to find out whether Jamal can still be stopped. But her pain and embitterment are too deeply embedded. Is there no solution at all? Kim begins to research on the other side. She meets David, another visitor to the disco. Like everyone else he too is a soldier. "Do you like being a soldier?", she asks him.

From David we learn something of the inner life of a soldier and learn how it is to be a member of the occupying forces. We experience the constant presence of threat in Israel and the belief there of being able to survive only through violence. We meet his grandmother who had survived the concentration camp in Germany and we hear of the history of the Jewish people which for two thousand years has been looking for a safe place, a place without enemies. "They want to throw us into the sea", David's grandmother shouts and Jamal's mother shouts: "They want to banish us."

"Enemies, what exactly does that mean?" asks Stella, the alien. "From my point of view they are all human beings and they all want to live. David's grandmother and Jamal's mother could end their hostility but they would have at least to listen to each other." The attempt at establishing a holographic frequency transfer fails; both of them are too deeply entangled in their hostile thinking. The international cartel becomes visible too, the powerful of this Earth who pull their strings in the background and sew antagonism in order to partition the world amongst themselves. Not only Israel and Palestine also South America, Africa, the entire world is under their spell. But only as long as we project power onto them – through our fear, through our beliefs of being powerless and through our indifference. The cry of the alien finally defuses the bomb. An international force for a new challenge, a deep connection to life and the mutual refusal of each individual to be enemies are necessary to end the war permanently. "In times past, all human beings were aliens", says Stella at the end. "We have to help them to remember."

Shaar'ladam – the gateway to God – in Harduf

Before the beginning of the pilgrimage the core group met for a few days in Harduf, an anthroposophic kibbutz in the North of Israel, in order to make the last preparations and to rehearse the play. A committed group had founded this community around the same time as we did our own. During the seventies they had come together to develop an entirely new way of living together. Many from the original core group are still living here today. They wanted to incorporate positive approaches into the kibbutz and they were decided to do it differently than did the generation of their parents. The teachings of Rudolf Steiner were an important inspiration to them. Their radical community idea has today faded somewhat into the background. The daily life in the kibbutz takes place in more or less traditional family structures. Many from the founding group told us that with regard to community development in Harduf they have more or less failed. Too much comparison and rivalry have come between them. The subject of money and also the unresolved issue of sexuality had been too difficult. In the meantime community life switched to a high social, spiritual, ecological and political engagement. Theatre, art and crafts, gardening, work with disabled and child education form the social web. Nevertheless, one can feel a communal spirit presiding over everything.

We were offered the hostel in the woods. Shaar'ladam, the gateway to God, is the name of this oasis, where a small group of people wants to live in total harmony with nature. The group of three men and two young women has been living in the woods for about half a year. Gardens and small houses were developed without any artificial intervention from machines. We had a large tepee at our disposal. It serves us as habitation and work space. The first night the inhabitants of this place stayed in the tent with us. This was not easy for us who longed for our own work-space where we could concentrate without interference. Our partners however were more than accommodating. After a talk the following day they decide at once to leave the "Dome" to us.

Quickly things settled down between us and we soon felt like one big family. One of the leaders here is called Rehi. He radiates a lot of heartiness and peace. He is the classical figure of a wise human being, in touch with nature, coming across positively to us almost like a character out of a novel. We feel a little bit like the nomads of old who have been sent on pilgrimage by God to return home to the Holy Land.

Harry

One of our central supporters in Israel is Harry Finkbeiner. Originally from Germany he has lived in Harduf since its foundation together with his Israeli wife and three children. What distinguishes him is that despite everything he has never given up. Full of compassion he stands up everyday for human rights in this country. He has kept an open mind. Due to his being very close to Judaism and Jewish belief he reacts with shudders and indignation at the injustices he sees occurring in this country. Because of his idealism he was during the first years unaware of the political background. Then all of a sudden it dawned on him and he began, along with his engagement in the kibbutz to become involved on the Palestinian side. "Israel contravenes its own constitution. The way politics are today we should have no right to be here." He speaks with a full engagement for human rights. If one is listening to him one might think him to be anti-Semitic. But he is anything but that. He dreams of a blooming Israel where justice and charity reign and the Arab population stands beside them on an equal footing. There can only be a free Israel when there is a freed Palestine. He stoutly supports this view.

In its origin the kibbutz movement was once engaged with a regenerative force affected by the secularized idea of paradise: one wanted to bring God's paradise to Earth. Many leftist students came from Germany to Israel to learn in the Kibbutzim. The nationalistic character of the movement, the military bent and the suffering and misery that went with it became only slowly clearer to the successive generations. Unfortunately this was also associated with the failure of the entire kibbutz movement. The idea of narrow nationalistic community thought changing into one with global awareness will probably only be written in the distant future. The foundation of a peace village in Israel where Palestinians and Israelis lay the basis of a peace community might though be a powerful start. The small village of Neve Shalom/Wahat al-Salam has made the first firm steps towards this dream and then at this point the healing aspects of the kibbutz movement can be taken up again.

Harry supports us unreservedly wherever he can. He bristles with energy. He has already organised many peace marches for Middleway, an Israeli peace initiative and he does not balk at facing the military, radical settlers or radical representatives of Hamas. He enters into contact with all of them and tries to speak to them. He is outspoken and does not mince matters. He expresses what he thinks. For this he is loved and consulted by many. His knowledge is in demand not only at a political level. Harry is also a healer and as such people come to him. From birth he had a lame arm and found ways to heal himself. This led him to become a chiropractor in order to pass on his healing knowledge to others. He firmly believes in inner guidance.

The cosmic tribe

On some evenings we share together beautiful fireside feasts in the pine woods of Shaar'ladam. I feel once more like a nomad returned from an ancient past who meets her cosmic tribe again. The new pilgrimage in the Promised Land begins. More and more people join who are ready to leave behind the tyranny of violence and opt for community life. I feel like a witness of an era where a new civilization is being born. Until late at night we sit around the fire where moving words are spoken about more truth and humane contact between us all. Aida Shibli, a young Bedouin and engaged peace activist speaks about her first contact with Tamera. I well remember the letter she wrote me which asked what difference it would make to her and other people in war zones if we, living in a secure peaceful place, build up communities for the future. In her search for real answers she wrote "Our families will continue to be killed, exploited and daily we have to witness innocent people dying."

I wrote a long letter back to her. I wrote about the field-building force and about my deeply held belief that it ought to be possible to develop peace at one place on this Earth. If this can be successful, it will then affect the whole. So, one day she came to Tamera. Since then her life has changed fundamentally. Between us we have developed friendship and cooperation.

Songs, laughter and deep conversations fill the evening. I let myself be touched by the beauty and depth of the Jewish soul in its originality and pureness. Alongside the brightness and passion of the Arab world radiates towards me. Aida's speech about her people touches the listeners. It seems to me that the Jewish soul matures by withdrawing into its religious denomination and quiet reflection, forever looking for places where it can be, undisturbed and free of persecution and the threat of annihilation. The Arab element however is looking for expansion, contact, community, passion, dancing and the weighing of strength. We speak of the original united family which let in the great rift which developed between the two peoples. We speak about Hagar, the servant of Abraham, who became pregnant by him. Later, when Sarah, Abraham's wife, also became pregnant, Sarah became very jealous. So she had Hagar and her son Ismael exiled into the desert. Is it not interesting, that the primary rift of this country has to do with a conflict about jealousy and strife? Is it not self-evident that we need entirely new patterns for the solution of these intimate, social structures in human history? Because these everyday conflicts of love pop up all over the place, we think they are normal. One declares the illness to be the cure! Since everyone suffers from the same illness nobody takes any notice of it. Hardly anyone would fathom out that these simple elementary situations of everyday life are the root cause of the global conflict and that therein too lays the possible source for a solution. I find it important that we do not overlook these very simple and elementary questions.

Nevertheless, it must never be overlooked that Jews and Arabs have for hundreds of years been able to live peacefully alongside each other. Only later when the international powers supported the sending of Jews to a land which had already for centuries been populated by the Palestinians did the conflict explode in this extreme manner. This is the political side of the conflict which, nevertheless, has the same origin, namely, the estrangement of the human being from its true loving nature.

Performing the play

We spend our time with rehearsals, with the planning of routes, and the painting of shields. We distribute the different tasks and form ourselves into a group. The days are more than full. The management team was fully occupied. For me this meant quite a change in my ways. As the leader I am challenged with the task of seeing to it that the group is not awash with organisational questions. What is when and where? Who meets whom? Which text has to be finished? What goes in the internet? Who collects whom? In between all this there are interviews with the prominent daily paper Haaretz and others. Daily the faithful Kate is on the phone for hours in order to prepare the appropriate contacts. Angelika Reicherter, the filmmaker, has arrived to accompany our path and to make a documentary record.

Again and again the daily morning attunements give us thoughts for the day which help maintain the creative power. For the first time I come into intimate contact with the Jewish notion of angels. I get to know the cosmic being of the angel Gabriel, the angel of discipline. What an inspiring imagination to let an angel of discipline take oneself by the hand! Up to now I have always considered discipline to be an essentially human characteristic. Indeed it is our task not to act purely from our own strength, but to allow discipline to bring us together. What a wonderful idea, to let this concept of discipline take us by the hand and to surrender the leadership to a higher power.

Towards the end of our five days stay the first public performance takes place for the inhabitants of Harduf. We announce it as a public dress rehearsal. Approximately 50 guests are arriving. The director of the theatre of Harduf, Jakow, gives the introductory speech. Afterwards Harry speaks.

There is much trembling inside of us. What will happen with the spectators when outsiders confront them with their own history? Will they feel patronized? Will it offend them?

But in fact the spectators become spellbound. We see them moved and forcefully struck by the play. We see tears flowing and, although I am on stage, I too can hardly hold back the tears at times. Our voices begin to tremble more and more. It is an enormous challenge to keep up the tension. At the end of the play we light six candles in memory of the victims of the war. Each actor leaves the stage after lighting a candle. Magic silence in the hall! When we created this scene we had not been aware of the Israeli custom of lighting six candles in memory of the six million victims of the Holocaust.

When the play was over the tension was enormous. One could have heard a needle drop in the room. Then the release of the applause! We move to a smaller room, and become completely silent.

For us too the play has every time something of a cathartic effect. We are then invited to a talk. We are overwhelmed by the positive feedback. It is a challenge for us to take in the many acknowledgments. Many are saying that the play has a healing effect upon the soul. Still one can see in their faces how they are touched. They thank us for the purity of the play; they thank us that we did not permit any cynicism. They thank us for the courage and the hope this play awakens. Mainly Jewish families are present. But also from the Palestinian side we receive acknowledgment, from a man who only recently lost two members of his family. We had not reckoned on such a positive response.

The next day the pilgrimage through the Holy Land begins.

Pilgrimage to the Sea of Galilee

The holy aspect of the land

We begin the pilgrimage on the Golan Heights in the Northern part of Israel, in the headwaters of the Jordan River and walk from there towards the Sea of Galilee. According to international law the Golan Heights belonged to Syria before they were occupied by Israel after the six-day-war in 1967 and annexed in 1981.

Our guide's name is Tamir Yaari, an Israeli, who, like no other human being, knows the essence of this country and its nature. The ascent towards the waterfall where the river has its greatest flow beneath Mount Hermon draws us into the frequency of being on pilgrimage. Quietly the land discloses the whole aspect of its soul. Who after all would know that this small country holds in store such fertile and powerful places for the true seeker? The water is loaded with high energy. Despite all this beauty the essence of war is continually present. We feel it everywhere. Like a cenotaph, a Syrian tank lies in the middle of a beautiful water basin where the water forcefully roars and gushes around it. In the war of 1967 it fell into the abyss. There it now lies telling its story. We hold a meditation and in front of me I see many lost souls devoid of orientation. Repeatedly the strong cue is received to maintain the contact with the ancestors during our peace marches.

Later we walk through the Golan Heights finding plantations of fruits and avocados. The stinging heat soon changes our mentality into that of Bedouins. Everything switches to an inner standstill. Quietly we put one foot in front of the other. All that exists is the present. Any irritating thought robs energy. One feels as old as eternity. Presently a turtle crosses our way. While taking a bath in a river, Vera was almost touched by a kingfisher which was being chased by a falcon. She has probably saved its life since the falcon's flight was checked by her when it had the bird almost in its claws. This gift of a few seconds gave the kingfisher time to disappear.

In an oasis with a water basin we find our encampment for the night. Tamir has been living in a natural cave for a long time. He has small kettles with him and provides us with tea and coffee. In the big kettle we later on prepare some soup with the vegetables we had brought along. Since we have to carry everything the food is frugal but tastes all the better for that. After a small gathering around the fire we turn in early.

The next day after the meditation at sunrise we set off into the early morning. Now it is the animals that lead our consciousness into the full presence. We see different birds of prey even some eagles amongst them and there are also marmots, gazelles, wild boar, cranes, jackal, all at close range. Snakes too and unusual grasshoppers cross our path. One gets the impression that all the creatures which live here want to show themselves to us.

The land of extremes

In the middle of a desert landscape we discover a hollow in the ground filled with hot water. It is magical to lie in the midday heat in a hot tub in the middle of the wilderness. A broad fountain of water shoots out of the earth. It is so hot that we cannot bathe in it. One and a half metres high the fountain shoots into the air with an average width of one metre. We learn that the water comes up from 1400 metres beneath the earth. This land lives from its extremes.

Very quickly we tune in to being a group. It is as if we were walking through time and space under the roof of eternity fathoming out each depths and each detail. Sometimes seconds appear to expand ad infinitum.

Days pass as if we would have touched them with wings. Boundaries shift and new spaces of consciousness open up. The inner realm is present in its smallest contours, nothing remains hidden, it appears to move to the outer realm like an involute body.

Dream and reality walk hand in hand. If we were to be asked who we are and where we are going to, I would now answer: we are wanderers from the past and the future preparing a new presence. Already the faces in our group have changed completely during the past few days. The pure life in nature has the power to effect the changes and the essence of human beings shows itself untarnished.

Shabbat in the desert

In a derelict former Syrian village we meet for the celebration of Shabbat. Rabbi Ohad Ezrahi and his wife Dawn, and Emma Shamba Ayalon arrive from Tel Aviv together with others who would have liked to pilgrimage with us. The bullet holes in the walls of the old ruin remind us of the war between Israel and Syria. Around us even much older ruins, of over 2000 years ago, remind us of times long past.

Boaz, an Israeli war invalid, has settled down here. "My house is your house" he hospitably welcomes us.

Outside, on a carpet, we have festively installed our camp. Simple food, a wood fire, singing and prayer unite the various human aspects which are assembled here. Ohad and Dawn powerfully lead the chants of Shabbat. Tamir speaks a simple prayer. In the meditation we look back on the past week and welcome everything we have experienced.

Six wild pigs appear and greet us from a respectful distance. Seldom have I seen so many animals as I have done during these last days. They seem to have become curious about the new paradise and the reconciliation between human being and animal. They are part of a large developing movement, the Movement for a Free Earth.

In the Stone Circle of Rugum Harliri

Our next goal is the old stone circle of Rugum Harliri. Shmuel Shaul is expecting us there. For many years he has been involved with the study of the landscape and the soul of the country of Israel/Palestine. He tries to include the contact with the Earth in his healing work with human beings. He is a man who seems to be known to me immediately. One meets with a basic feeling of: "Ah, there you are again, finally!"

Together we develop a little ritual which is to connect us to the ancestors of primordial times. Many groups begin with an outlook on Israel's history by addressing the migration of Moses with Abraham and his descendants. Only a few look at the much older history of the tribes and the cultures which before had peacefully lived in this land. They adored nomad Gods and Goddesses, Baal or Astarte, asked for fertility, rain and protection. The rituals served to celebrate Creation. They were the religions of Creation which shaped the cultures of that time. Only much later religions of redemption came into being which made the human being look up to the one august God. While today the reconciliation of world religions is more often than not the main subject for discussion, the questions of "When do we reconcile ourselves with our earlier past?" and "When will we reconcile ourselves with the "Geist" of the Goddess?" are left untouched.

In the midst of pastures and cultivated land lays the age-old memorial noticed only by few people. A ring similar to a labyrinth has been built from countless middle-sized stones. In its centre there is a sort of dome inside which the feeling is of a womb.

While on the arched roof the group chants an Israeli mantra that means: "I am the being, I shall be" each one of us enters into the approximately 7000 year old cave-like room below the earth to formulate his or her personal prayer. To us, the mantra seems to last forever, vibrating as a cosmic sound in the ether. While we sing all sorts of inner resistances crop up and enter my consciousness crystal clear. "It takes too long. It is too cold. It is too holy. I am tired. I

113

want to sleep" the small battle rants and raves within me. It seems to me, as if I could read in the faces of the others about what is happening inside them. But by and by we all, even to the last of us, surrender. At first there is surrender, followed by joy and finally comes the power. Forcefully the chant swells and thereafter a large exhilaration spreads amongst the group. The tiredness and the exhaustion of the long walk have totally disappeared. For a long time we stay at the fire talking.

We lay sleeping on our mats for about two hours. Soft sounds of sleeping souls fill the muggy summer air, but we are then woken up by sudden rainfall. At first quietly and friendly, then more and more heavily! No roof in sight! Astonishingly the entire group reacts with cheerfulness and serenity. Humour and cheeriness quickly lighten anything that threatens to become too heavy. When the rain stops again we try to dry the wet things by the fire and wait for the first morning light. No thought of sleep anymore. Despite heavy rain clouds the rising sun is showing herself in full glory.

In the tracks of Jesus

We walk and walk. Endlessly today's path spans ahead of us. Vera radiates and bubbles with humour. Again and again I can clearly hear her bright laughter and that of Janka. Every one of us comes in touch with his or her limits and the power that is hidden behind them. Each one of us, at different points, is challenged to extend his boundaries. In the distance we see the Sea of Galilee and we walk towards it. We become aware that we are walking in the tracks of Jesus of Nazareth. I am astonished and glad how this far away past touches me, as if it had been only yesterday. We are in a festive mood and harbour feelings that are both known and familiar to us.

On the way we pass a large enclosure with turkeys. At first I am shocked about this type of mass animal farming and then it gives way to astonishment as in hundreds the turkeys come towards the fence in front of us. Expectantly they watch us. Tamir makes a gurgling sound. At the same moment they all together make a peculiar sound which swells up almost like a full orchestra and sounds as if a large audience was cheering for us. An incredible scenario, never seen or heard before!

While we approach the Sea of Galilee it becomes quieter in the group. Almost divine feelings overcome me. I am in a trance-like state, not quite free of pain, since during the past weeks I had developed typist's neuritis. But it is not difficult for me to overlook this small sting of pain. The path runs on endlessly. Tamir was noticeably out in his estimation of distance. Every time we thought we were about to arrive, the path kept winding on for another few kilometres. Laughingly we notice that each new corner adds on another five kilometres. Many of the paths are full of water and cannot be recognized as such anymore. At one point we wade for about 700 metres through water which reaches up to our thighs. The group is amused since I wade quite unperturbed through the water with my boots and clothes on. I am far too tired to want to change anything. It is as if my feet had taken over the walking programme themselves and I follow them obediently. In the background the bright laughter from Vera, Juliane and Janka can be heard again as they practice walking on the water!

In the night we find shelter underneath some palm trees and eucalyptus trees. Again we are woken up by the rain in the middle of the night. We move closer to the tree trunks and arrange a small living room underneath a palm tree, astonished how much protection it would provide. Sonja is steadfast, stays out lying in the rain and calmly asks what time it is.

Reception of the new pilgrims in Tagbha

Early in the morning of October 31st we set off for Tagbha. This is the place where our pilgrimage is open for anyone who wishes to participate. We have formulated a public paper in which the ground rules for the pilgrimage are announced. All participants commit to walk with us in the "Geist" of GRACE, independently of any world view or religion they might adhere to. During this pilgrimage we are all disciples of GRACE.

I shall quote some of the spiritual guidelines which we had already published in our letter of invitation. They are meant to remind us that we have come in the name of GRACE.

Spiritual guidelines for the pilgrimage

- From peace comes the force.
- I am part of the community and I live according to the principles of solidarity and compassion.
- I honour and obey the rules of each place I enter and I leave each place more beautiful than when I entered it.
- I nourish thoughts of trust. Danger arises out of thoughts of fear. I therefore deal consciously and carefully with my thoughts.
- I am part of the community and respect the rhythm of the community.
- I am thankful for mirrors from the community. I learn from my mistakes and from those of others.
- I shall commit myself to a communal space of stillness each day and to choose those forms of meditation and prayer that fit with me.
- I take full responsibility for my thoughts, my words and my actions.
- I do not allow myself to act from egoistical thoughts and to lead unnecessary discussions.
- I help wherever I can and ask for help when I need help myself.
- I lead a simple life as regards sleeping, eating and drinking. Here too, I follow the monastic rules of the community.

We arrive at the Benedictine monastery of Tagbha which is located directly on the shores of the Sea of Galilee. It is the place of the multiplication of the bread, the place where the famous feeding of the 5000 took place. Friendly monks welcome us. The same evening our first public theatre performance is to take place. The rainy nights left their toll and have affected my voice. Tried by the forces of nature we stand on the stage in the evening. Two singers Michal Talya and Jutta Wurm, one from Israel and the other from Germany accompany our performance with their songs.

On an open-air-stage we act with full concentration in front of approximately seventy spectators. Many Israelis and Palestinians have asked us to stage the play in Israel. This encouraged us. International peace workers tended to warn us that bringing the play to Israel would be a risk. We have to be prepared for much anger and indignation. Now, for the first time we face the hour of truth. Harduf was more or less a "home game" since the people who meet there are anyway all engaged in the peace movement. We feel relief as we notice that even though our play arouses heavy discussion among the anonymous audience it also meets with positive resonance. It was often commented that the play incorporated a certain "consciously created naivety", especially with regard to the difficult topic of conflict, but that it was able to open hearts which had been closed for a long time.

One of the spectators is Haya Shalom, who like my self was nominated for "1000 Women for the Nobel Peace Prize 2005." Coming totally from the political movement, she had her problems with our play. "loo many stereotypes", she said, and that in reality everything is much more complicated. Nevertheless she is visibly touched and stays with us during the first day of introduction.

We also get to know David Lisbona an engaged man from the Israeli peace movement. He calls himself a Zionist who is deeply moved by peace. Amongst other things he is also a co-founder of the group Middleway. In the course of the coming weeks he will join us from time to time and will become an ever more intimate friend giving us important information and often acting as a supporter in the background.

On the following morning, on November 1st we welcome our new co-pilgrims. At the lake shore we hold the first joint morning attunement. Again I am touched by the closeness of Jesus. It felt as if he were sitting amongst us. What a historical place! A goodly sized group of 50 people has come together. Not all of them will be with us for the rest of the way. After a "geistig" introduction where we familiarize the new participants with the "geistig" rules of the pilgrimage and the basic thoughts of GRACE we go to a small cave above the lake for a meditation. Here too it is as if I could feel the power of Jesus. I see him in front of me as he often must have been sitting here in his search for the connectedness to God, whom he called Abba, dear Father. Every pilgrim was asked to reflect upon his own decision and to see whether there were any further questions regarding the pilgrimage ahead of him. Afterwards we move a few metres down to a roaring waterfall which gushes directly into the lake. Here we bathe and baptise our new group, ask for physical health and protection and strengthen ourselves. These were two entirely different energies we came in touch with one after the other in short succession. One leads to quiet reflection where as the other one vitalises and energises the whole body with elementary power.

In a sharing circle in which everyone has the opportunity to talk about their concerns, Haya Shalom extends her most heartfelt thanks. She says that during this day she has regained something which she had long lost - the connection to a simple spiritual source. The gist of what she said was: "The unsentimental way you pray, helps me to be able to pray again."

We go to bed early. The next morning we shall start out on our path. The focus now is on forming a mutual group body. We are apprentices together and learn what it can mean to be on the move in the name of GRACE.

On the Way to another Life

The group-body

Blessed by the rain and in the new formation we pilgrimage for the first few kilometres on a country road, at first silently, later walking in pairs talking about the questions we were given. At the front someone is always carrying the GRACE shield drawing behind him a colourful snake of human beings moving through the desert-like countryside.

The first challenge is to establish a group to arrive at a basis for common harmonic vibration. Each participant arrives here with his personal history, with his hopes and with his injuries. Some of them have come to Israel for the first time. Very different views of the world are held by us. Everybody is represented, from relatively orthodox Jews, to anarchists, political hardliners, feminists, and Buddhists as well as young students whose attitude is characterised by an openness towards the world. The youngest amongst us, Joanna, is 18 years old and Alice with her 70 years is our tribal elder. As of now we start the morning by counting the group members so that we can be sure no one gets lost. The leaders impress on everyone to be alert, keeping altogether by forming a long snake and that we look out for the people in front and those behind us. This exercise in awareness seems to be a little too difficult right at the outset. The cosmos imparts a teaching. Two people are not with us at the first break. Equanimity is our first exercise. Search parties are sent off. After a good hour the two surface again. At some point our snake had suffered a cut. In deep conversation, not seeing anyone ahead of them they had marched straight on past a parting of the ways.

Our path leads us through the Arbel valley. From here a steep ascent begins passing caves and cliffs. The first day's route amounts to 22 kilometres which is quite a challenge for the newcomers. At an ancient synagogue we hold a ritual. Everyone speaks a word into the circle which he associates with peace. Tamir sings a psalm. His voice echoes from the surrounding rock faces. Way below us lays the Sea of Galilee. Even now, though still far away from us, its special energy and intimate contact with Jesus' deeds are accompanying us on our way. It leaves a deep imprint on my soul.

A small group of international women joins us for a few hours. This is to happen often during this pilgrimage. We have to adapt ourselves to the fact that we are not a closed communal body of pilgrims but are open for Israelis and for people of other nations that happen to be in the country. This time because time was short we did not manage to really get to know each other and exchange ideas. Later we shall get better at it. In the evening the women depart again somewhat disappointed.

First arguments

During our first lunch break heavy discussions flare up amongst our co-pilgrims. The subject is the purpose of the wall. Joel, an American orthodox Jew, passionately represents the view that the wall has avoided suicide attacks and that the wall supports the peace process. Harry is against it and speaks in a dedicated way about his experiences with Palestinians. The wall represents an acute infringement of human rights. He cannot support this violence in his immediate surroundings. Joel gets more and more excited and emphasises that we are not informed correctly and that we have to look at it from both sides. How often have I become the witness of such heated debates, which ultimately never lead to anything! Finally I stop it with my little bell of awareness. I ask for true listening and say: "As long as we are still searching for arguments to refute those of the opponent, we only add fuel to the emotional war. On this basis we shall never come to peace because we are not truly listening. All of us have arranged our own truths. What we take to be truth is the result of our socialisation. Let us not begin with our views of the world! We have been taught something which we want to believe in. Now we are here to open up our own walls and to consider afresh. Peace work begins with true listening and true questioning."

I am grateful that the group immediately accepts my intervention. We undertake the following walk in silence to let what has been said resonate in us.

In the evening we arrive at our nomad's tent in the middle of nowhere. Some of our Israeli friends have put it up in between some fields; and they will keep doing this for our night encampment throughout the pilgrimage. With its ornamental patterns it provides a simple shelter for those of us who find the open sky a bit too exposed. At the fire there is a hot soup and a circle of "deep listening." Moving words are articulated. Slowly different fates of members of our group are revealed. Joav, a quiet and somewhat shy Israeli says: "Already now the pilgrimage dismantles the wall inside of me." Then, with a gentle voice he begins to sing an Israeli song. The group, one after the other, joins in and quiet humming fills the air. It is time to bed down our weary heads on Mother Earth.

Being a guest with the Bedouin

The next day we walk through Arab villages in the direction of Shibli. This is a Bedouin village in Israel that has been named after the Shibli family. It is situated at the foot of the legendary Mount Tabor. The siblings Aida and Mustafa Shibli are part of our group. We are invited by their family to perform our play and afterwards stay for the night. We are received in the large Bedouin tent and royally entertained. Today is the end of the Muslim time of fasting, the Ramadan, the first day when Arabs are allowed to eat again to their hearts content – a celebration day for all Muslims. It is the custom that the young people go from house to house and ask for alms. This is to remind everyone that they are responsible for the well-being of the poor and they are given food.

We are all very tired. Alas, there is no time to go further into this.

The same evening our performance is to take place. Building up the stage, arranging the tent, saying hello to people – time passes by quickly. No time for little aches and pains or any moodiness.

Astonishingly many guests arrive, many of them from the peace movement but also inhabitants of Shibli are amongst them. A great number of them do not speak English but they come all the same to see the play. As fast as lightning the tent is changed into a stage. Although many children crawled around among the rows of seats, still during the play you could hear a needle drop. The pictures are elementary and constructed in a simple way so that they can imprint themselves into the soul without having knowledge of the language.

There is a follow-up talk. At first spellbound silence. For the first time there are many Palestinians in the audience. An Israeli breaks the silence. He gets up and with a trembling voice offers his thanks: "I feel that I have been seen. I am this soldier David which you portray. I was an officer. Through you we are able to see what had become of us after all these years of conflict. Please carry on, we need you."

Others express their affinity with Jamal, the suicide attacker in the play. Repeatedly the feedback is given that the reason that this play is so touching is because it is so pure and in a certain way innocent.

The father of Aida and Mustafa, who in his Bedouin garb radiates composure and dignity, also confirms that it has touched him. He is one of those who do not understand English but has nevertheless grasped the core of the play.

In the morning he joins our meditation circle. He wears our kaphir, a traditional head dress, on which it says in all languages "We refuse to be enemies." It is very unusual for him to sit with us in our meditation. From his viewpoint we belong to another religion and for a Muslim it is not customary to attend the prayers of others. He asks Aida to translate my prayer which I speak for all to hear. "He has never before done anything like it", says Aida overjoyed, translating each word carefully. It is an elementary text of meditation which is intended to lead us "geistig" into the day. Additionally I give thanks to this place and thanks for the hospitality.

Then he starts to speak. At first he tells a story from his tradition which is to reveal that Islam in its core is also a peace religion. Then he expresses all his respect for us. It is a moving moment for us. He is certain that we shall be successful since our purity can be felt and because we come with our hearts open. "May God protect those who come with an open heart." Surely resistance will be met too since we bring a very new message but also Mohammed and other prophets initially encountered resistance. It is clearly noticeable that we carry in us a wisdom which finally will generate trust. He regrets that there is this language barrier between us since he would wish to tell us more about the story of his Bedouin tribe and would also wish to hear more from us. While he speaks he begins to cry. Tears are a constant companion on our way. All of us cry most days at some point, it is as if a large river of tears opens up compassion and prepares the power for renewal. I perceive the words of this man as a great blessing. I feel an overwhelming thankfulness for having received the respect for our work from the side of the Arabs. I feel our selves seen in our endeavour and our struggle and I do not take this for granted at all.

On the way to Nazareth

Our way now leads us to Nazareth. We walk in the streaming rain. Everywhere, in the villages, Arabic prayers drone from loudspeakers. Often we love these sounds, though today all we want is to escape from them. It feels like continuous brain washing. Although we do not understand a word of them one feels they are associated with hostility, and with stirring up feelings against the enemy. The voices of the speakers often sound very fanatical. Unconsciously all cells draw together. One wants to get away, somewhere where there is silence.

In the village we see children playing with pistols everywhere. Ben is lightly hit by a small stone from a slingshot. Nothing serious but it creates an emotional climate that can easily lead to inner irritation. We walk half an eternity along a rural road. All along the curb of the road we see the bodies of animals that have been killed. Suddenly Vera bursts into tears. Her feelings pour out of her. "Nowhere here have I even seen the slightest attempt at peace. This land is not holy at all! How can there ever be peace here if the human beings are so careless with their immediate environment?"

Sometimes I ask myself whether I expect too much of the young people. For once it is not an easy experience to watch with wide open eyes what we humans are doing with this Earth.

In Nazareth we enter the old Arab quarter. In its alleys into which Jewish Israelis rarely dare to venture, a young Israeli has opened up a hostel especially for pilgrims. What we are presently doing is exactly in accordance with his vision. He greets us most happily and tells us that he has always dreamt of Israel/Palestine becoming a free country where people on their pilgrimage approach Jerusalem from the North in order to get to know the path to God.

En route Mohammed Shabili joined us, a 56 year old Palestinian who for 30 years was a guerrilla fighter at the side of Arafat. Two years ago he changed to the peace side. "For 30 years we have fought and it did not bring us anything except that we killed one another. Now I want to try it with peace. It is difficult if one sees the injustice but there is no other way." That is the way he talks. Shortly before Arafat's death he went to visit him once more and explained his thinking to him. Arafat gave him an order to take the path of peace. Today Shabili works and deals with Israeli and Palestinian politicians of all denominations negotiating cease-fires and trying to convince them all of the need for peace. The meeting with him is too short to truly get to know the man behind the words. He promises his support to all of us but I do not know whether we shall see him again. In the evening another theatre performance takes place.

This time our venue is a public stage, a sort of cinema with professional lighting. About 100 people are in the room, Benjamin is disappointed. He had hoped for a much larger audience here in Nazareth. I am much more detached. Shmuel was astonished when he heard that in Tagbha 60 people had attended. This, he says, is in no way normal in Israel. We again met with a lot of resonance and agreement. Both Israelis and Palestinians extended their thanks.

Training for non-violence

In Nazareth again a new group of pilgrims joined us, most of them being young people. The youngest one is now Freya who celebrates her 16th birthday during the pilgrimage. Charly Rainer Ehrenpreis, my long-time companion from Tamera accompanies the youth group. They will walk with us for a while and then help with the olive harvest in the West Bank.

The next day training for non-violent action is offered by Michael Rafael, an experienced instructor, for all those who wish to walk through the West Bank. He comes up with all sorts of possible scenarios of danger: "How will you react? What is violence to you? How do you behave in the face of a situation of violence? What do you do if one of your leaders is taken prisoner?" The participants are confronted with many such questions.

Under his leadership the group has the task to work out guidelines to which the entire group will have to adhere. I am mostly there as a spectator. I can see how fear creeps up in some of their faces: "Now it will become serious." I am grateful for Michael's support as it is good to be clear about where one is going.

My task now is to remind the people not to identify with their misgivings, although it is good to know the potential scenarios of war in order to be prepared for possible difficulties. Nevertheless, spiritual work focuses on our not feeding the misgivings but in strengthening the power to trust in our inner guidance. More often our own unconscious fears create a difficult situation. The combi-

125

nation of both our approaches seemed to have strengthened the group. Above all it was important that the group worked out on their own the guidelines for participation, although in their essence they corresponded very largely with our own given rules. Each thought that we create ourselves enters deeper into our cellular memory. Although I go into the unknown I have the feeling that we are well prepared.

At El Megiddo

We carry on to El Meggido, an age-old ruin of an Israeli town, which today is an important memorial. One battle after another has been fought here with each conqueror putting up new architectural signs of his power. This place is a memorial to the history of war which can be followed right through to the present day.

On the way we are accompanied by Amit Weisberger, an Israeli, who during two years travelled by horse and cart from France to Israel together with his wife and child. As a young man he was touched so much by the history of his country and its actual political situation that he could not but be bound to set an existential sign to express his will for peace and his solidarity with the people of Palestine. This journey has fundamentally changed his life.

Some days ago my inner voice had warned me that we must not sleep outside today. Thanks to the efforts of Aida we were offered a schoolhouse in a nearby kibbutz where we could spend the night. Sure enough it rained heavily. Thanks to the Goddess for her protection! When we are out in the nature for a long time we develop a fine sensory awareness which puts us in touch days ahead with warnings so that we are protected on our way.

At the schoolhouse we get to know Ofer Israeli. He knows a lot about survival in nature and for years has been living in close intimacy with the elements. He knows every plant in the land, knows how to feed himself in the wilderness of the country and how to build shelters. He is interested in a peace research village for the Middle East. "But please without the religious front", he says vehemently. He says he has already tried out such a lot and that it always failed because of terrible religious fanaticism. It is not, he feels, about unifying religions but about overcoming them. "It is thanks to world religions that for centuries we have had these terrible wars. Oh, these incessant debates of whether to celebrate Shabbat or not. It is an impertinence that the Palestinians have to continually endure the religious celebrations of those whom they feel to be their occupiers. It is a sign that we are all ready for a real new beginning."

I am glad for his forceful words. How often have I thought in a similar way, when during our peace camps, I had to settle who could speak which prayer and for how long so that no one felt hurt. Myself, I am convinced too that sooner or later all religions will transform themselves. However, if we do want to develop a peace village, there is for certain no way to avoid dealing with those who wish to practise their beliefs, everyone in his or her own way. Peace work in this country must fully address religion, its dark side and the side of pure belief. Those who refuse to address this subject will always be confronted with closed doors.

Performance in Umm el Fahm

Our path leads through woods and wadis, over hills and through Arab villages to Umm el Fahm. In front of a kindergarten we sing a children's song and are invited to a coffee. Moving contacts!

The first accident on our journey happens. Alice, our tribal elder, slips and breaks her arm. Wonderful, how the group reacts, quickly and calmly. Also Alice, herself, takes it calmly. I can still today see her as she lay there night after night with her arm set in plaster held upwards, and always with a quiet smile on her lips. I admire this woman and what she takes upon herself despite being over 70 years old.

Umm el Fahm is the largest Arab town in Israel with almost

50.000 inhabitants. We are put up at a sports centre in the gymnasium. With much effort Aida saw to it that a performance takes place at short notice. 250 seats, the hall keeps filling up. There are for certain 200 people in the hall, many of them are young people. This is our test of walking on fire in the Arab region. After the performance the people give a standing ovation. During the ensuing questions I am challenged to the utmost. I could have taken it as criticism. People came up with topics in some of which they did not feel themselves adequately identified. But I quickly realise that really what concerns them is simply that they want to be heard. We perceive them as human beings who are suffering from injustice but they want to know whether the actors are people with compassion. All those who talked so vehemently did however thank us afterwards.

It is the 8th of November. Today we undertake to walk silently in the direction of the wall. The day of the meditation at the wall draws nearer. May the Goddess be with us! May peace prevail on Earth!

Historic Significance of November 9th

Background of the wall in Israel/Palestine

November 9th is one of the planned highlights of our pilgrimage. It is a historic date at many levels. It was our intention to arrive this exact day at some point of the Israeli wall on the border of the West Bank and to hold there a solemn vigil.

The West Bank or the West Jordan Land is a large part of the Palestinian autonomous territory. It is the area west of the lower Jordan and the Dead Sea. Since the six-day-war in June 1967 Israel has occupied the West Jordan Land. In the nineties agreements were passed to turn it step by step into an autonomous region under Palestinian administration. Because of the violent escalations between Israelis and Palestinians since the year 2000 this plan for autonomy has been gravely jeopardised. The building of the wall since 2002, mostly unnoticed by the Western world, is the last result of this conflict. It is a violent intervention in the fate of countless people. The most popular argument for the building of the wall goes like this: "It is being built as protection against terror."

The reality says something different. The wall separates Palestinians from Palestinians, towns from the land and it separates farms from the water sources, workers from their places of work. It is made of reinforced concrete and with its height of eight metres it is double the height of the Berlin wall. Outside of built-up areas it turns into a high-security fence. After its completion it will be more than 700 kms long – double the length of the "Green Line." Only few people are aware that a large part of the wall does not follow the Israeli borders as recognised by the UN in 1967, but expands far into the Palestinian area. Many towns and villages in this way are cut off from hospitals, schools and from telephone, electricity and water supplies. A large part of fertile land has thus been annexed to Israel without the public noticing.

The wall separates the West Jordan Land into 81 parcels. Over

200.000 Palestinians have been expelled from their land through the construction of the wall. 160.000 people live in areas which are fenced in all around – "behind barbed wire with watch towers, ditches, double fences, pressed into a system of passes by a military bureaucracy which watches over each person's coming and going" – so writes the Israeli journalist, Amira Hass. In July 2005, the International Court of Law in The Hague summoned Israel to "immediately stop the construction of the installation of the barricade and to tear down those parts which against international law have been erected on Palestinian Territory." Nothing happened.

Another detail that we were also informed of during our pilgrimage: About 12.000 Palestinians were literally shut out of Palestine by this type of politics; they are now forced to live squeezed in between the wall, i.e. the insurmountable high-security fence and the Green Line. Although the line cannot be seen, those who are caught crossing it are sentenced to prison. Are these measures for the protection against terrorism? Those who walk through Palestine and witness how many of the farmers have lost their land, how many relatives and families have been separated from each other, how children who used to go on foot to the next-door school now have to drive up to 35 kms by bus in order to reach their school, are made very aware that a time-bomb has been set ticking. For those who have no hope in life anymore it is a last satisfaction to leave this planet with a cry of revenge.

Does not the thought seem close that in a more just world there would be no terror? Is not terror always a result of suppressed life?

I ask all Israelis, for whom it is difficult at times to read such lines without feeling incriminated or judged, to not immediately react. I am not writing this out of any hostility towards the inhabitants of Israel. I write all this in order to unmask a structure and to show that this approach draws everyone ever deeper into war and misery. There can be no peace until such time when we leave behind forever the entire system and its thinking.

November 9th, 1989 in front of the Berlin Wall

On November 9th 1989 I too became a witness of the opening of the Berlin wall. It had been a well thought out barricade of concrete walls, three to four metres high, or of metal-grid wire fences reinforced with ditches of up to five metres deep, trip wires, running tracks for watch dogs and surrounded by signal and watch towers. This was the way the East Berlin and the GDR were separated from West Berlin and the German Republic. Under the pressure of the non-violent mass-protests of the GDR inhabitants the government of GDR opened up the wall on November 9th, 1989.

I experienced the opening of the wall at the so called "Check-Point Charlie" one of the most well-known crossing points. Quite by accident I happened to be in Berlin at that time together with co-workers of the project and Dieter Duhm and I was to give there a speech. The joyous news made us formulate a statement about the opening of the wall with lightning speed and pass out the hundred of thousands of copies.

It said "The revolution in the East has to be followed by the revolution in the West", in the hope and in the belief that the enormous power of change in the East would be matched by the most courageous spirits of the West in order to overcome together as new comrades the walls and atrocities of the capitalistic system.

The reality was different. Quickly capitalism managed to take over the power of change of the GDR movement. It was terrible to see how this change was swallowed up by a system that little cared about the humane background. It all petered out and we had not more humanity but "more value, more market and more consumption" the motto for the survival of capitalism.

Nevertheless, at the same time and in the background committed spirits quiet and determined kept on working for the realisation of a "Concrete Utopia".

The opening of the Berlin wall was a historic event which on November 9th we wanted to commemorate by holding a meditative vigil in front of today's Israeli wall. It was important for us to set a sign for feeling connected with the larger lines of history and their potential for healing. The fall of the German wall is one of the few current examples in history where a non-violent revolution was able to lead to victory. This is only one of the lines of significance which connect us to the historic date of November 9th.

November 9th, 1938, the Third Reich "Night of the Pogrom"

The second essential connection leads us further back into history. On the night of the 9th to the 10th of November 1938, the Night of the Pogrom of the Third Reich, in belittling terms also called the "Night of Broken Glass", the first big hit of the Nazis against the German Jews was carried out. Hundreds of synagogues were set on fire, many Jewish citizens murdered – the numbers range between 90 and 400 – and more than 30.000 human beings carted off to concentration camps.

With such an account I can hardly carry on writing. I have to retreat and remain in silence for a while to let myself be touched by the fact that this atrocious insanity is true, which I can here only refer to in sober words and which we like to read over in the books of history. And this part of history is not yet in the all too distant past. We are compassionate about the fate of others as long as it is bearable for us and as long as we can believe in some sort of consolation. But we have almost no possibility of reaction when we hear what had been done to human beings in the concentration camps.

Never before have I been touched in such a way by the atrocious works of fascism as I have been when visiting the concentration camp at Mauthausen during my pilgrimage through Austria. This then is the human being. The cruelty human beings are capable of goes far beyond what I am able to imaging even up to this day. The wooden barracks of Mauthausen still today resonate with the living history of a past whose reality could hardly be looked at by any of the survivors. To view this massacre is just too horrible. Look at the people who are reduced to almost only bare bones, look into the eyes ripped open wide with fear and fright, see the carts filled with the dead bodies of starved people being daily removed from the chambers. And see the commanders who gave their orders for torture, subjugation, murder, mutilation and sexual assault. Quickly the observer is so overcome by nausea he wants to turn away. Only too quickly the mind is looking for some kind of soothing distractions. Consciousness is apt to draw a veil of oblivion across all the atrocities of history.

They were your fathers and grandfathers who had lived and acted in this war, there is no use turning away. Those whom you loved and respected were participating. They were human beings. Quite normal human beings! Victims as well as perpetrators were equally prisoners of an infinitely larger mass hypnosis. Today we are called to recognise this. Only then can we begin to end war.

Claude AnShin Thomas, a Buddhist monk and veteran of the Vietnam War pointedly writes:

By taking up arms I was directly responsible, and the killing only stopped when I was honourably discharged and sent home with numerous decorations, including a Purple Heart, a decoration for injuries received. However, when I began to put together the grenade splinters of my life again and discovered the heart that had been broken by the war, I understood that justified killing does not exist, that there is no separation between good and bad violence and that real morals and honourableness do not exist in war. War has never any morals. It is simply the expression of suffering. Acting that is generated by suffering.

Through our presence at the wall we want to bear witness to this underlying part of history, which will cause more harm until it is consciously recognised and abandoned by the vast majority of human beings.

133

Night Vigil at the Wall

Arrival at the wall

We leave Umm el Fahm with 42 people including nine Israelis who have decided to enter the West Bank together with us. Yusuf, a member of Middleway is leading us. He remains surprisingly calm when he receives a phone call and is informed that his wife has given birth to their third child in Tel Aviv. The Middle East: I know of no other place where the two extremes of life are so much a matter of course and lie so near to each other, birth and death are part of everyday life.

Our path takes us through wadis, olive groves and various villages. The tension is high. What will happen to us at the wall? Will we really get into the West Bank? The telephone rings almost continuously. Kate, Klaus and Benjamin are untiringly busy on their mobiles. Repeated new information could easily entrap one into becoming nervous but a higher force lets us remain calm. It is a unique venture for a group of pilgrims including Israelis to want to pass over into Palestine. Officially Israelis are strictly prohibited from entering.

After a long march of silence and accompanied by some members of Middleway we arrive in Baqqa al Garbye at the wall shortly before sunset. For many of us it is the first visit to the wall. Like a surrealistic work of art it protrudes into the landscape, separating the Arab town into two halves. We have dealt with the wall such a lot already that it looms into our world almost like a legend.

A residential house was integrated into the wall and serves now as a military station. Immediately in front of the wall we meet Jamila, a young Arab woman. She tells us the story of how the wall separated her family.

Our two Israeli friends have put up the tent right next to the wall in the grounds of demolished Palestinian houses. We assemble in

the tent. A young inhabitant of the town who speaks German supports us all he can. He even brings us a lamp and an electric cable.
Klaus and Kate are in full action. Many thanks go to them. Part of
the group settles down in a nearby school. Tamir and others play
with the children. The very same children, who before had been so
friendly, all of a sudden start to throw stones and the windscreen of
Joel's car is smashed to pieces. He has joined us today by car. Is it
an accident that of all things it happens to Joel? Joel is an American
Jew and orthodox Judaism is his spiritual home. Again and again
he warns us against too much one-sidedness and contributes with
important information about the Jewish body of thought. His
whole inner being is aligned with justice. Repeatedly he argues that
the construction of the wall serves peace. The longer he stays with
us - and with short interruptions he will be with us throughout the
whole of the pilgrimage - the more his view of the world caves in.
"What I am seeing and experiencing here is not part of what we are
taught", he says with growing shock. With magnanimity he accepts
the smashed windscreen and in the evening speaks moving words
in front of our Arabic visitors. Nevertheless this broken glass is a
warning to the Israelis and no easy start. With how much blind
hate will they be confronted on the other side?

Slide show on the wall

At sunset we get together in the tent. I begin with an introductry
talk. Shortly afterwards we soon receive visitors. Israeli Arabs and
Palestinians circle our tent. They bring water, tea, coffee and sweets.
Representatives of the town; a Palestinian whose house has been
demolished on the day of his wedding; a doctor; the deputy mayor,
they all begin to talk.
The young Palestinian who always carries photos of his demolished house with him is asked whether he could live together with
the Israelis who had done this to him. He says: "I would sacrifice
my house for peace, if only it would be the last act of destruction

135

that was to happen. So many human beings have already had to die. Peace is the only way", he says despite all the sadness he radiates.

Meanwhile the video beamer has been set up. How often, in our visions, have we seen ourselves projecting images of peace against the wall. How many sceptical voices have warned us and explained that this would be impossible and that we would be immediately chased away with tear-gas. We stayed firmly with the vision.

If we do not allow any internal images of hostility we shall succeed, was our sentence of empowerment.

Now it became true. Disturbed by no one, greeted by the inhabitants of the town with coffee and regal hospitality we look at pictures of our pilgrimage, photos of the wall and visionary pictures of a peaceful land. One picture is shown over and over again and reaches deep into the soul. It was taken during our action at the Berlin wall. A beautiful woman hands a flower to a soldier through a small opening in the wall.

This picture carries within it a deep sound of soul. Surely, to a soldier there is no bigger adventure than that of war. The even bigger adventure of the future though will be the path to love, the path of the man to the woman and vice-a-versa. In the future, mothers will not let their sons go to war for their homeland, since they will know that there are other lives and other perspectives of love.

In between these scenes, the photograph of our *cosmogramme* repeatedly lights up on the wall. It is a simple delineation designed by Marko Pogacnik, geomancer and landscape healer. It stands for the overcoming of the wall and accompanies us during the whole of the pilgrimage. Marko Pogacnik wrote:

The cosmogramme does not refer to a certain place but to the landscape as a whole. Compared to our blessed planet, Israel/Palestine is but a minute speck on the surface of the Earth. This rounded place, a life organ of the Earth which now is separated, is an expression of the inner separation of contemporary man from his own wholeness: within itself the feminine is separated from the masculine as are reason from intuition and the heart from wholeness. This cosmogramme sings the song of reunification.

We know that we are presently doing something that is strictly forbidden; but all the same we feel well protected. It is a magic moment
and it opens up to us the power of vision.

At this point the vision lightens up in front of my eyes: next time
there will be thousands who will attend this meditation. The small
budding cell of a new peace force could give to both sides of the wall
the endurance and potency which is necessary to penetrate the wall.
Few catalysts would be needed to initiate such a movement. With
sufficient endurance, precision and determination it could even be
possible in this land to overcome the concept of the enemy and to
launch a non-violent revolution. However, only with the full support
from the international world! Peace in one country is no longer only
a local affair. We are participating globally in all that is happening in
the regions of conflict on this Earth.

The deputy mayor of the town is most moved and asks us insistently that next time we announce our arrival. They would then
mobilise many forces in town and would receive us officially and
act together with us. Now that we are slowly picking up the vibes of
this country, its sound and its rhythm, the vision begins to bud that
it could be a non-violent event with thousands of pilgrims. How
often have I dreamt of the inhabitants of both sides form long lines
on either side of the wall, of the Israelis coming together and burning their passports, a gesture of their newly won freedom which
shows that they are no longer content to have their longing for a
homeland misused by a government which tramples human rights
with its feet.

The Palestinians too dissociate themselves from any Islamist and
terrorist slogans. Symbolically one takes up the primordial form of
nomadic life, knowing that this land belongs to no one. But one is
determined to create adequate places for those who are looking to
make homes here.

The night in front of the wall

Meanwhile Tamir lights a fire. We talk altogether for a while. This evening we hear incredibly sad stories, but nothing is escalating, no hate, no emotional explosion. Shared songs open our hearts. Healing can only happen through direct human touch. Late at night most of us retreat to the nearby schoolhouse to get some sleep. Benjamin Vera, myself and some others stay in front of the wall throughout the night.

I am wide awake. Continuously my eyes rest on the wall. In the moonshine the entire thing takes on an almost romantic shine. I feel connected to the beauty of the desert. Jackals are even able to bed their heads down on a garbage dump and there find the comfort of the cosmos. But they can move on the next day. They are not stuck in a prison like the people on the other side of the wall and exposed to continual indignities.

It could be that this wall, as bad as it is, will set in motion an act of consciousness in many people and awakens forces that could ignite a peace process. As a result of all our "geistig" preparations I sense it as being part of a legend, as if we could override the reality of this wall through a powerful "geistig" act. While I sit fully awake and meditating in front of the wall dawn is coming up. Punctually at six a.m. and shortly before sunrise many guests arrive. Many engaged peace workers from the peace movement have heard of our venture and have now come to meditate with us. Three camera teams came, two from Israel and one from Danish television.

We know that at the same time other groups in other places are getting together in order to accompany us. Marko Pogacnik puts on a peace march through Ljubljana, Maurizio Martinelli assembles people in Venice, one group with Bernie Glassmann, Sami Awad and Rabbi Ohad Ezrahi meditate at the same time in Auschwitz, a smaller group in the concentration camp of Mauthausen, at Tamera in Portugal, in Vienna, in different places in Germany, everywhere engaged meditations for a realistic peace alternative in Israel/Palestine are taking place.

The meditation

The wall is protected by a fence. Parallel, between the wall and the fence, a military road runs along where Israeli military jeeps patrol regularly. There, immediately in front of the wall where normally no one is admitted we want to meditate. An iron gate in the fence about three metres high is the border crossover. It is still closed and separates us from the wall. While we wait we sit down in a circle in front of the gate and I slowly read the text for the later meditation point by point. My whole body is trembling. Despite the noise and the honking cars the concentration is magical. Even the soldiers who take up their watch posts behind the closed gate cannot hide the fact that they welcome us.
I read with a firm voice:

1. See on the one side the Palestinian people with their pain, their longing for freedom and their cultural heritage. See on the other side the Israeli people with their culture, their injuries and their century-old longing for protection and home. See the old story, the roots of the conflict. Abraham, ancestor of both peoples, had a son Ismael by Hagar. Then later Abraham and his jealous wife Sarah sent Hagar and Ismael into the desert. It started with a love conflict. Imagine that Abraham and Sarah find a new solidarity and a solution in respect of Hagar and Ismael. They know now: A God of peace and love would never agree that they should fight each other. Together they take care for their sons and their education. They overcome the wall.

2. Imagine that representatives of both people walk slowly towards the wall, accompanied by friends from all over the world. Their intention is to overcome the wall of separation. Mothers from both sides extend their hands to each other united by a strong decision to not any longer let their children become victims of violence and war. Men come from both sides, silently sit in a circle, firmly united by a decision not to participate any longer in

139

wars of hate. From now on they will take over together the responsibility for their country. Imagine that there, where now the wall is, Israeli and Palestinian farmers create gardens together – with olive trees as a symbol for long lasting peace. Doing this together they get to know and respect each other's humanity.

3. Imagine that the construction of the wall stops and the parts already built disappear. Imagine that peace workers from all over the world together with Israelis and Palestinians start to act together with a lot of artistic spirit: *We sell the wall.* Knowing that nobody has the right to possess this wall, that it violates peoples' rights and human rights and that its construction consumed huge amounts of money, now selling it would serve humanitarian needs. The wall will be taken down piece by piece and at some places it will be transformed into works of art or memorials about the history of war and separation.

With the profits hospitals are set up where Israeli and Palestinian doctors work together in the spirit of healing. Universities and peace schools are built. Here the foundations of peaceful cultures will be studied. The money will be invested into joint ecological projects, research into water supply, reforestation and pilot projects for solar technology.

4. Imagine that in mosques and synagogues, in Christian churches and in schools the memory of the original sources of peace is regained. People return to the source that overcomes all hatred and animosity. Christians, atheists, Muslims, Sufis, Jews and pagans build together the new spiritual temple of our time. Also the ancient gods and goddesses of the nomads of old are invited to be part of this new covenant.

The daughters and sons of Abraham recognize each other again and join together with the common purpose of making their land a Holy Land. They carry this decision into their human relationships, into their contacts with animals, and with nature. They carry now the common responsibility for the Promised Land as a place of peace. When peace can be realised here, it can be realised anywhere in the world.

5. Also in governments and in leading positions of the economic and scientific world they start to remember their responsibility for the destiny of the whole country – not only for one people. They know: There cannot be a free Israel without a free Palestine, and there cannot be a free Palestine without a free Israel. New leading forces turn up. New ideas for solutions arise. They take part in the destiny of the whole Middle East. They take care that refugees can return to their country or that they find in dignity a place for a new home. Nobody will any longer be considered as an unworthy being. Imagine that the arms industry will no longer provide weapons but instead will deliver humane technology that brings fertility to the country for all its inhabitants. "Swords become ploughshares". The international world supports the reconciliation with all its means, as they know this to be their responsibility. They also do not deliver tanks any more, but instead they come with the unwavering will to cooperate for peaceful solutions.

6. The terror of fascism begins to heal as the souls of the former victimizers – of dead ones as well as of the ones still alive – see their mistakes and their deep guilt. They genuinely ask their victims for forgiveness. Imagine that all the ancestors recognize their wrong doing and their fanaticism. They realise through tears, what they did to each other, not knowing that those whom they considered to be enemies, are, in reality, members of their own cosmic family. They acted in the belief that they found the one and only truth. Now they extend their hands for reconciliation.

7. Imagine you are given into your hand the seed for a future culture of peace, *a cosmogramme*, a letter of life for the process of reconciliation. Imagine that you plant this seed now into the

earth here at the wall. You take care for it, you send light and you water it. Imagine how from this seed a new power grows, how the knowledge for a free, sensitive and peaceful world is generated. Imagine how the seed opens up and starts to blossom at different places on earth. Switch on your light and make yourself into a force that will not rest before peace is realised on earth. We take on the responsibility to overcome the walls of separation in ourselves in order to make peace on earth possible.

8. Imagine how rejoicing peoples on both sides welcome the dismantling of the wall. They see each other as friends. Their differences do not create animosity any more but shared interests instead. Together they have started to create a new culture. May it become true that we all find our own ways to celebrate and live this one source of life and love. May we all rediscover in our own manner the sacred core of life and celebrate it. In this sense we light up the light for peace in the Holy Land, peace on earth and peace between all beings.

Blessed be this process.

Altogether we are about 80 people. The gate is still closed. We begin to sing and some start painting. Talks develop and beautiful encounters with waiting schoolchildren who have to pass the gate every day to get to their schools, with people on their donkey carts who transport olive branches, with workers of both sides. Tea and coffee is being brought. After two hours finally the soldiers come and open the gate. At first however they open it only to the waiting Palestinians.

Further patient waiting! I admit not one second of doubt that we shall arrive on the other side of the wall this day. Finally we receive the liberating news. We are allowed to go through the gate in order to meditate in front of the wall and thereafter we are to enter directly into the West Bank. In a flash we pack everything up. And as now the door is finally opened up to us, one person after another goes to the wall and sits down. Each with the *cosmogramme* in front of him sits for a good hour in silent meditation. I play the flute and then from the loudspeakers we hear the well-known Israeli song "Zaman el Salaam" composed by Yair Dalal.

One of the woman participants writes in her diary:

Surprise that after the chaos of the morning I experienced the meditation as being very intense. The concentration was there immediately as we sat with the cosmogramme in front of us and our backs to this wall which makes visible the separation and the pain that exists in this country. As I sat there the lines of the cosmogramme start to swim in front of my eyes, they become alive and begin to flow into each other like waves. Instantaneously it was clear to me that this wall, this situation here has to do with my own innermost sphere, with the most intimate, with the innermost of every human being. The hope and the certainty rises inside of me that one day all walls will fall and I find a prayer of high precision and resonance. Thank you for the possibility and a special thank you to Sabine.

Then all of a sudden the call comes. The soldiers ask us in a friendly way to now pass the check point. The long awaited moment has come. We enter the West Bank.

Entry into the West Bank

The reception

Not only atrocities happen already for so long.
I have seen the love, already for so long.
See the tears, the anger, the hope, the blazing heat,
and what is happening in the faces of children.
Already for so long.
(English translation of a German song by Hannes Wader)

The sounds of the guitar trail away. We listen to Charlie's songs which afford our hearts and our tired limbs a few moments of rest. Then the moment arrives - the long expected moment has become reality. The special moment that a while ago was still only dreamed of like a vision, has now become true: We enter the West Bank. After a long night's vigil we are all a little overtired.

A group of men receives us on the other side. A small lorry drives up. We are asked to load up our rucksacks. One of the men, Fayez Owdi, is to accompany us during the next few days. At this point we do not suspect that in the time ahead of us a very deep bond of friendship will be woven between him and ourselves and that he will guide us through nearly the entire West Bank. There he stands in front of us, a man with big black eyes, black hair showing traces of silvery grey, with his striking face marked by the thin lines of fate. The large moustache accentuates his character and gives him a very masculine bearing. He is 56 years of age. He is not one of those people who seem to be instantly familiar to oneself. He is a peasant and has grown up in the area of the present-day West Bank. His family has lived there for generations. His attitude is formed through an education in the Islamic world. For a long time he was active as a Marxist in the Palestinian resistance movement. Large parts of his land were taken from him. In a touching manner he talks of young people who, to his dismay, play with the thought of sacrificing their lives for the liberation of Palestinian.

After first words of welcome we set off equipped with shields which show that we are on a pilgrimage in the name of GRACE. Immediately Fayez leads us to the wall and on the way shows us various completely demolished houses. He leads us just the same as he has probably often before led groups which had come from Europe, first showing them those places where the immense misery of the country strikes the most. Here the wall runs through Baqqa al Garbye, across the former market place. All shops along the broad road leading up to the market place are closed. There is no one left who could buy anything, since there is no longer any through traffic.

Confrontation and first encounters

The faces of the members of our group, especially those of the Israelis who are walking with us, have become as white as chalk. Shock and fear is mirrored in them. Fayez is full to the limit with stories of the suffering in this land. To Benjamin and my self it is a challenge to lead the group and yet at the same time to have to cooperate with a totally new guide whom we do not even know. "Stop the occupation" is the big demand that screams at us with totally unvarnished directness.

I already see now that many of the Israelis are coming up against the limits of what can be reasonably imposed on them. A first identification takes place with evil which here expresses itself without any reservations, then resistance sets in by playing down all that is being said as far too one sided. The process is always the same. I ask the participants to now practice the art of listening and to keep being a witness and noticing what kind of effect Fayez' vehemently spoken words have on them. For the present time it is not so important whether it be all true, the important thing is to hear his injury and indignation.

145

I feel that the big challenge of the moment is to give to the Israeli pilgrims the protection they now need to be able to handle the experiences of the coming days. One of the co-pilgrims from Switzerland suffers from dizzy spells – too much sun and too many issues all at once! We order a taxi to take her to the next pilgrim station.

Late in the evening, tired out by all the impressions of the day, we arrive at a Palestinian family. Children, women and men of all ages surround us. Scenes occur which I will never forget. We have so far not yet publicly announced that there are Israelis with us. Here, under the protection of the house we dare to do it. It is moving to be allowed to become a witness of how those, who for years had only known hostile media pictures of one another, are now discovering humanity in each other. One can feel the potential solidarity and friendship. At first suspicious, they eye each other with curiosity. At the same time a festive dinner is being prepared on the floor - vegetarian Arab food. Slowly we see how the men venture into deeper dialogue. Our host, Yousra greeted everyone with: "My house is your house." When she came to Michal she learnt that she is an Israeli. For a split second she hesitates, we hold our breath. Hospitality succeeds: "My house is your house." Now both have a lot to say to each other. Michal, who has already done a lot of peace work with Palestinians inside Israel, now hears how it is to live as a woman in Palestine, to be the mother of eight children and with a husband who is out of work. And Yousra shakes her head, how can a grown-up woman not be married? Unfortunately my son is only 16 and too young for you, she says, and laughs mischievously. Months later through a fund raising drive, Michal will get the money together so that the daughters of Yousra can complete their studies.

Then night falls. We still do not know where we will sleep. I try to explain to Fayez, how important it is to us to have an opportunity to meet as a group in order to speak about all that has happened. "Yes, no problem, come, come", he says.

We are led through a dark alley of the town. It is getting darker and narrower. One has the feeling of coming to the end of the world and then he opens up a huge iron gate. There is a little court-yard and an even smaller room in which only a few people can be put up. No electricity. So there we stand all 50 of us. Ben and myself are challenged to improvise quickly. For Fayez the simplicity of the place goes against the tradition of hospitality. He wants to organise a bus and drive us to the next village. Only after much persuasion can we convince him that we want our pilgrimage to be as we find it and that we shall manage perfectly well in this place. To us it seems most important that the group meet now together after the night at the wall and the many impressions of the day.

A dramatic night

In the middle of all this chaos, Uri, an active Jewish anarchist, arranges a meeting for the Israelis. They most urgently need to talk among themselves. Some were appalled that I publicly announced that there were some T-shirts with "Stop the wall" printed on them and that those who purchased one would support Palestinians who had hardly any money.

Some felt too much under pressure in having to follow a politi-cal statement. Again the warning comes: "You are far too one-sided." Many are in a state of shock and are frightened. Green Hamas flags are all over the town; we are in an open unprotected place; this was too much for some of the leaders of the group who are part of a clear political front. When Fayez in the dark had opened up the huge iron gate and led us into the dark courtyard, even I thought that now we would be kidnapped and become the bait in a deal to free political prisoners! It is now of the utmost importance for me to remain unaffected and not to identify with the reproaches of the Israelis. The circle is so important. Many times I perceive the behaviour of the Israelis as overly sensitive. It is difficult for me to understand what makes them identify so quickly with the fact that they are Israelis. A human being is a human being. This is what I think. However after I have listened to their various fears and reactions, I can more easily understand their deep feeling of being in an extremely dangerous situation.

Lisa is trembling with fear. Deeply shaken she is crying continuously. She repeats over and over again "I wanted to know all this. But it is too much. I did not know all this. What can we do? We have to do something." Joel remains outwardly calmer, but one can see that his view of the world is beginning to shake. Daily, he encounters situations which in no way correspond to what he has been taught by the teachers he reveres so much. I appreciate him very much as he always strives for truth and justice and does not hesitate to differ from the opinions of the majority of the group. If at the beginning many had avoided him for precisely these reasons, he is now more respected and liked, particularly for the thoroughness with which he looks at the issues.

An almost sleepless night follows. I am lying in the courtyard. We had offered the small room to the Israelis in the hope that they might feel more protected. Shortly after I fell asleep late at night a group of Palestinian men, smoking cigarettes, enter the courtyard, debating loudly and heatedly. They position themselves right at the foot of my sleeping bag. Being roused from an uneasy sleep, associations of criminal situations do indeed flash through my mind. Gloomily the characters stand in front of me. Immediately I am aware of being afraid of what their behaviour might trigger among the already terrified Israelis. Again and again I try to signal to the newly arrived Palestinians to please leave and above all to be quiet. They nod but soon after the noise level swells up again. Excitedly they make me understand that they are here to protect us! The very thing that has triggered scary thoughts in me is meant as a protection for us! Finally around 4.00 a.m. it becomes quiet.

Encounter with a Palestinian and an Israeli Soldier

Control of the soldiers

The next morning we set off for a long way through the olive groves that are typical of this region. In between, our organisers are on the phone a lot. New people continuously want to join us or leave us. They are being held up at the check points, not being let in or out. Our team of organisers is challenged again to its limits. I am very grateful that despite everything they never forget the spiritual frequency of the pilgrimage of GRACE. This is probably one of the deepest secrets of our success. May the Goddess be part of each phone call!

We are walking through an olive grove. The sun bathes everything in a colourless light, illuminating it all with brightness as if it were set in an eternal world. We have not been on our way long when a jeep with three soldiers comes towards us.

The following experience has imprinted itself very deeply on my memory. It sits deep in my soul and will come up again and again and remind me of this elementary experience. I became a witness of how human beings are able to instantaneously let go of old behavioural patterns and open themselves up to something new. Through this a new vision and a possible new reality radiate into our life.

The soldiers want to control us. With cool, official faces they ask us why we were walking along here and tell us that it is forbidden to enter the security zone.

As we talk about what we do their formal working faces start to crack. Somewhat disbelieving they look at us. They are used to politically engaged international groups which on and off show up in the West Bank. But we are earnestly going our way on foot

149

through the whole country in the name of GRACE, and they have never met with something like this before. They become more and more curious and the talk takes on human traits. Finally they let us carry on.

The Goddess and the pomegranate

After a while we come to a fountain. Happily Fayez shows us how the farmers scoop up the water in these oases. We take a rest in the shade of an olive tree. It is the peace emblem of the Palestinian world. I feel like starting a talking circle. Here under the silvery-grey light playing on the olive trees and the place's immense sacred frequency, a talking circle could prove itself worthwhile in bringing alive in all participants a humane tomorrow.

For some time already it has been my concern to initiate a talking circle where the participants have the opportunity to express what is moving them. Up till now there has not really been a true opportunity to talk. What moves the young people? What takes place in the German pilgrims who know how the fate of this country is connected to the aftermath of the Holocaust? When will the Israelis speak of how they feel?

Joel gives me the pomegranate. It is to go from hand to hand and will serve as a symbol of our mutual esteem and respect and of our willingness to listen to the person who is holding the pomegranate.

The talking-stick-circle, or the so called "deep listening", is one of the simplest methods I know to leave behind the ping-pong of discussion and to afford each other the respect and awareness which is needed to really listen to each other in a circle of people who are relative strangers to one another.

I open up with a prayer and am reminded of the Goddess with the pomegranate which festively illuminates the whole situation. How the soul asks for such moments where it is lifted up beyond suffering and pain and hopelessness in order to strengthen anew the forces of self-healing. Unpretentious simple rituals which are not soaked in any defined religion or ideology can always support a group to find itself and to build up mutual vibration. Such deep listening can produce miracles.

I know that the hearts of all participants are bursting and that it is high time we talk so as to avoid any unnecessary emotional scenes.

Visit of the soldiers and first talks

Admittedly life often plays a somewhat different tune than the one expected. Just as we start a jeep draws up with the same soldiers that earlier on had stopped us, and the faces of all our participants mirror tension, curiosity and mutual concern. I am determined to protect this talking circle and go up to the driver's window. I explain our situation to them and that it is very important that we are not disturbed. They ask if they may watch. "Watch? That I'm afraid is difficult, but you can ask the group whether you might participate." I surprise myself with my answer. They readily get out of the car in order to join our circle.

One of the participants begs us to consider: "How are we supposed to speak the truth with people in uniform sitting with us. They stand for everything we want to overcome."

"Let us decide to see the human being behind the uniform", I suggest. The group agrees. The soldiers sit themselves down.

Now the pomegranate wanders from hand to hand and the individuals talk, moved by what has touched their hearts since entering the West Bank. Israelis express not only the fears they have lived through since they arrived on this side of the wall but also how deeply touched they have been by the Palestinian hospitality. Some have seen and experienced so much that they now need a day of rest.

Many admit to the circle that never before had they let themselves be touched by the misery of this world. Apart from pain they also feel added strength and a new responsibility. Some simply pass

151

on the apple without talking. After a period of silence one of the soldiers finally breaks through his inner limits after obviously having struggled with them for some time. He did not know what to make of us. "Shall I really let myself into this? What do they think of me? They will despise me for being a soldier. They connive with the Palestinians so that the anti-Jewish front is strengthened." Such and similar thoughts are to be read all over his face. But now the moment has come, he breaks through an inner taboo, takes the pomegranate and begins to talk about his situation. "I do not like doing what I have to do. I too do not think that the Palestinians are our enemies. But as long as acts of terror take place we have to protect our people. I try to behave here in a friendly way. Sometimes I even give the children something to eat. But my experience has been that shortly afterwards they throw stones at me. Why do the children throw stones at me after I have given them something to eat?" Somewhat insecurely he ends his searching words.

Readiness for reconciliation

Afterwards the pomegranate wanders on through the circle. Nobody speaks for quite a while.

Now Fayez takes the pomegranate. He rolls it to and fro in his hands visibly struggling for words. His eyes shine powerfully as if one is able to read the entire history of this country in them. Fayez, a Palestinian man with his own history, taught not to show feelings, a Marxist, resistance fighter of the Palestinian movement "Stop the Occupation" is obviously moved. The muscles of his face are trembling.

It is almost certainly the first time in his life he has sat in such a spiritual circle, taking the time to listen without interruption to the points of view of others, and to top it all, to do this in the presence of Israeli soldiers in uniform. If they saw him his comrades might accuse him of being a collaborator and despise him for sitting in our circle. But Fayez is too much a seeker of truth to let himself be prevented by such thoughts from pursuing his intuitive search for a solution. He keeps looking at the young soldiers. The circle is absolutely quiet. Everyone is waiting expectantly for him to speak. Slowly and hauntingly he begins to talk to the soldiers.

Very profoundly he explains why the children throw stones. He is at pains to talk with great restraint but then one sees how a wave of feeling wells up in him. He breaks into tears and struggles for each word. "Listen, you are young, you do not yet have a wife and children. But I am sure that your mothers and fathers feel as I do when my sons or my daughter leaves home. The children begin to sympathise with Hamas because they want to do something for their country. Can you image how I feel when I have to witness this? Can you image how we all feel? For generations we have been living peacefully side by side. Why now do we have all this and for so very, very long? Can we not slowly begin to accept that we are not able to carry on like this? In this way the endless murdering will never come to an end. Why do we not at last simply stop? We could stop it, right now."

His words have a strong and insistent effect. Nearly all the group openly let their tears flow.

We become quiet. It could just be as simple as all that. Nevertheless the way out of the mess seems impossible. Between them stand the walls, walls of judgement and prejudice, walls built with countless injuries, walls of world views, religion and ideology, walls of political slogans and regimentation.

Because of these walls all that is humane, beautiful and true is being pushed into private niches. Only sometimes a crack creates a small opening shedding light on all who are near. And this releases great illumination. It is a crack that brings with it the readiness for reconciliation and the readiness for a new beginning.

Further on our way through the villages, in between loudly honking cars and many waving Palestinians, Michal talks to me of her feelings. "I see you have already adapted to this place. You take the honking for a friendly gesture. But I jerk nervously each time." She, who is very courageous in her peace work, now expresses her many questions and doubts. "Where is the path? If the Arabs perceive us as weak they will drive us away and we will be back to the old situation where there was no place for us on the Earth."

She tries to describe how the settlers feel but in everything she says I hear her own search for a new identity. "We need deep healing", she says with quiet seriousness.

We reach Tulkarm and come to a meeting place of the Palestinian administration. In the town we see again everywhere the placards and flags of Hamas. Michal faints from the accumulation of everything, the fear, the sun, the many new impressions!
But as I get to her she is already laughing again.

Arabic night of festivities

In the evening we are put up at the hostel owned by Fayez a little outside Tulkarm. He has prepared a large party.

By now, after this day of shared experiences, Fayez seems like a close friend to us. In his village he is the "father" of a huge family clan. Originally he had once been a rich man. Between our young people and his children moving contacts take place. His eighteen year old daughter has expressed her desperation very convincingly to some of our women. She is anxious to do something to end the injustice that is being done to her father and her whole people but does not see any possibility. Originally she wanted to become a journalist but there is no training available for this. Now she carries the picture of the founder of the Hamas on a chain round her neck. The talk between her and our women becomes more and more intimate. When she heard about Tamera and the study centre for peace she is totally excited. Entirely new perspectives open up for her. She lights up in the talk and asks whether she might visit us. All of a sudden a new perspective in life opens up for her.

We feel the huge responsibility and the possibilities which lie in our work. May we obtain the necessary strength and the money needed so that the work that has been begun can be realised on a larger scale so that the youth of this world has a chance again.

I yearn for sleep. But the later the evening the more animated everyone becomes. More and more dancing groups are presented. Fayez turns out to be a skilled dancer as well as teacher of a youth group. One dance after another is being performed and finally all of us are seduced by the typical Arab dances. It is a real celebration of encounters, one with the other. Outside in front of the door another moving meeting takes place between our young people and the youth of the village. Many of our young men are taken to the homes of the Palestinian young men.

I am offered a small suite for the night. For the first time in many nights I find a good rest. I enjoy it to the full.

Despite all the turbulence and fears I feel protected and guided. I am thankful for the peace and quiet within me. Despite all the fears, resistance, hopes, heartfelt openings, fainting, broken arm and difficult police controls our ship is now well set on its course and sails towards a higher goal.

We Shall not Remain the Same

The secret of community

The faces of our pilgrims are not the same anymore now they have been on the other side of the wall. They have clearly experienced something that goes deeper than any normal daily experience. None of us will now be the same person as when we left home. Some keep switching between laughter and tears.

One major challenge for most of us is that of being continuously in community. Our night camps are mostly in large public assembly halls where we usually have to lie huddled up in the cramped space. Generally there are only one or two toilets for us all and a shower only in exceptional cases. I am impressed how the participants who had hardly any community experience have managed to adapt. Without grumbling our group takes in its stride whatever is offered. For the moment we have become a well functioning tribe! Private interests appear almost like peculiar relics of a world gone by.

Our way leads us through the village of Jayyous. The village is located six kilometres away from the Green Line but as ever the wall separates the farmers from their land. We are welcomed by the mayor and various representatives. One of the farmers gives a moving speech about the situation in the village. We don't have much time to spend as this day we have a long march ahead of us. Various men and some children accompany us. Some took our GRACE-shield and begin to loudly sing: "PLO, Israel no." They are unaware that Israelis too are walking in our group. How do they feel? Will we be able to provide the protection they need? I exercise myself in the faith of God. Determinedly I explain to the children and youths that the slogans they have are not a good idea and that they should invent positive slogans. I emphasise that we are on a pilgrimage to look for solutions for both sides involved. I suggest to them that they might shout: "For a free Palestine." They look at me somewhat astonished but accept my objection.

We walk for many kilometres along the fence that separates Palestine from Israel. Fayez positions himself in front of an olive tree and sings a prayer. A cheerful and joyous spirit prevails amongst us. It is astonishing how much basic joy for life these people can muster despite all the suppression and their suffering.

We shall overcome

We arrive at Qalqilya. This formerly rich Palestinian town used to be frequented by Israelis who liked to shop in its ample markets with its reasonable prices. It is only 17 kms to Tel Aviv. Today 45.000 inhabitants live in Qalqilyas as if in a ghetto. The town is surrounded on three sides by the wall. All access roads are controlled by the Israeli military. A Palestinian police car drives in front of us for our protection. Today is the anniversary of Arafat's death. Honking cars, with banners printed with a variety of slogans, drive through the streets. We are expected at the office of the peasants' union of the Palestinians Autonomy Authority. Many speeches are held. Something in the soul begins to oppose all these speeches. It is difficult to keep listening to the same repeated accusations. Longingly the soul is looking for fresh approaches to solve the problems. To learn to show sensible compassion is a high art. Ahmed Azar is there, a member of the Fatah, who sat in prison for over 22 years. He describes his political path. Another speaker explains very plausibly and factually the reasons for the construction of the wall. He particularly outlines the ecological background and emphasises that all the main water sources are to be located on Israeli ground.

At the same time there is an underhand attempt to deprive the Palestinian Autonomy Authority of its power by dividing the country up into many small parts none of which are accessible to the others. A country without water and without free internal access has hardly any future. One literally takes the water out of the mouth of the deserving.

Joel is shocked. He is no longer able to reject these arguments. Even before, he never had a ready answer when asked: "If the wall has been put up for the sole reason of keeping suicide attackers away why then does it not run along the Green Line?" Now the long term planning behind the line of the border is explained. A major challenge awaits Joel when he returns to his Jewish friends in the US who all hold the same beliefs he used to hold. He will not be the same as before. He has seen too much. He will possibly feel he is now an outsider. He will also have to be able to withstand many questions and even attacks if he decides to stick with the truth. Which of his friendships will endure given such drastic changes in his view of the situation?

After the many speeches we sit there all a little tired and a little at a loss. What more is there to say? What would give some real hope? I feel like singing a revolutionary song but want it at the same time to be a soft song. Being a woman I have the deep inner desire to let something soft illuminate this hardened masculine world. We begin to sing the song: "We shall overcome." It is the first one to spontaneously enter my mind.

We hit the mark. Enthusiastically the men join in. We take each other by the hands and sing verse after verse. I am touched. Never before had I sung the song "We shall overcome" with a foreign mayor in a foreign town.

Peace march through Qalqilya

When we took off from Qalqilya we were met at the next turn of the road by a large gathering of people equipped with banners. They wanted to join us. Now we meet the next challenge. I greet the waiting men and have them translate the banners for me, knowing full well that there are many people for whom the keyword "Israeli" is enough to set them hating. With only a few words I explain the purpose of our pilgrimage and that we do not wish any confronta-tion because we want to encourage the Israelis to build up a resistance movement. For this they need from the Palestinian side a readiness to cooperate.

"Do you sense any type of violence right here?" asks the deputy representative of the ministry of the interior who today is our escort. No, the men with their banners stand there in a determined but friendly manner. Over it though hangs the latent atmosphere of tension and the strangeness of it all compels one to be careful. We have a megaphone and through it I announce what is happening here and what is written on the banners. "We are all invited to go together for part of the way."

Some time ago we had decided to always move as a group should we ever become part of a large assembly so that in this way we would be able to distance ourselves from anything that would not be in accordance with the purpose of GRACE. This rule however is long-forgotten and the group is now all mixed up with demonstrating Palestinians.

I walk ahead. Once again our path leads us up to the wall which on this side is sprayed all over with graffiti. Anger, longing and creative fantasy are freely expressed here. From afar we see the Israeli watchtowers looming far above the wall. A ghostly sight! For about one kilometre we walk along the wall. A farmer shows us his huge farm at the outskirts of the town which has now been cut into two halves by the wall and the fences. If he wants to cultivate his land he has to pass through a gate which is many kilometres away and only open at special times. The authorisation which he needs to cross over can only be obtained at a time when he is normally supposed to be planting or harvesting. One can easily understand how humiliated he feels. Even the eyes of the latest to join our group are now fully opened to the fact that this wall serves other goals than to protect against potential violent criminals.

We proceed very slowly. At the edge of the town the gathering of people is reduced one by one to its original group of pilgrims together with a sprinkling of Palestinians. We leave the town through a tunnel beneath the wall. After a few kilometres we come to the house of a Sheik. Festive tables have been prepared for us and we are heartily welcomed. Lentils and onions and many trimmings for the pitta-bread are offered.

Chairs and mattresses are carried into the street. The old Sheik counts 121 children and grandchildren of his own. His oldest son is a Sheik too. The night before in Qalqilya he talked to us about the many religions in a most humorous way. Our young people played circus with the many children. Quickly it took on the shape of a small village festival. The group is happy in this place. A little breather and good human contact soon remind us that life can unfold its beauty even in the hardest of prisons as soon as human souls are allowed to reveal themselves.

The Egyptian television has arrived. Benjamin and myself give interviews. I am no longer afraid to speak in clear terms. I have to express what I see. Two of our Israelis also speak publicly, which I find very courageous.

At a check-point we say good-bye to some Israelis. They need a break in order to cope with all the impressions they have had, but nevertheless they want to come back later. We, who remain, share with the Palestinians the humiliating situation of having to stand in line for hours every day.

Olive harvest in Salfit and the cosmic blow

Towards the evening we reach Salfit, a Palestinian village with many Israeli settlements located on its surrounding hills.

Two days of olive harvest lie ahead of us. Sometimes the access roads are only open to Israelis. That makes the olive harvest a cumbersome undertaking for the farmers. Again and again they are attacked by aggressive settlers. International harvest helpers are invited for protection.

We are welcomed cordially in the rooms of a political meeting house which serves as a hostel to us at the same time. Again pictures of Arafat are hanging all over the walls, a very common sight. We sit in black seats at the conference table. The Palestinian television must have reported on us as we are clearly already known. My eldest daughter Delia has joined us. Much joy of seeing each other again in the middle of Palestine!

The next morning it turns out to be that our help with the olive harvest is very badly organised. Benjamin and myself have our hands full trying to avoid the worst of the chaos. We learn that there is not enough work for all of us. Uri tells us that Rabbi Arik Asherman, founder of the organisation "Rabbis for Human Rights", is also looking for international helpers for the harvest. Quickly we organise a group that is to join the rabbis. On the bus ride to this place I was dealt my "cosmic Zen blow."

The bus stops at a checkpoint. We have to change vehicles. I am fully occupied with a talk about organisation when on getting up I knocked my head giving myself a heavy blow. Everything turns around and I sink into a chair noticing that blood is streaming from my head. I have knocked a hole in my head by banging it against an overhanging toolbox. I see my pale face in the driver's rear-view mirror and notice how everything seems to be getting blacker. My inner sensor remains calm and I tell the others quite calmly what has happened. I know instinctively that I now have to try to prevent the emergence of a field of fright. Benjamin acts with concentrated strength. He is a credit to his name of "son of the right hand of God." As soon as I close my eyes I see a lot of light. It feels as if a lot of long dead souls are dancing around me.

Repeatedly the catchword "Nablus" comes up and I see how from here we could tie a string of light leading upwards. In the state I am, Nablus appears to be a key place in the processes of turning war into peace. It was in Nablus where the great injuries in the realm of love occured which finally led to God's wrath and to devastatingly cruel wars. This is the heritage of the patriarchy. Meanwhile I lie in the last row of the bus with my head in Vera's lap. Sabina, the nurse who travels with us, holds my feet. Vera out of support and compassion succumbs to a faint too! Although I am only semi-conscious I still have my humour with me.

In a taxi Sabina returns with me to Salfit. It is suggested I have the wound stitched in a nearby clinic, but I know that all I need at the present moment is peace and quiet and want nothing that would nourish within me any fright or panic. I feel slightly sick and giddy which tells me that I must have a light concussion. Sabina looks after me carefully so that I can entrust myself totally to my inner world of images. God has ordered me to rest and I surrender to it. If I want to come up quickly my circulation does not play along and I feel sick. It is a tall order for me to have to let go and to trust that the group is well led without me. Benjamin Vera, Rico and Klaus do it wonderfully.

One is prone to fall in love with Charly when he puts all of his strength into the singing. In certain situations he might well unify a whole world through it, so powerful is his voice. Everywhere he warms hearts. In one of the forum circles, while I lie in the next door room, Vera declares her love both for him and for me. She talks about what it means to her and to her own hopes that Charly and I already began to realise our dreams at the age of 17 and that we remained faithful to them despite all the difficulties. Gratefully I hear all this though only half awake and dreaming. Just now a large part of my perception appears to be happening on a spiritual plane. I dream of Arafat who wants to run into the arms of Sharon but Sharon does not notice him. In this dream I am surrounded by dancing souls, some of whom move in a space of light-giving forgiveness and are looking for the connection back to Earth while others drift about without any orientation. One room is totally closed and dark. It is my duty to bring light to it.

I dream a lot of spaces of meditation which are shared by Palestinians and Israelis. We create a string of light towards the ancestors. The field on Earth becomes lighter as remembrance, reconciliation and healing occur. I let the images come without judging them. In one of the dreams I see myself with an opening in my head through which the light is streaming.

The group of pilgrims enjoys the two more or less quiet days of the olive harvest by being in direct contact with nature and the people. I lie in bed and recuperate. During these days we bid farewell to Fayez. He has to fly to Lebanon at short notice. When he hears of my accident in the forum circle he asks everyone to get up and to join him in prayer: "I am very sorry about what happened to Sabine", he keeps repeating. It is very unusual for a Palestinian to have a woman as a leader. At some point during the pilgrimage he took my arm and put it around him and said: "Now you are like my mother." At this point we formed a contract of trust. Fayez has become part of our cosmic and motley family. He says that he has accompanied many groups but that he never before had experienced anything as deep reaching as this. Charly sings for him the song "How can anyone ever tell you, you are anything less than beautiful." Tears begin to run down on Fayez' face as Mustafa translates the text for him. Almost all of us have to cry too. He says: "Crying is a cleansing of the soul and the spirit." He has given all of his heart in accompanying us, always taking pains to bring some order into the Palestinian chaos.

During the sharing circle we also learn that one of our harvesting groups experienced a confrontation between settlers, police and soldiers. This seldom happens when people from abroad are present. Nobody though suffered any damage.

The 16 year old Ludwig Schramm talks of a deep experience he made. He witnessed how a Palestinian boy, a proud rider on a donkey kept hitting the animal. Ludwig's reaction was one of deep compassion with the donkey. At the same time a lot of anger and hate about the boy came up. He was appalled about his anger and felt that he could not undertake anything with this attitude. Through talks in the group his anger gave way to a greater understanding of the boy, for his life under occupation and his notion of being a man. Altogether everything came to a good ending.

At the close of the olive harvest all participants got together once more to exchange experiences. Ludwig managed to speak about his vision of non-violence without judgement. With this he was also successful in reaching the boy who promised not to torment an animal anymore.

163

Our youth group will help with the olive harvest for another week. The others move on in the direction of Ramallah. Bidding farewell, one of the farmers of this region shakes hands gratefully and says: "When we shall be freed, we shall come with you to the other countries, to Colombia, to Iran, Iraq wherever you want help with the large liberation movement for a free Earth." A heartfelt farewell.

The Miracle of Anata

Anata - the "no self"

Anata (Anattà, Sanskrit anatman) is a term in Buddhist tradition and means "no self." It was Buddha who, like no other, gave us the teachings of "no self" and the experiences that are connected to it. I was not aware of this when I first came in touch with the term. Here in Palestine Anata is the name of a place where injustice is crying out to heaven.

The "no self" may well be the reason for the small miracle that became possible in Anata. With myself still very shaky from my accident, we all reach the boundaries of what our souls are able to bear and there is no space left for the agitated thoughts of the ego. At first these may rear up once again. With all the strength they can muster they want to activate the latent body of pain. Afterwards all becomes quiet. The inner needle points almost to standstill. At this point the human being will either stay quiet and resign or surrender and hand over the reigns to the "no self." Afterwards all that is left to be done is to become a silent witness until at some point a higher force ensues which takes over and acts through us. This is Anata – the "no self."

In Anata we hear stories and become witnesses of human suffering that surpass by far what a human being is able to take in. The little Paletinian town is located only ten kilometres away from Jerusalem.

Opposite, on the neighbouring hill we see the luxuriously built settlement of Jewish settlers connected to a well constructed net of roads. The inhabitants of Anata can only watch this life from afar. For them this is the other world, inaccessible to them. All they know is that everything is taken from them so that those on the other side have a good life. The wall that is built around the centre of Anata keeps them away from their land, their fields and from access roads. At the outposts of the town large stone boulders block

165

the way; the inhabitants can leave the town only via one single road controlled by a checkpoint. The town is suffocating. Today the wall surrounds the town to the extent that inhabitants cannot even use their former rubbish tips. The rubbish is now burnt repeatedly in the streets leaving behind a horrible stench.

The daily drama

Our quarters are in the town hall across from the school. Words fail me! When entering the schoolyard one can see the humiliation all at once – a huge wall goes right across the yard! By this measure, 800 school-children are squeezed together into this tightest of spaces. We, the outsiders, are privileged. It is embarrassing to be here as a spectator. It is rather like watching animals in a cage. Anata is an example of how human beings force other human beings to live lives subjected to complete inhumanity.

The supposed main wall is being built 100 meters below us. The wall through the schoolyard has apparently been constructed to protect the building site of the main wall from stone throwing children. However, it can hardly escape anyone that this wall has not been built for security! There is no need for the main wall to be built that close. It could just as easily have been run through the valley below. But, down there are the important water resources!

A whole group of teachers surrounds us and talks to us insistently. Still today I can see them in front of myself, see the faces torn with anger, fear, desperation and hate. Here the precisely functioning psychology of victims and perpetrators has become set in a firm pattern. "In the mornings the soldiers arrive to provoke the children to throw stones. Every day they come with gas, not tear gas, something much stronger", one of the agitated teachers tells us the never ending story of suffering and indignation. Everyday they witness the same scene: soldiers on their watch walk along the wall, the children, primarily the older ones, pick up stones not being stopped by the teachers who stand nearby watching silently.

Throwing stones is the only remaining weapon to demonstrate their cry of indignation to the world. Soldiers following their orders fire some shots of warning. The hate of the boys grows and they throw the biggest stones they can throw. If a soldier is hit on the head these stones can cause ugly injuries. At this point the soldiers retaliate with tear gas or what ever other gas it might be. Desperate and with added anger and indignation in their hearts the most courageous ones amongst these Palestinian boys carry on fighting - a futile battle until they have to give up.

"One day our pupils will provoke the soldiers so far that one of the children will get killed, all the more reason for the school to be closed down", says the teacher. Some of the Israelis still maintain that one might be afraid of the unpredictability of the children. Desperately, they look for explanations which might serve as an excuse for the other side. But it is so obvious where the anger comes from, and it is also obvious, even to an outsider like my self, who would have the power to end this misery.

An outcry of indignation

Despite much knowledge of human psychology the outcry of indignation persists! Why does the world permit this injustice? Why does nobody intervene? Why is there no mass movement to end this craziness? Why does Germany remain silent rather than act with solidarity in the face of all of this global injustice? Out of the fear of anti-Semitism? Are not all Arabs Semites? Would the Jewish people not be helped much more, if they were only to reflect on their original, humane State constitution?

Daniel Barenboim, together with his friend the late Edward Said, built up the West-Eastern Divan Orchestra and in so doing set a courageous example. In 2004 he conducted a concert in Ramallah at which highly talented young Israeli and Palestinian musicians performed together, as well as with musicians from all over the world. The creation of this orchestra alone is a quiet revolution. In his speech during a prize giving event the famous Jewish conductor recited from the declaration of independence of the State of Israel in front of the Knesset.

"In 1952, four years after Israel had declared its independence, I came to Israel from Argentina with my parents as a ten year old boy. The declaration of independence was to us an incentive and inspiration to believe in the ideals which turned us Jews into Israelis. This remarkable document states the following commitments:

The State of Israel will pursue the development of the country for the well-being of all its citizens. It guarantees freedom and equality according to the visions of the prophets of Israel. It will also guarantee social and political rights equally to all its citizens regardless of religion, race and sex. It will guarantee the freedom of belief and conscience, the freedom of speech, education and culture.

The founding fathers of the State of Israel, who had signed this constitution, committed themselves "to stand for peace and good relations with all neighbouring states and peoples."

This speech of Barenboim raised a lot of indignation amongst the members of the Knesset. What would the consequences be if the Israeli people were to remember these guarantees? If it no longer were to identify with the interests of a government then it is in no way better than the one in office during apartheid in South Africa? Some time everyone has to have been in Anata. Every one has to see this with his or her own eyes. It should be obligatory for every German secondary school class to visit a region of crisis in order to see for themselves the effects of global violence and then to study its implications. Also on the Israeli side of the wall, the soldiers who have to obey the often absurd orders are almost still children. Are there no other, more sensible jobs for them to do, rather than having to utterly lose their hearts, their beliefs, their hopes and their fervour to a system of violence? Who, after all, is in a position to withstand all this and still retain hope and strength?

Too long the world has been asleep

Those who start to see will also understand the deeper meaning of global peace villages. To change from a system of violence to a system of peace we at first have to recognize and to develop. It makes no sense to wait for governments to act. Dauntless we can seize our possible freedom. With microscopic precision the first course settings need to be executed, which will then have an effect on the whole. The system which makes the machine perform differently still needs to be invented. If the prototypes function then it will work worldwide. I keep seeing pictures which are almost romantic and at the same time militant. Let us put away our passports which tie us to a false nationality, to a false collective dehumanisation? Do we want to end up as soulless machines drowning in a system of consumerism? Let us start from scratch. *Neti neti,* this is not who we are! This is not the human being! This is a worldwide and insane aberration which can but lead us jointly to our own destruction. Nobody will survive this system without losing his heart. Like lemmings we rush towards the same fate. We still take refuge in believing that misery is something that only concerns other people and we still like to believe that all is clean in front of our own main doors. Still many of us console ourselves by believing that bad karma is the reason today for people living such a destitute and painful life. However, it concerns us all. This avalanche of violence cannot be stopped if we do not rethink decisively.

"Too long the world has been asleep" says Hamdan, a young disabled Palestinian who, with his crutches, accompanies us for a few days. "Are we not human beings too? Sometimes we feel abandoned by the whole world." The gratitude for us being here and listening to them is huge.

We sit in the town hall and need a space to have some peace and quiet. Continually the door opens and shuts again. Continually the phones ring. Palestinians come and go. Nevertheless, we are able to form a circle for "deep listening." Some villagers who come to join us at first are laughing, but then gradually becoming more and more curious. Without being asked the first ones take it on themselves to ask newcomers to switch off their mobile phones or else to make their calls outside. Again and again I am astonished at how this form of talking takes on a natural magic and authority and I am grateful for this.

Today we passed through two checkpoints. Many in the circle try to find the words for the dismay they feel about what they have seen. Words adequate for what touched them seem to fail every one. Today, I too feel this as strongly as never before. The whole group appears to be almost paralysed. Some almost dissolve in their tears, others have no tears left. It is as if some sort of lingering resignation is overtaking limbs and spirit even the entire body. It affects the breathing. It affects the voice. One hardly wants to move. Some are grateful for the opportunity to speak in the circle. For others all they want to do is to leave.

A prison within a prison within a prison

Mohammed Alrifie from Anata tells the story of his stud farm and racing stable. At the age of 17 he started to realise his dream. He built up the farm. Three times it was destroyed and with it his dream in life. Now for four years some of the horses have been standing in a tiny space, a prison within a prison within a prison. We have heard many stories of human suffering on this day. Astonished I notice that the majority of the people in the circle are nevertheless deeply touched by the fate of these horses. "Maybe I like animals more than people", says Andreas, a young Swiss journalist. A small group had visited the stable of Mohammed. Full-blooded Arabs stand in narrow cages on a rubbish dump in the middle of the town. They are visibly suffering and one of them continuously repeats the same movements, pulls up its head and lifts up its right hoof as if it were again on the race track and about to go. "My horses suffer as I do", says Mohammed, their owner. He had put all of his money and all his love into this project which was repeatedly taken away from him. With this project he wanted to demonstrate non-violent resistance offering young people a perspective. In 1997 his house was destroyed for the first time. He had a heart attack. Israel wanted to buy his land, but he declined. He rebuilt the house and in 2000 it was destroyed again. And yet once again. In 2001 the bulldozers were at the front of his house ready to tear it down. His one thought was to open up all the stable doors in order to save the horses. Of the 40 horses that he chased out only 20 later came back. Where should he go with them? For four years now they have been confined there. Meanwhile an Israeli settler has built a stable on Mohammed's land. And after all this Mohammed can still say: "I do not hate the Israelis. This is not the end of the world. One day, even if it takes a thousand years, the land will be returned to me or my descendants."

This is one of the many moving stories. Repeatedly the participants in the circle express their dismay about the fate of these animals. One is under the impression that this is just about the limit of suffering that they are able to abide. Some Palestinians find the talk about the animals strange. Astonished one of them asks: "Are not human beings more precious?"

Indifference, the creeping fascism of our time

I am alarmed. We cannot leave this place without leaving some sort of a mark. In Anata, clearly a peak is reached for the group of how many stories of suffering they can absorb without either falling into unconsciousness, closing their hearts or succumbing to a raging anger. Since we are in the West Bank we only hear the one side of the story. People want to vent their anger and begin to hate those who inflicted all this suffering. The enemy lives over there on the other side. How will it be for us when we cross over and visit the settlers on the other side and get to hear their stories? Crystal clear I observe a psychic process in us human beings which I have

171

so often noticed before. People who for too long have helplessly had to witness human suffering react with an automatic mechanism of hate and indifference in order to protect themselves. They search for clichés so as to be able to vent their feelings. But as long as one is not acutely threatened, indifference is the easier way. One insulates oneself. One chooses a smaller horizon in life where fewer unresolved questions and problems can crowd in. "Indifference is the creeping fascism of our time", says the former priest Hans de Boer in his book "Blessed commotion."

Once more I lie awake most of the night on the hard tiled floor and cannot sleep. I want to give birth to a new idea for tomorrow. How can we leave a seed of hope behind in this schoolhouse that amounts to more than mere consolation? I surrender into the hands of the Goddess knowing that behind everything the Sacred Matrix reigns, a force that always and everywhere designs a pattern of solutions. May this force act within me and bring forth something new. One must have become a witness in order to truly understand.

Sowing the seed of hope

Although I still feel worn-out and my head is not in order, a force comes to me whenever I need it. This strengthens my spiritual trust. In the morning I recognize a radicalization in others too. Michal Raz from Israel who lives near the Dead Sea where she intends to build up a community says: "We cannot just leave here as if we were tourists. We have to leave a mark to show we are serious about our peace work. This visit has lasting consequences for me. Everyone ought to reflect about his or her future contribution."

I explain to the group that I want to go over to the school and ask the teachers to invite the pupils to assemble in the schoolyard for some sort of joint action. I go to the school together with Dhyan who speaks Arabic and has a wonderful way with children. We ask that we may speak to the children and sing a few songs with them.

The teachers are surprised but agree to it. Our entire group of pilgrims is invited to come along. Taking our GRACE placards with us, we go to the schoolyard and stand in front of the wall. Several school classes come and we form a large circle. Now we have to become creative! Dhyanis marvellous at doing this. He strikes up an Arabic song. Each child is asked to say his name out loud. We do it too. Each person is welcomed into the group with loud applause.

I notice that some of the pilgrims are embarrassed. "This is naïve. No help at all. This is like being at the kindergarten." Nonetheless, I have to be very clear now and without any false considerations follow my inner guidance accurately. Yes, I do give in to all the naivety I can. Today it appears to be my elixir of salvation. There is no time for either outer or inner discussion. I am asked to create a situation of joy with all the force we have at our disposal.

"The presence of joy generates healing power also in the midst of the deepest of troubles", was the first input I received in the morning. I remember well the question put by my teacher of religion. He asked us whether from our viewpoint Jesus had been naïve. At that time my answer was a definite yes. "Yes, he must have been naïve otherwise he could never have gone against the current of those times as he did and make all those miracles happen." In difficult situations I often resort to this memory. It gives me strength and I consciously choose naivety as a form of action which is still able to reach our childlike souls beneath all of its irritation and disappointment.

"If you do not become like the children..."

Today, to be like a child was like a call for help of my injured soul and was an invitation to others to do the same. Totally unplanned, scene after scene unfolds. I suggest that with our hands we form a large ball of light and push it into the middle of the circle. The children participate with growing enthusiasm. With much concentration we push the ball of light towards the middle, and having arrived there, we stretch our arms and hands towards heaven calling out "Salaam", the Arabic word for peace. Again and again we repeat this ritual.

It baffles me how easily a situation of enthusiasm and joy can be created, and yet also one of concentration. The same children that the day before threw stones are now concentrated on pushing a ball of light into the middle of a circle and calling out Salaam.

This is followed by an improvised speech. I talk about non-violent revolution. I speak impromptu and directly from the heart. I want to sow a seed of hope to encourage the children and prevent them from throwing stones after the armoured cars and tell them that this will only aggravate their situation.

As we arrived in the morning many in our group were afraid of the unpredictability of the children and the likelihood of more stone throwing. It is incredible, the kind of authority a wild hoard of boys can exert on the soul and in particular on an Israeli one. Here in Anata the image of the enemy, of stone throwing children - which is spread throughout Israel - is more than confirmed. For one moment we open the door to another reality. We also tell the children that there are Israelis here among us. Later, one of the teachers, visibly moved, tells us that this is an encounter of a different kind, one where the children do not meet with Israelis in uniform but with Israelis who have come to play with them.

An image comes up in my head: Young people from Tamera, after their 3-year studies and with enough community know-how, come here in order to create an example, which demonstrates how human beings are able to experience absolute freedom even when living in a prison. Instead of throwing stones they would no longer react to the soldiers marching by because they have found something more interesting to do. Withdraw the attention which is normally extended to the enemy and you deprive him of his power. The clear and cheerful laughter of the children would make the soldiers on the other side more than curious of what is going on behind the wall. They would be reminded of their own adventurer's soul. One would make technological experiments together, for instance to produce autonomous energy supplies; one would regularly deepen the aspects of community and solidarity. And maybe, as time goes by, one would invite the soldiers to participate in the experiment.

Violence can never be the answer

While our action rouses enthusiasm amongst the children, my appeal to stop throwing stones met with brief indignation from some of the teachers. Agitated they stand in a tight group around me. "How can you take away from the children the only weapon they have left? It is what endows them with the last spark of strength, courage and pride? We have no other weapons. And we have to fight. Otherwise no one in the world will hear our story." Slowly and with stern words I explain to the teachers why I have to motivate the children to resist non-violently. "Violence can never be the solution. All that violence does is to forever create more suffering. I do not want to see these children die. To stand up to armoured tanks with a stone is futile. Do you want one of the children to be killed? Clearly the Israeli side is the one with more power in this game. They will present your stone throwing children to the public and explain to it that you are terrorists and that one has to protect oneself against the likes of them. But there is a higher strength. Non-violent resistance, well trained, can bring about real miracles." I talked to them about the success of the Carnation Revolution in Portugal and of the opening of the Berlin wall. In both of them no blood was shed. "We will do everything that is possible for the international world to hear of your suffering", I explain to them as well as I can. They listen attentively. They recognize that I do not talk from a hostile point of view but out of support. The farewell is warm. It is a never ending task to effectively loosen encrusted patterns which are made of a concoction of fear, anger and revenge. Peace workers of all countries, unite! This isolation of people behind walls has to come to an end.

Where do we go on from here? During the brainstorming earlier this morning we have collected a lot of ideas. Who is willing to help so that these may be realised?

A new strength grew inside of me. With absolutely no pre-planning I have been prepared to let "Anata", the "no self", act through me. I have the impression that we have left behind more than the

175

symbol of a ball of light in that schoolyard. With our appearance and behaviour we have created a crack in the daily violent routine of Anata. The endless repetition of attack and counter-attack was interrupted for the first time in a long period of time. A new field of information, a new possible thought and behaviour pattern has briefly loomed into the grey everyday life, creating a small crack in the hypnosis of fear and anger. On this day many held back energies pointed in a new direction and found a new outlet. This experience will leave behind a deep impression in the souls. Surely, this peace experience is not strong enough to change the prevailing field of violence. Probably, in the days to come, the same old scenes will repeat themselves in Anata. Too new and too unusual the other possibility of life looms in the old world. Nevertheless, we have left something behind in Anata, something that will unfold its healing power by itself. An opening has been created. It is similar to a stream. At first there is a small opening. This might finally lead to the stream to take an entirely new direction. New thoughts create a new reality. The inner wall has received cracks. Through these small openings the pupils were able to perceive the people on the other side. They did not look into the faces of enemies. Rather they looked into the faces of Israelis who are engaged, full of compassion and willing to help. We cannot resolve everything by means of our own strength. My feeling tells me that in Anata a new field has been created for growing the plant of peace.

The journalists and engaged networkers in our group draw up and send out on the internet an international appeal for support for Anata. Already the next day, first reactions arrive from schools in Switzerland and Greece.

Many weeks later we hear that a peace conference of war veterans has taken place in the school of Anata. Is it coincidence? I see this as part of the larger wave of life and call it: "The miracle of Anata."

Zaman al Salaam.

The War Game in Bethlehem

Bethlehem, an abode of God

Bethlehem. In the barn in Bethlehem the Christ Child was born. Still today the church song from my childhood rings in my ear:
"There he lays, miserable and naked, the creator of all things."
Recognised by no one, despised by the prevailing culture, the son of God came to see the light of day. When shall we be able to recognise the children of God and build befitting shelters for them?

As long as our culture is not able to provide a home to this divine light it is better to bed our head down with the refugees and the dispersed. Under the bridges, on stone floors of assembly halls, in places where people reflect upon justice, may there be my home. May those places be my guideposts where life itself finds its unconditional right of existence.

Here I find more home and protection and cosmic security.
When will recognition become successful?
When will not only the human being be raised to be God, but when will a divine culture see the light of day?
When will our houses become the true abodes of the divine nature in the human being?
When will we build houses in which truth and trust reign, where an open spirit is shown towards the guests who seek us, where there is festivity and celebration in honour of Creation?

O Bethlehem, abode of God,
behind all your facades of war,
behind the tanks and hidden bombs,
where even those who barricade themselves in your Church of Nativity are being shot at,
behind the murders and the bloodshed

I have not lost the glow of hope,
which guides me,
and I am ready
to listen to this inner voice
and let myself be led by it.
Give us shelter
and let the power of love illuminate so that it will never expire.

Holy Land Trust and Sami Awad

In Bethlehem is the seat of the Holy Land Trust, which is a Palestinian organisation for non-violence and also our most important partner in the West Bank for the organisation of the pilgrimage. Its director is Sami Awad, a wonderful person, with whom friendship and cooperation is becoming ever deeper.

Sami Awad, 34, is a Christian Palestinian and the son of refugees. Already his family was committed to the thought of non-violence. His uncle, Mubarak Awad, is a symbolic figure of the Palestinian resistance who had to emigrate to the United States to avoid going to prison. Sami's family, originally from Jerusalem, was expelled from there during "Nakba", the Israeli banishment of the Palestinians in 1948. For many years they are not allowed to enter Jerusalem. Sami's father, a Christian preacher, lived in a refugee camp in Bethlehem and later went to the United States together with his wife, where Sami was born. Together the whole family eventually returned to Bethlehem. In the eighties the Intifada began. "It was a Palestinian uprising which was mainly non-violent", says Sami Awad. "Even though, the media mainly showed people throwing stones. The Intifada made it clear to the world that Palestinians exist and that their situation is unbearable."

As a young man Sami Awad followed the ideals of his uncle Mubarak and distributed flyers for non-violent action. Several times he came into conflict with Israeli soldiers. In order to avoid going to prison his family sent him to the United States, where he studied peace and conflict resolution. He returned to Bethlehem as a trainer for non-violence. His pupils are police, politicians and even entire villages.

Sami Awad: "My work consists of empowering people and communities to act non-violently. Many Palestinians at first believe that non-violence means to accept the injustice and not to resist. But non-violence is a much more powerful tool to end the occupation. Gandhi was an example of this. The more one is able to free oneself of fear the more one is able to really act non-violently. What is a greater victory and needs more courage, to shoot a soldier or to make him lower his gun? How often have we stood unarmed in front of soldiers and looked into their eyes and how often has the soldier burst into tears and had to be replaced?

From Sami Awad is the following thought: "To end the occupation is a bagatelle compared to the task of afterwards building up a free, peaceful and democratic Palestine."

He counts on the strengthening of the original Palestinian village societies which have especially suffered under the occupation and with the construction of the wall. "Here lie the roots of Palestinian society and it is these which we have to strengthen." Sami Awad counts on close cooperation with Tamera with regard to the Plan of the Peace Research Villages so that in Palestine, too, it will be possible to develop modern examples of an ecological, self-sufficient and communal village life. His understanding of Christian charity also touches me.

"The source of non-violence is love. We are only able to love others if we love ourselves. Love begins with the acceptance of oneself. We have to find the point within ourselves where we can fully accept ourselves as those who we are, i.e. our capabilities, the colour of our skin, our culture and our age. This is where our power to act begins and the power of non-violence."

I am very happy that we got to know this non-violent, visionary Palestinian spirit and I am curious about the many possibilities for cooperation which will develop out of this friendship.

The refugee camp "Ayda-Camp"

In Bethlehem there are four refugee camps. We find a hostel in the "Ayda-Camp" that we got to know during our trip to Israel in 2002. Together with Rabbi Jeremy Milgrom we visited this place at the turn of the year and for the first time heard the stories of the refugees who live here. Even children have been shot at by the soldiers of the occupying forces allegedly because they had thrown stones. A young man by the name of Mohammed, with whom we then had celebrated New Year, talked to us of his dream to create a place for children and youth right here in the refugee camp.

He said to us: "I do not want to witness how our children and youth lose the joy and curiosity of life and forget how to laugh. I want to hear the children laugh."

It is impressive how many things here have been further developed during the past few years. All the rooms of which the young Mohammed had dreamt of do now exist. One feels the immense engagement within the refugee community.

At the beginning there were only tents, later huts and narrow alleys where people who were displaced for generations lived together in the narrowest of spaces. The centre, built out of own resources, is a living example that even in a prison one is able to create one's own freedom. Over all the newly built rooms there presides the spirit and living proof of a conscious effort to leave behind the war and the suffering. There is a little library, a room with internet connection and a small museum that displays the history of their ancestors.

The eight metre high wall soars up directly next to the refugee camp as a daily reminder of the occupation. Soldiers patrol regularly, many of them almost still children themselves, prompted and educated for war with all its cover-up, and deception. Shocking to see that on both sides they are but children, at whose expense the drama of global war is played out.

O Mother of life look, through my eyes:

What has been done to them! Not to judge have I come but to see and recognise, to cry your tears and to draw new power from them for the absolute NO to this system and its structures.

No children shall die anymore on the battlefields, no matter from which political party, religion or view of the world they may have come. The cry for more justice, the cry for life is more embracing and more powerful. I struggle with GRACE, for the victory of life over death.

A somewhat smaller wall divides the centre from the rest of the camp and has been painted by the children together with their young educators at the Ayda-Camp.

Their story is here told in pictures. Created with a lot of dedication and precision one sees the paintings of Palestinian women and men with tents who are forever being displaced and attacked by soldiers. Where are these children supposed to find their source of trust? From earliest childhood they know nothing but the history of persecutors and those persecuted. In one of the paintings one sees a large identity card on which in big letters is written:
Father: prisoner
Mother: murdered
Place of Birth: refugee camp
The painting bears witness of a fate that these human beings share with a large part of the world's population, forgotten and ignored by affluent Western society.

At the moment I do not bother about the question of guilt, since the victims of this system, which in itself is wrong and does not offer any solutions, are to be found on both sides of the wall. And they have been victims for centuries. We bear witness as much to the pain of the Israelis as we bear witness to the injuries done to the Palestinians.

Is it not astonishing that despite the degradation Palestinian refugees have endured for generations, despite their indignation and anger, a copious humanity and love still prevails? Is it not a miracle that after the seemingly never ending humiliation, degradation, torture and agony and after having lost all their rights, that not even more acts of terror and bomb attacks have taken place? To me it appears like a miracle, it proves the fact that apart from all the suffering and all the desperation there does exists an untamed will for more life, more love and respect which wants to find its true course. A rift seems to go through humanity, while one part chooses revenge and terror, the other chooses, maybe still quietly and unnoticed, a deeper level of compassion, love and humanity.

The tales of the inhabitants of Ayda-Camp go to one's heart. Nobody who has the opportunity to meet them will remain untouched. It is impressive to see how they create hope for their children in this tight space and with small means. They demand that their land which was taken away generations ago be returned to them. They are ready to share their land with the Israelis but they want to be seen and acknowledged in their origins and in their tradition. They demand their rights be given back to them.

I am sure they too would gain new insights in the name of GRACE if only they had the opportunity to meet with Israelis, with their "brothers from the other side." Many of them might then see that it would not necessarily have to be their own land that they receive back, because people from other countries are now living there who were themselves in turn once displaced and to whom the land in their sights has been legally awarded.

Injustice turned to justice

Injustice was turned into justice. The readiness for a real new beginning is the precondition for GRACE. We bear witness to a talk between an inhabitant of the refugee camp and the Jew Hila Cohen, a beautiful young woman, whose family originates from the Yemen coming from there, to a country pledged to them as the Promised Land. Generations of her family had been searching for a place where they would be allowed to pursue their way of life without either being punished or persecuted. In deep fascination she and a Palestinian refugee talk about their path and their fate.

I am grateful to have been allowed to witness such an exchange as it has possibly taken place for the first time under this roof, namely one with much respect and great compassion. Only occasionally did I intervene to help it along.

If someone wants to witness people who despite all the misery and all the injustice do not lose their capability of humanity, happiness and love, then he or she should visit Ayda-Camp or many other places throughout the West Bank.

On the Israeli side of the wall little is known of this. The "brothers and sisters" on the other side of the wall are made to believe that the refugee camps are breeding grounds for terror and violence and that for this reason they have to be controlled and sealed off ever tighter. Concepts of an enemy are being kindled here which do not have anything to do with reality. Seldom, it is the other person that we truly hate. Rather it is the totality of the projections that have been taught to us that lead to hate, the image made of others without ever before having been in contact with them. If for 24 hours we were to seriously try to walk in the other's shoes, our perceptions would change enormously.

Hate is born out of projections and out of a culture which has been created from closed hearts. The sons of Abraham and the mothers Hagar and Sarah must inevitably meet again and recognise each other and then maybe if not to love each other, then at least to accept each other. There will be no free Israel without a free Palestine.

The war game

In the evening we perform in a large modern hall in Bethlehem. The tension in the audience transmits itself even to us up on stage. When in our play the figure of the Palestinian suicide attacker calls out: "I want revenge", they applaud. For a moment the actors are startled but calmly carry on playing until the end. The tension in the hall is high. Many are enthused but some do not agree with the peaceful message. Some young Europeans, helpers in Palestine, are outraged because Jewish history is also portrayed. A young French woman exclaimed angrily: "The Palestinians cannot be expected to suffer because of the Holocaust!" On the way back to the refugee camp, a young inhabitant of Ayda-Camp expresses how much the play has touched him. He asks: "Were you truly allowed to perform this play in Israel? And they did not throw you out? It is superb that through you our situation is being brought home to them."

In the morning after a two-hour talk at the refugee camp we leave to catch a bus accompanied by twenty children and youths. Surrounded by the mingling voices of the young people, by rucksacks stacked around in the street, by pilgrims gathering their last items, and with the GRACE shield in my hand I start off in the direction of the bus. I am still a bit weak from the blow I had received on my head. All of a sudden, in seconds the total situation changes. What just a second ago had been cheerfulness and calm had suddenly changed into upheaval panic and people running. Elias, one of our hosts, tells as sternly to go back.

"Soldiers", he says somewhat resignedly, "because of the kids. Just wait."

About 200 metres away I see soldiers walking to and fro. Shots can be heard. Now quick decisions have to be made. The question of how much we function as a group imposes itself now. I decide to move as fast as the wind in the belief that as an international group we could calm down the situation. Briefly I explain to Elias. Outwardly but not inwardly calm, I slowly move forward shield in hand. The others follow.

The bus is not there anymore. Probably it has moved off, as the situation has become too uncomfortable for the driver.

Now, at close quarters and behind the corner of a house I see three soldiers with guns held high. Opposite them is a group of children. May be that they held some stones in their hands but nobody saw any of the children throwing them. The children were about to form friendships with some of the Israelis in our group. The bus drives up again from the other side. A loud shot can be heard. Like kids playing at war a whole load of soldiers with guns ready to aim come running around the corner. But this is no game anymore, this is becoming serious.

At this moment everything in one's own system of cells is transferred to war and its own magic and authority. It feels known from way past. What one might have been afraid of subconsciously all of a sudden becomes fact. Nothing functions as it would normally. The consciousness which sets in at such moments is a completely different one from the one we know in our every day situations.

Inwardly it appears to me that right now two parallel worlds exist. I see the fear, the commotion and the panic, and am aware of a readily available behavioural pattern that exists inside of me. Next to that there is another force which remains as a calm witness. Calmly I go towards the soldiers and tell them that these children are peaceful and determinedly ask them to stop as all they are doing with their behaviour is to provoke violence in the children.

One of the soldiers appears to me like a man possessed. Fanaticism gleams in his eyes. Clearly it is not reason that is reigning here. He is completely absorbed in this game of war and nothing will change him.

"Go, go, your game is over", he answers brusquely with a threatening gesture.

Behind the wall I see more soldiers with their guns ready to shoot. I stay put for a while, until Elias, the trainer for non-violence, quietly asks us to get on the bus. They are most familiar with this type of situation and I do not want to risk anyone in our group being hurt. Therefore I ask everyone to follow.

Even to this very day I relive this whole situation in my mind. I ask myself whether I acted correctly. The group is in a confused and agitated state. Everyone has a different impulse to react and I am grateful that after the initial turmoil they are ready to follow me. I appreciate from this situation that the group's work on spiritual guidelines for the pilgrimage had been worthwhile.

A wrong reaction, a small unconscious or provocative action and what had just before appeared to be peaceful turned into violence.

You can do peace work for twenty years - war happens in a second and is able to destroy everything.

One has to be aware of these latent energy processes when passing through war zones. It is in this place that the inner shifts must occur which often can save lives. Would I have been alone I might not have got back on the bus. All of a sudden one is challenged by the question: What does it mean to end war here and now? One wants to neither act like a hero nor like a coward. One wants to act in a way that is healing. One wants to understand what exactly the small shift entails that is capable of ending war.

Visit to a military station

In the bus, over the microphone, I briefly explain why we have decided to leave. I respected the wishes of Elias who is a lot more familiar with the situation in the country and I listened to him. Inwardly it feels as if a higher power guides me when at such moments I have to quickly decide to trust as there is no time to be lost. Each second is very valuable.

After everything has calmed down a little we decide to drive immediately to the military station in the hope of shedding some light on the situation.

Daniel Lang, an Israeli pilgrim, has arranged the visit for us. His 19 year-old brother, who is doing service at this station has declared himself ready to arrange the necessary contact with one of the officers. A young guy with a radiant face comes towards us in front of the big gates. What a beautiful human being! He could well be the David from our play "We refuse to be enemies." What if he were to receive his formation not in a military camp but instead in a global station for the learning of peace for the protection of all beings? What if the taxes would flow into the construction of peace stations? Let us not fool ourselves. Peace has to be learned and studied as much as war does. Shall those controlling the globalization of violence go to war themselves rather than sending young people!

A young officer bids us a friendly welcome and explains the story to us from his point of view. It is harrowing to hear how he faithfully recites the propaganda of his State. He trusts the decisions of his government which are meant to serve the wellbeing of its citizens. He is not willing to challenge things. Would he still remain who he is if he were to pilgrimage with us for three days? Hardly any of the soldiers or the officers are aware of the actual living conditions of the people who live behind the wall. One is prone to even believe in his credulity, although his "not knowing", i.e. his "not wanting to know" is shocking. According to his words he believes that they are serving to protect against acts of terror. To the question, why does the wall not follow the Green Line, the accepted border of Israel, he has no answer other than to say that the State is looking for just solutions and that it is not the task of soldiers to scrutinise the decisions of the government. "This country is at war and thereby it cannot be helped that innocent people are affected too. There is nothing more unpleasant than to be on duty at a checkpoint but it is necessary in order to protect the State." We ask him to explain to us the situation we experienced in Bethlehem.

Very soberly he outlines his point of view: "I am sure that one of the children has thrown a stone. Everywhere, where there are many children, soldiers are instructed to stand alert since one wants to avoid that Israeli soldiers are wounded. It is their duty. This appears like war but in fact no one is attacked."

He does not seem to know or does not want to know what this does to the souls of Palestinian children and the anger, desperation, and blind hate this creates in them. Does he not know that Palestinian children know no other Israelis other than those who aim their guns at them?

I tell him our point of view. I talk to him of the suffering and the misery we have seen on the other side and that this injustice only breeds further violence. I also ask him whether he is aware of the concept of the enemy which is built up in Palestinians if they only know Israeli people as soldiers and never as human beings.

He listens attentively and one can see his face changes colour now and again. But he is on duty and he will not tell us what he really thinks and feels. This would go against his professional ethos.

The officer emphasises repeatedly that they are on duty to prevent violence. He does not feel that it is correct for soldiers to refuse service, since it is primarily through them that a peaceful solution is possible. If it is known that someone was unnecessarily violent he is immediately discharged.

It was possible to defuse the bomb

After half an hours` talk we leave the situation, in turmoil over all that we have seen and experienced. One can hardly distinguish between sadness, resignation, anger, disappointment, helplessness and exhaustion. Everything mingles into a conglomerate of undefined feelings.

Daniel, who identifies with the Israeli side, speaks out vehemently: "Few of them are correctly informed. Understand that it is not the soldier that is our enemy, the enemy is the ignorance. This ignorance is not only displayed by the soldier but by the international world too."

Uri, who for years is fighting for the rights of the Palestinians, is angered: "This was exactly the situation that Sabine talked about in her parents' generation. All of them said that they knew nothing about what happened with the Jews. They have to know it though, and they are able to know it too. We have to make it clear to them that they have no right to be here. I could have shouted: Go away! I am ashamed at times to be an Israeli."

Both of them cite important arguments. At some point though, their talk is no longer serving a better insight. Emotions have taken over. All of a sudden Daniel and Uri stand confronting each other and shouting at each other. The nerves of the group are laid blank.

"Stop!" I call intervening and feeling reminded of the scene in our play when Stella, the alien, was able just in time to stop the bomb going off.

"We cannot proceed in this way. If we are not able to make peace among ourselves how should they? Let us try to understand how we can end the war." I suggest one hour of silent marching.

This was our last stay in the West Bank. Only a few kilometres away from the narrowness of the refugee camp we all of sudden find ourselves in the midst of a beautiful, wide natural landscape with terraced gardens, water sources and woodlands. The group walks quietly along their path and into the dusk. I am still too exhausted to walk as a result of my accident and let myself be driven to the encampment for this night.

We prepare our camp at a place in the country with a source of water. Exhausted I sleep deeply for an hour. All the pictures of the last week pass in front of my eyes. Not one of us will be leaving this experience without being changed.

It is Shabbat. Ohad and Dawn arrive together with friends in order to celebrate Shabbat again together with us. In quiet reflection we look at the happenings of the past week. Their powerful chants help to lighten our feelings.

The next morning, rather like monks, we sit opposite each other in early morning light. "Who are you and what do you want" is the name of the game that in a ritualised way will give us the opportunity of an exchange. It is about intensive talking and listening. "What will you do with the experiences you made?" "Do you believe in a possible solution?" We put these and similar questions to each other. We sit opposite to each other in two long rows. One side speaks the other side is silent and listens without reacting. New decisions are sprouting in the souls of those who have become witnesses.

It is astonishing which kind of forces nature offers us in help. Gaia Earth, I lay my head down onto the bed you provide for me. Nobody shall be allowed to lead a war for a country that does not belong to anyone. Gaia, Mother Earth, in your name we are on pilgrimage, so that in a not too distant future Bethlehem may bear its true name rightly.

Visit to the Settlers

A wrong attitude towards time will always create war within us

After the dense atmosphere of Palestinian towns and villages, of refugee camps, checkpoints and the wall we are once again wandering in nature. We have left the West Bank and approach Jerusalem. It can clearly be felt how the entire group is regenerating. Something internal is visibly coming to a rest. Now, when walking, we have the opportunity to delve deeper into the experiences and to understand more. We can become witnesses of our own thoughts and feelings. How often are we afraid that something is done to us which in all truth we do unto others? This is an essential point which decides whether there is war or peace within us. To live in awareness helps us to perceive our own speed and to thus make time our friend. How often do we proceed far too quickly and pass from an experience just made to something new before even a fraction of what has just happened has the opportunity to enter consciousness? A wrong attitude towards time will always create war within us. Many of us are still moved by noticing just how fast we ourselves are ready to react if only we are agitated, attacked or find ourselves in a difficult situation.

No one can hide it, each one of us breathes with relief that we have now left the West Bank. At the same time we are very conscious of the injustice since the inhabitants of the West Bank do not enjoy the same privileges as we do. They have to stay permanently there in the situation which we as guests shared with them only for ten days. What quickly became too much for us is their everyday life. How can we ever give them advice? No, we can only share, perceive and help where it is possible for us to do so. Help through self-change, help by addressing the sick part of the side from where we have come. The one side can only heal when the whole is healing. It is not a part that is ill. It is the whole that is ill. On the one side of the wall the illness has become obvious, on the other it is there wanting in its latency to enter consciousness in order to heal.

An awakening to a greater kind of human being

A feeling besets us so as if we had to leave a loved-one. This time the loved-one is not a person but a whole country with its customs, its living habits, with its beauty and its urgent call for help. It leaves behind a feeling of sadness but also of determination to do something for all those whom we have to leave behind on the other side. We want to tell the world what we have seen. We want to talk about the humanity and the beauty which we have experienced in the West Bank but also about the infinite sadness, of the anger and about being neglected and left alone. How many people in the Western world are afraid of being left alone! Could not then many of them be healed if they were to decide to no longer leave alone those who need us so urgently? True love does not run away when things are getting difficult. It is precisely here that love abides its presence and healing power looking for the channels of self-realisation.

Overall I sense the mood within the group to be something of a miracle. They participate in everything, living in the simplest of circumstances without grumbling. Where does the group take its strength from? We have not only seen misery, many have also experienced human solidarity and closeness in a way that has hitherto been unknown to many of us. There was no time to circle around oneself. There was no time to entertain thoughts of aloneness. Some have taken a big inner step, an inner twist - an awakening into a greater kind of being a human being. Can people change? This pilgrimage gives me a clear answer: Yes, under new conditions we can change. The community has become our haven. Everyone arrives punctually for the morning attunement or to the joint talking circles. Everyone is grateful for these meetings. All in the group can feel the healing power of the common "Geist" and of the listening. True communication and contact become possible if we adopt the habit of not interrupting each other. One can feel the effect of mutual respect. We all experience the healing power of being together in a higher spirit, made possible by the group through truth, compassion and creativity. That we were able to deeply touch so many people must also have been due to our mutual "Geist". It was a special vibration we radiated. The people felt this and it created trust. A functioning community is able to produce miracles. Alone this would not have been possible.

Visit to a settlement

Since I am still too groggy to walk for longer stretches I experience the pleasures and pains of our work from another angle. I have latched myself onto Klaus and his organisation team and ride with him in the van. I prepare sandwiches for breakfast and distribute them at a resting area to the passing group. After arriving at our encampment I begin to prepare the soup for the evening. I find rest for about half an hour underneath a pine.

We have something important in mind. We had decided at least once to plan a visit to a settlement. Today about 400.000 people live in the Israeli settlements – all in areas that "legally" belong to the Palestinians. The settlements are the biggest cause of dispute in the Israel/Palestine conflict. Their security serves as an argument for the fragmentation of the country through countless checkpoints, walls, roadblocks and separate settler roads which are prohibited to the Palestinians. In large parts of the peace movement it is frowned upon to even talk to settlers since their presence in the West Bank is considered to be an injustice which has to be removed before any kind of negotiations can take place. The settlers however see the reality differently. Many have come here, to the land of Abraham, for deeply felt religious reasons. Others came because the State had offered them reasonably priced living space and because they were not informed properly in their countries of origin. Many stand out for their militancy and extremism. While Israel cleared its settlements in the Gaza Strip in the summer of 2005 there were still settlements being built in the West Bank.

All previous tries to get in touch with settlements or orthodox representatives of the Jewish faith have so far failed. Complications cropped up every time. It appears to us that the settlers and the orthodox live apart, not wanting to be disturbed they retire from a world which they only see as a threat. So as to not leave Israel with an unbalanced view our Jewish friends had insistently asked us to include in our planning at least one visit to a typical settlement. In actual fact a second pilgrimage ought to be made, one which would lead through the various settlements in the West Bank.

Michal organises a visit for us to Alon Shvut. The inhabitants of this settlement are willing to receive us. Since we have to undertake to travel a long way, we have decided to make an exception and use a car. With a small group we drive there while the rest of the pilgrimage group spends the evening at our encampment. The settlement is surrounded by high security fences. We pass a control station where all people entering and exiting are thoroughly checked. Each visitor could be a possible terrorist. As the settlements are located in the occupied territories which legally belong to Palestine resistance against the occupants has to be taken into account. After having been checked at a heavily protected military post, the first thing that catches our attention about the settlement is its appearance, of streets being just like European streets. Clean compact cars, front gardens, only few people on the road, all completely calm. This is the direct opposite of the Arab world where there is a lot of hullabaloo in the streets and most people live in very humble quarters.

We meet the settlers in a room that has been designed in the memory of a murdered settler. On the wall there is a picture of a young man who was shot by Arabs ten years ago.

We are given a hearty welcome by a man who has clearly participated in peace camps before. He stands out through his openness and his willingness to hear other voices. Many of the settlers we met today we liked straight away.

First perceive what you see

David Lisbona, whom we got to know at the Sea of Galilee comes from far to support us in this talk. We hear now the stories of nine settlers. Michal introduces the circle. She asks that we listen to each other without interrupting. Each of the settlers is to speak with regard to three questions given to him and relate what is important to him.

One man interjects that he would first like to hear from us what we think about settlements. Some of us begin to speak. Soon ideology fills the room and dispels the human "Geist" of courtesy and trust. It is human encounter, not political statements that opens hearts. I have made it a basic rule for me to put aside my personal judgment whenever I enter an unknown place. "Perceive at first what you see. Remain open to the possibility that your personal view might change enormously through this encounter. Then say what you have perceived. Afterwards you can form your own judgement, while knowing that it is never final."

In an unobtrusive way, David Lisbona, demonstrates his experience with "peace circles." He asks that we do not waste our valuable time wanting to convince each other. Now it all depends on listening to each other. "We want to know who we are, where we come from and what our human concern is." Sensibly he puts forth this idea and it is immediately accepted.

What follows now are very innate and very touching tales. Next to some distortions and irritations I see the Jewish soul in front of me, the Shechina, looking for the house of God that she can live in. It is as if our hosts were surrounded by a certain aura. A touch of melancholy, of poetry and longing surrounds them. They live in the Promised Land as if they were the immediate descendants of

194

Abraham awaiting the imminent return. We touch, although at first on the surface, the heart of a community with its own history, with its belief, its pain and its moving generation-long search for God. From their point of view this is the land that God had promised them and to which they had been faithful over hundreds of years despite persecution and disappointment. Persecuted by the world, violated and disgraced. Those who had been dispersed in the Diaspora have now been called back to "their" country, promised by God. By no means all the settlers come to this land due to religious motives. Here though we encounter this archetypical aspect of religious search. They come from various countries. One of them had lost all his close relatives in the Holocaust. At this place and with a deep will to found a religious community they have come together again. One feels that it is almost a pure classical, innocence particularly amongst its young members which is so touching. They came not to hate. One feels the spirit of the community in this people who have been so persecuted, and so misunderstood by the world and which is held together by their belief. But not all of them touch me with such immediate purity.

With others I have to enter into special peace work since I notice how within me I am so ready to react with antipathy. One of them is a rabbi. His voice rings with the fanatical undertones of a human being who through great injuries has moved towards a shocking fanaticism. His conclusion: "What is happening in this country is no human question it is a national issue. Naturally on the human plane injustices happen but they cannot be avoided in a war. I lost my entire family in the Holocaust. We need a place where we can live and not be persecuted. In order to manage this, the measures sometimes have to be drastic. God will exercise justice. A place is needed where we are allowed to practice our religion without being persecuted, a place which we do not have to permanently share with other religions. You do not know how it feels to have to continually listen to the Arab prayers through the loudspeakers. The Shechina is the abode of God. We need a place that is kosher and not clouded with all this alienation. This is the land that has been promised to us for thousands of years. We now have to show strength otherwise we have no chance to survive."

He is getting more and more agitated through his speech. His voice reminds me of a Islamic sermon which we heard from the loudspeakers in conjunction with the Friday prayer read by a fanatical Sheik. Without understanding the words one hears the hate against the enemy and the determination to fight to the last. "Eye for eye, tooth for tooth."

A Jewish woman journalist is similarly angered when she speaks. She has made the effort and travelled from far away and during the first ten minutes is indignant of the fact that we walk through the West Bank for ten days and only take one evening to spend with the settlers. Without asking who we are she launches an attack. She feels threatened and attacks as a matter of principle. We try to explain to her why that situation arose but her indignation leaves no room for understanding. She begins to speak in a never ending avalanche just as we have also heard on the Palestinian side where the feelings of injustice abound. It is the language of the oppressed and the persecuted which is never heard.

"No one understands our religion, our belief. Everywhere we are dispersed. All along we have been antagonised. When we came here the land was not inhabited. We have made it fertile and inhabitable. What you were told about the Arab world is simply not true. They will do everything to get us out from here. They want the whole land for themselves. The checkpoints only serve to protect us from terror. They will always hate us, no matter what we do. And they are firmly decided to wipe us out. We went into the desert to create space where we can live. Now that we have made everything fertile they want to have back what does not legally belong to them."

The basic feeling of having been treated unjustly rings through each detail of her speech. But as we keep listening to her for a while without interrupting she bit by bit becomes softer.

A characteristic of all accounts is the statement that there is no place for the Jews where they can be undisturbed and free from persecution. Most of them however say it with an open attitude free of the utter hatred of the Arab world. A young poet is also amongst them. He says pensively: "I believe that everything which we experience today is still a punishment due to Sarah and Abraham sending Hagar and Ismael into the desert. We have to find a way where the brothers again reconcile themselves. God wants us to be able to live together in this land."

An older inhabitant, who used to have a high rank in the military, says: "If we are not prepared to compromise we shall never have a chance for survival."

A young portly man relates in detail how, when they were children, they used to be friends with the Bedouin children. Ten years ago his brother was killed, just like that. Since then the fronts have hardened. He very much longs for friendship with his Arab brothers, but the situation is becoming more and more difficult.

"I want to love them but I hate them at the same time. I see no solution", says another. His girlfriend is moved. She looks like the archetype of a young Mary Magdalena who is looking for the path of the Lord. She would really like to pilgrimage with us. We ask the young poet by the name of Eliaz Cohen to read one of his poems. Shyly but with a firm voice he begins to read in Hebrew which we have later translated.

Poem about Ismael

Ismael is casting stones at me.
"Words," he cries out,
are harder than stone, and where were you
when I was cast out at dawn
with just a skin full of water and wrath.
Our sons, Ismael cries out,
shall jostle in our midst
and serve each other,
shall bear ladders, angels and children

casting memories at each other like stones.
Arab boys provoke me.
Throwing me back three thousand seven hundred years,
running naked, the hills arching their green torsos against our bodies,
sheafs of envy our mothers thresh,
almost unconsciously, for Ismael and me.

His second poem is a poetically formulated story:

"Do not uproot my olive tree"

When we were children, a tremor of excitement would go through my body every time we reached the threshing floor. Right there, in the no-man's-land between our houses in Elkana and the entrance to the neighbouring village of Masha five ancient olive trees stood. The adults had told us that they had been there since the times of the patriarch Abraham. Several of us children would try to surround the thick spliced trunk. Black leftovers of olives from the harvest were all over the floor and got stuck to our autumnal sandals. One of the trees, I recall, we had learned to enter, penetrating his interior in order to become One with it.

Not far from there, at the edge of the threshing field, would we stand and raise our eyes eastward: From our vantage point the land of Samaria opened up before us - its hills and valleys, the small villages nestled in it, the first budding settlements.

This land of the olives! Some weeks ago I took my children along to visit the threshing floor's ancient olive trees. I was greeted by a giant concrete wall in the face of which I became a child again, looking up from below. The view of the land called to me from beyond the wall. The modest houses of Masha seemed to still be there, as were the mountain ranges. But it was not possible to see them. The land is being cruelly dissected in front of our eyes. I am not making a political statement right now – and not because I am afraid to. It's simply that the pain is much deeper and more personal. The landscapes of my childhood are being expropriated in the name of "personal security."

In his photography Gaston has caught the two symbols that are cur-
rently fighting over the land – the olive tree and the wall. Becoming
rooted and being separated? The old and the new? In front of my
mind's eye I see, in somewhat different times, how we form a wall of
people, hand in hand – Palestinian villagers, the children of the set-
tlers, leftist activists and rightist believers- to conquer the wall in the
name of the "not uprooted olive tree of solidarity."

What would happen if we now had the time for some weeks to
jointly look day by day for a real answer? I have to think of the
artists of the time of World War II who also did not have any
other possibility than to express their hearts in paintings and
poems. Here in some of the settlements as in the Arabic villages a
totally different seed of peace is ready to blossom if only we develop the necessary form of community and of deep acceptance for
each other. This does not work without the support of a committed "third party." For them it may be easier since they do not identify with the enormous collective pain which has grown during
thousands of years. They see behind it the potential of a large
hitherto unfulfilled love. Isn't there a large potential of love in
each situation of enmity that wants to be discovered?

Afterwards the inhabitants thanked us very much. We created a
warm atmosphere and they were not used to being listened to.
Shocked but also with hope I leave this place. One would best want
to invite them to come to a peace camp in Tamera. I can imagine
that this would lead to many openings. Our host thanks us most
heartily. He keeps saying: "The work you do is wonderful."
He also says that he is impressed by the Christian way but he
could not understand why Jesus had said: "If someone hits you on
the cheek then hold out the other one to him too." I tell him of my
commitment to the non-violent path and explain to him that I
believe that this path, if gone all the way, will be more powerful and
effective than the fighting with weapons. However, this thought is
only to be understood if it is free of thoughts of powerlessness and

bravery. The power of non-violence is generated by a soul that is not injured and as such wants to awaken the memory of wholeness in his or her counterpart. In its core each soul has an uninjured point and cannot be injured. There one is at home with God. "How long already have people killed each other because of their views?" The longer I am in this country the more I feel confirmed in my belief of the power of humaneness and non-violence. I talk to him of the vision of primordial utopia and catch myself using the words out of our play: "We have to help that they can remember."
Remember the peaceful possibility to live.
Remember the being we are.
Remember we are all *one* common family.
No one of us has the right to take life.

In my heart I have decided to look deeper into the path and the essence of Jewish settlements. How about a human experiment: rather than clearing the settlements one would invite the Palestinians from the West Bank into the settlements? It would be the duty of both sides to share with each other their sorrows, their fears, their joys and their longings. Maybe they might discover that they are fighting the very thing that they originally wanted to love in each other.

At present such an approach already exists. Neve Shalom/Wahat al-Salam is the only village in Israel where Arab and Jewish families have chosen to live together and where the children share one classroom.

Entry into Jerusalem

Neve Shalom/Wahat al-Salam

Our last important station before Jerusalem is the village of Neve Shalom/Wahat al-Salam. From far off the little village can already be seen. It is a unique place in this country. The name derives from Isaiah, 32,18: "Then my people shall live in a tranquil country, dwelling in peace, in houses full of ease."

It means "Oasis of Peace" and was founded by the Dominican monk, Bruno Hussar. Neve Shalom/Wahat al-Salam is the only peace village in Israel which is inhabited by both Jewish and Palestinian families. It is located on a little hill near the motorway between Jerusalem and Tel Aviv and below in the valley one can see the Christian convent of Latrun. It is impressive how the small community, despite all the resistances in this country, has been successful in creating a positive public stand. On their path they were exposed to mounting resistance, both externally and internally. The history of the origins of Neve Shalom/Wahat al-Salam is a good example of how the study of outer resistance can strengthen the development of character and of projects. Strong individuals live here together and are fully engaged in their stand for equal rights and entente between the two peoples. Since 1979 a bilingual primary school exists with a kindergarten and a secondary school. It is the only peace school in the country. They provide access to an appreciation of both cultures for the children from the village and its surroundings. The "peace school" is a supra-regional institution which brings together Arabic and Jewish youths as well as adults from all over Israel and other countries to meet together and to attend seminars and courses for better understanding.

The Palestinian Eyas Shbeta, founder of the peace school, is married to the Jewish Swiss-Israeli, Evi Guggenheim and they live here together with their three daughters. Together they had visited us in

Tamera. Their book "Oasis of Peace" tells the moving life story of their lives. In this they describe the political situation of this country, the history of the origins of Neve Shalom and the conflicts in a marriage in which two totally different backgrounds had to come together. Evi and Eyas were also instrumental in bringing our play to Israel. We like to cooperate with them.

Our group was put up in the gymnasium. Evi invited me to spend the night at her house. Once again I was very connected to the weather spirits since already weeks ago I had received the inner call that we would be well advised to have a roof over our heads in Neve Shalom. There is some organisational back and forth as Neve Shalom is rather expensive for our budget. Finally we were offered the gymnasium for free. And it rained cats and dogs! Bucket loads of water shot from the sky. If only it would happen like this in Portugal!

I invite our group to a forum. I want everyone to be able to express creatively the emotions that have accumulated within us during the past days. Artistic expression and creativity are often excellent methods to free oneself from the build-up of anger or ill-humour and to prevent one identifying with it. I invite all those who want to, to go into the middle of the circle and to portray their present situation. It is the art of creatively enacting one's inner processes without all too naturally and in an everyday manner connecting them to the people sitting around and to express inner feelings without hurting others and without entering into the ping-pong of discussion.

This form of community communication is a much tried method for us to be able to let off steam. It clears the air among all concerned. Gratefully many in the group take advantage of this opportunity.

Benjamin, on whose shoulders rests so much of the responsibility for the group since my accident, gives a wonderful performance on the issue that as a German he has forever to try and to hold the balance between incessant reproaches of either being too "pro-Palestinian" or too "pro-Jewish." I use the opportunity to add a short and humorous performance on the issue of non-identification.

Music that creates peace

On November 21st, at 8 o'clock in the evening, another one of our performances takes place. Many people come from near and far. Enthusiastically Evi says that there are between 200 and 300 people. Maybe there were not quite that many but it is even so a wonderful audience. I give a short impromptu talk about the purpose of this pilgrimage.

Afterwards the world famous Israeli musician, Yair Dalal, comes up onto the stage, alone. For some moments it is absolutely quiet. Then, the gentle sounds of his instruments fill the room. He enchants everyone with his violin and his small Arab *oud* and his own plain voice. While he sings it is as if he were to tell his own personal history. He is both a Jew and an Israeli Arab with Iraqi origin. For this group in the Israeli population the hurt is doubly painful. Since their childhood they grew up with the division. They belong to both groups the Jewish and the Arabian which are at war with one another. It must feel a bit like growing up between divorced parents and yet wanting to love them both. Either one breaks under the pressure of this psychic conflict or the consciousness awakens to a higher level, to a new synthesis. Yair is faithfully following this path and has become well-known for it all over the world. His music is absolutely touching, peace generating and grandiose. His music speaks with an enormous soberness and shows with precision his connection to both cultures. Yet there is nothing spectacular and overly virtuoso included in order to prove his mastery. It is this magical simplicity which so touches the heart of the listener.

Dreamingly we listen and connect lovingly with the soul of this country. I see the desert in its light-flooded transparency in front of me, I see the minute flowers which somehow manage to live in the sand; I see the camels and with them a majestic silence of a timeless dimension streaming into my soul and bringing the gift of the power of perseverance. The jackals and the desert lynx transmit both the power of speed and quiet alertness. I see wandering

Bedouin and veiled women. I see soldiers with the faces of children and boys throwing stones, crying mothers, angry men. I see orthodox Jews in front of the Wailing Wall and Palestinian men praying at the Dome of the Rock. The land unfolds its unique flowering soul but behind it all I hear the sadness, the pain and the never ending hope of a life of true humanity. The heart of each one in the group opens up. Afterwards we perform our play in great peace and quiet.

Even Gideon Spiro, a courageous and radical journalist from Tel Aviv, is touched. When I saw him I straight away realised how much I like him. My heart jumps for joy. A few years ago he had been a guest to Tamera at one of our first peace camps. In his somewhat dry manner he describes how touched he was to see scenes of his own history in the play. A former parachutist with the military, he participated in the Six Day War in 1967, and he was part of the original "shaken ones" who later engaged themselves in the founding of groups of conscientious objectors like Yesh Gvul. Outwardly he is a little rough but he has a big heart.

People from Switzerland have arrived, among them Sundar Dreyfus from the Schweibenalp. Also the bandleader and the singer of White Flag are here. I got to know the two at the outset of my pilgrimage in Lucerne. This is the way circles are closing. Both are very touched by the play.

Afterwards we meet in a small circle at the guesthouse with Ohad, Dawn, Aida, Yair and the theatre group. A wonderful opportunity for talking follows. The idea and the vision of the Peace Research Village shine forth before us. One has the feeling that it is as if by sheer accident the essential carriers of the idea have met up. It is after midnight when we finally go to bed only to have to get up again at six in the morning to pack. Again and again I am thankful to the group for their full and wholehearted participation.

Now that the high tension is slowly ebbing away we notice how much we have seen, held and brought about. Now the soul needs rest, rest, rest to digest all that has happened.

Our path leads us further through the Jerusalem forest. From there it is another eight kilometres to Jerusalem itself. Darkness is approaching when we finally arrive in the little forest of Hirbet Himmame, which is seen as an oasis of power by many Israelis.

Maybe I would have acted just the same

Only a few hundred of metres from here Yad Vashem is situated, the famous Holocaust museum. I had already visited it during earlier visits. Most of the others make use of the opportunity and visit the place despite their tiredness. After ten days in the West Bank where we have mainly listened to the Palestinian side, it is vital to also be able to see this aspect. No one remains untouched. Now is a special moment, after the experiences of the last week, to be able to hear on the one hand the taped speeches of Hitler and on the other hand to hear the voices of those who were the witnesses of this gigantic annihilation of human life. With tears in her eyes, Irma, a very enlightened and politically engaged veterinarian, speaks in the circle about her experience: "I feel deeply ashamed to be a German. I could not speak German in there. Right up to this day I still cannot understand that all of this did truly happen. The processing of our history has not been completed yet, not by a long way."

A journalist comments in her diary: "If anything within me might be tempted to think that the Israelis are now doing exactly the same to the Arabs as once was done to them then such thoughts too are impossible given this absolute and unexplainable cruelty which we Germans perpetrated only two generations ago. Of course we "knew" but now it is written in our hearts once more. Peace work can never build up on accusations from either one of the sides. Peace work is healing-work."

In the meantime Benjamin and myself retire to our quarters. On our way we encounter a very upset man. It is Gabriel Meyer, the founder of the initiative "On the way to Sulha." This is a peace initiative which was set up at the beginning of the second Intifada. They organise meetings and camps with Israelis and Palestinians. *Sulha* is the Arabic expression for reconciliation. The initiative uses traditional elements of conflict resolution which are still alive in many Arab villages. In the case of a conflict in a clan all concerned meet and listen to the different opinions. At the end, when an agreement has been made, the peace is confirmed with a strong cup of Arabic coffee and this according to tradition settles the conflict once and for all. The Sulha-Initiative gets different population groups at many levels together for talks. Thousands of people are brought together for creative festivals.

But at the moment though Gabriel rants and raves, gesticulates wildly and complains that no one had ever thought to inform him of the time and place of this event. We sit down at the warming fire. I only know that today it is up to me to play the role of peacemaker. We inform Gabriel that it was not we who organised this evening and that we were assured that everything would be ready for us. Soon we share humour and human warmth. He went to fetch his guitar and begins to sing some songs in a very lovable way. Gabriel is a man with a big heart and talks full of enthusiasm of his meeting with the Dalai Lama.

It is already dark. Poles for the tents are being carried through the woods. Since we could not obtain permission to drive in, everything has to be carried from far away. Somewhere in the dark we can hear someone calling loudly. It is our friend Ibrahim Ahmad Abu El-Hawa. On many of our trips to Israel and Palestine he had been our host. In his hostel the Mount of Olives in Jerusalem he welcomes travellers throughout the year from all over the world. Now he needs helping hands to carry things since he has come with an incredible amount of food. Once again, and with every refinement he has cooked an Arabic vegetarian meal for us all.

"There is something else but not for you" he says mischievously trying to hide a bag. "This is for the people who are not from

Tamera." He has smuggled a plate of chicken legs into our vegetarian kitchen. Our love of animals while tolerated is met with
astonishment. To us an Arab kitchen without meat is wonderful
but to the Arabs however it is something almost unimaginable.

Torches and candles are brought out of the theatre box to bring
some light into the darkness of the tent which our friend Amit like
a little miracle worker always manages to put up in ever more
astonishing of places.

In the middle of the turbulence Jürgen Kleinwächter arrives,
friend and engaged solar researcher from Germany. Delia and Vera
went to fetch him from the airport. Hearty welcome! He will be
accompanying us for a few days.

After a festive dinner we assemble for a little event. The circle is
opened up by Daniel who has organised the evening for us. He has
invited some representatives of the Israeli peace movement to
come along. There are 60 to 70 people in the room. Daniel is especially concerned that we get to see and understand the Israeli side.
He has brought with him Michal Yaa`kovson, a 26-year-old
woman. Three years ago she became the victim of a suicide-attacker in a bus and by a miracle she survived. Already years ago we had
met her here in the Jerusalem forest, a beautiful young woman.
Now she sits here again in our tent and talks. For two months she
had lain in a coma and the doctors had given up on her. She fully
understands the Palestinian suffering but she implores us to make
an effort to understand the Israeli side. (In the chapter "The question of guilt" I look more closely at this.) Everyone listening is
struck by her story. After intensive days in the West Bank where we
have been made very aware of the suffering of the Palestinians, we
now feel closely the experience of the other side. This young
woman wanted nothing else but to live. Just like the Palestinians
do. The soul has to understand anew: This is not so easy. It is not
possible to divide the world into victims and perpetrators. Healing
does not result from accusation.

A big silence reigns in the tent. Only few questions crop up. After all this, one needs the time to be deeply attuned to consider possible ways of healing. Michal gets up, unostentatiously bids us farewell and leaves. The representatives of the Sulha-Initiative already want to pass on to the next part of the event, but something within me rebels.

I think: "This is not the way to deal with the stories of suffering in human beings. We must be careful for the stories of suffering not to become subjects of consumerism." Delia comes up to me. "Mama, we cannot let her go just like this. She needs some sort of a feedback from the group or maybe a joint song", she says. "Shall I go after her?" I am grateful and proud about the way my daughter is actively cooperating and being compassionate. Michal does have to go but she is thankful and glad about Delia's sympathy.

A good talk unfolds with the representatives of the Sulha-Initiative. Gabriel seems to me like an "alien" with a big heart. Surely he is a future cooperating partner. Until late into the night one can hear the murmur around the fire. I lie outside underneath the starry sky in the shelter of a tree and sleep, despite it being very cold. This was our last evening before the great finale.

The next morning we meet for the last sharing circle, this one on the top of the little mountain where we had spent the night. Thanks, contact, agreement on new action and cooperation are all part of the talk. This place, Hirbet Himmame, means "antique place of the doves." It is a place with great visionary power. From here one can see Jerusalem and its hills.

We do not enter Jerusalem by the thousands. Neither do we have a donkey. Nevertheless we do feel a little messianic. What we cannot offer in terms of assembling large crowds, we bring in terms of human depth. We carry the seed of hope and the belief in a possible solution in our hearts.

Quite a few people joined us to walk the last kilometres. Women from Middleway, Haya Shalom, inhabitants of Harduf, Michal Talya, Rabbi Ohad and Dawn, Michael Raphael, Sundar Dreyfus, the founder of the Schweibenalp in Switzerland and some others who already feel part of our "tribe of pilgrims."

I feel very calm inside. It is hard to realise that this will now be the last day of our pilgrimage. Of course it feels special to me. Although during the last months there was not a day which did not feel special. Strangely I do not have the feeling of moving towards a big goal. Rather I feel the sentence and the experience that has settled in my heart: The path is the goal.

The policeman who guides us through Jerusalem obviously originates from the hippie scene. A long grey beard and braids give him a very special look. It seems to give him visible pleasure to handle the traffic for us so that we can enter Jerusalem unhindered. Coming to the Jaffa-Gate my mobile rings and we hear our friends in Tamera singing: "We shall overcome." And so our common song sounds across more than four thousand kilometres.

It is an important part of the task of our times to find adequate rituals to express what we feel inside without it becoming too much kitsch or having too much old religion stuck to it. Nevertheless we need an expression of the sacred wonder of the overall happenings. Some prefer to retreat within themselves quietly reflecting, while remaining rather more cool and sober on the outside, while others are looking for a more outward, more ritualistic form of expression. Those in leadership have the high task of bringing together both sides. Personally I would have preferred to withdraw fully into silence and to connect to the universe in all its quietness so as to be able to look from a distance onto the stage of life and give thanks for the incredible guidance and protection which we have had the grace to receive on our path. Instead there are many farewells, hugs, touching words, songs, tears and jokes, too. Slowly we realise that the pilgrimage is indeed over.

An hour later the core group which started out on the journey through this land made its way to the old city to the Ecce Homo. This is a little hotel managed by Christian nuns and located in the

Via Dolorosa. Finally, our station for the next few days. And what a station at that! The place has become part of history for me. I can hardly imagine a better location to draw the first conclusions of the pilgrimage. The hotel received its name from the famous words of Pontius Pilate: "ECCE HOMO – see what a human being!"

The last performance

We sit on the large terrace with our diaries and talk over all that has happened. In front of us the Dome of the Rock and the many rooftops of Jerusalem. There is little time left to take all this in. A quick shower, into the bus, and off we go to our last performance at the David Yelin hall in another part of Jerusalem. It is a hall worthy of our last performance. To us it is a last challenge to befriend ourselves with Middle Eastern mentality and to practice inner peace work.

However the stage which we wanted to build up is occupied and being used for sound-checks by the band which we engaged to play at the end. All attempts by Kate and Rico to persuade them to clear the stage are of no avail. More than an hour passes while we wait. Ben, Vera and myself stand somewhat concerned and not a bit lost at the edge of the stage asking ourselves how we will ever be able now to build up the necessary concentration. Ten minutes after the official beginning of the performance the stage is still not cleared. The bass player comes towards us and asks what is the matter with us and why do we make such faces? Visibly aggressive, he turns on poor Benjamin who up till now had been in a good mood and snarls at him: "Which part do you have in this show? You seem to be staring around with a heck of a lot of hostility at the world." Calmly I try to explain our situation to him. But he snaps back at me: "Ok, ok, I can see you don't want to talk to me," and takes off in a huff. I try to see an aspect of God in him and sure enough after a little while I succeed and see the humour of the situation. The hall has already filled up. Jürgen Kleinwächter sits on the floor gesticulating and surrounded by young Israelis who want to talk to him about solar technology. All of a sudden things move quickly. Change, set up the stage, fix the microphone, costume and then curtain goes up.

It turns out to be one of our best performances. In any case the thanks and the resonance are overwhelming. I am especially thankful to see that settlers are in the audience, too. Our play seems to have the power to soften hardened attitudes and to touch and reach out. One of the lady settlers said that she would like to have a film of the play to show to her students. The pilgrim group surprised me with the gift of a warm shawl for cool evenings which they presented to me on stage. One woman whom I had already met in Switzerland gave us a donation of 300 dollars. We are grateful for the large flow of thanks we received this evening. It gives courage to keep going on the path. One thing is certain: the pilgrimage will continue, how and whatever has to be done next.

Following our performance Gabriel is showing a film about the Sulha-Initiative. With his forceful voice he begins to sing a simple song. Wonderful, very loveable and humble! He enchants the audience with a Sufi-song and everyone joins in. The following concert is an appropriate end to it all. Half of the audience begins to dance. The energy keeps growing. Although it is late, enthusiasm and joy abound. I forget my concussion and begin to dance quite wildly with my two daughters. At the stroke of midnight a birthday is announced: Joav who was on the pilgrimage with us is given a birthday cake with 32 candles. After the lights went out in the hall I see the last musician coming along. It is the bass player who had beefed at us earlier on. I go to him to make peace.

He embraces me.

"What kind of people are you, I have never experienced anything like it, so much power and so much energy and so much peace and engagement."

"Well, then you will maybe understand now why I needed some concentration", I say, and he laughs somewhat impishly ashamed. "I am very sorry about that."

He is from Peru. Later that night I give thanks for this evening and utterly tired out I fall into bed.

Part III:
Ending the War

The Issue of Guilt

After the pilgrimage, after a three-day meeting with the core group that wants to develop a Peace Research Village in the Middle East and after a short stay with Bedouin in the Sinai I flew back to Tamera. It has been a four months absence. Although the entire sum needed for the Aula had not then yet been raised, my inner guidance called me back home. In the meantime the foundations for the building had been laid, the construction started in February and in May Monte Cerro was launched as planned. I was happy to conduct the opening event of the newly built Aula. It is a straw bale and clay construction with a wooden frame. Young forces have taken on the responsibility to lead Monte Cerro. The pilgrimage was part of their formation. More and more I am able to retire from direct leadership of Tamera trusting that I will still be called to important meetings and training sessions. I shall now be able to concentrate myself more on the further development of the international community.

After compiling the entries from my pilgrimage diary into a book, I continue to be concerned with the question: What is the core issue of the Middle Eastern conflict and how can it be healed? What are the correlations of outer wars and inner conflicts that are generated by our way of living? The third part of this book deals with these issues.

Before coming to the issue of guilt I have to go into the subject of information. The question of guilt can only be clarified if we are correctly informed. Information arouses our emotions.

We were shocked to notice that most people in Israel do not really know what is happening in Palestine. Likewise in Palestine people know little about the fate of the settlers who have come there from many different countries, most of them displaced persons themselves hoping to finally regain their homeland and their deep religious source. They have been brought up since childhood in the consciousness that this land had been promised them by God. On either side the media reports are biased and create a basic emotional vibrancy.

When as a young girl I asked adults how the cruelties of the Hitler era were possible and why did they not do anything against it, their usual answer was: "We knew nothing about all this."

Yet they believed in the inflaming speeches and the cheap propaganda. If one hears the speeches of Hitler or Goebbels today one asks oneself all the more: How was this mass hypnosis possible? How was it possible not to see through this insanity?

The principle of wrong information does still today have its effect as it did at the time of fascism, a little more subtle perhaps, a little less obvious maybe but still just as hypnotizing. Through the consolidation of the established media programmes and that of the large newspapers real news is seldom disseminated.

It is like 30 years ago during the Vietnam War. It was not until 1967 that the public was properly informed of the extent to which it had been deceived by false media coverage about the war and how that hid from us the truth about the extermination of the Vietnamese people and the methods used for this by the US.

I kept being shocked by the fact that Israelis are able to live in the immediate vicinity of the wall, and lead a life as if war did not exist in their country. Will they, too, say in years to come: "We did not know anything about it?" This question however is not only applicable to them. In the information age we are no longer able to say that we did not know anything about it, no matter how great the distance between us and the war might be.

"All they have to do is look and they would know everything", calls out one appalled observer of the situation. The generation of our parents could have known it too had they only wanted to.

Not until we have observed the inner psychic processes in ourselves, which lead to not-knowing and suppression, will we ever understand the workings of this mass hypnosis.

As soon as fear infiltrates us or a bad conscience takes hold of us and we feel guilty about something we have done, the mechanism of not wanting to know the truth then sets in. This mechanism functions faster than our conscious thinking and shuts down the programme of truth latent within us to be accessed.

One then grasps for all sorts of possible world views, ideologies, group affiliations, the development of cliques, political party memberships, all this without realizing that we are doing this to protect ourselves from the truth. This is especially effective as a group mechanism and because in a group it can be more easily hidden.

If many hold the same opinion, one is easily persuaded that the group view is true. Who after all is capable of keeping alive his inner light, to keep asking and illuminating the dark places where everyone else has stopped to want to look at it long ago.

It can get pretty lonely and dangerous out there, and common sense warns you to be careful and you are then soon willing to go with your habits and align with the opinion everyone holds to be true.

Added to this is the great longing to belong to a group. One does not want to be an outsider and to have all your friends disagreeing with you. Therefore, one adapts! It can easily be observed how people all of a sudden can change when they move to live somewhere else. From one day to the next they move into a different social setting and almost immediately their thinking and their views of the world are changed. The wish for group affiliation must never be underestimated since it is a fundamental aspiration.

If someone were to come now and make you aware of the essential truth yet in so doing opening up an old wound, then everything in you begins to fight back. Immediately you would go on the defensive. Otherwise your whole system might collapse and you would be exposed naked to the truth which you fear so much. In this system the question of guilt is easily solved in this way and it holds everything together. The system always needs a culprit and the guilty are always the others. This is the mechanism which works exceptionally well and is what keeps wars going. This mechanism has held many an empire together.

The guilt system requires someone being in the right and another being in the wrong. It exists by having at its centre a truth of which we are afraid and against which we have to protect ourselves with the propaganda of world views. It exists and feeds on the fear of separation.

Furthermore this thinking leads you to the justified conviction that it is permissible to lead a war against evil. Some people, either as victim or perpetrator, have to pass through the most painful experiences in order to see through this mechanism within themselves and before they are finally able to leave it all behind. Therefore peace can never be achieved within such a system. If we want to end war – both in the world and within us – we have to recognise and end this mechanism.

It would be very comforting if we could say: Bush is the one who is guilty, Hitler is guilty, Milosevic is guilty, Israel is guilty or the fanatical Islamists are the ones to blame.

I quote Dieter Duhm:

Could Adolf Hitler have developed his satanic plans if it had not been for his father Alois who had humiliated and hit him? Would Alois have been able to hit his son, had he been able to live joyfully and lovingly with his wife Klara (mother of Adolf Hitler)? Alois too as a child had not harboured any evil. Would Vladimir Putin have been able to mount his atrocities against Chechnya if he had had a loving and caring mother? Would the dictator Milosevic of Yugoslavia have been able to sow his terror if he had not witnessed the suicide of his parents? Would Saddam Hussein, the son of a peasant, have made his violent career if he had not grown up in such a hard milieu?

I wonder, would Bush have had to reach for the fatal mixture of alcoholism and religious fanaticism, if he had not been soaked from infancy with American double standards of morality?

In his book "Future without War" Dieter Duhm illuminates these backgrounds further:

Alice Miller has researched and described the circumstances behind well-known perpetrators of violence. Even with the most brutal of killers the old Mignon-question can be repeated: What has been done to you, you poor child? You will understand that this is not a matter of sentimentality but of a collective fact basic to our present civilisation, namely the drama of alienation, the drama of failed love relationships, the drama of homeless children, the drama of the pain of separation and human abandonment. These are no longer private problems but part of the social and human drama of our times. Behind this worldwide epidemic of merciless violence stands the experience of a pain which cannot be dealt with in any other way.

This is the global core issue we have to deal with today. The question is: How do we stop and overcome the pain of separation and the fear of loss or abandonment? Or, formulated positively: How do we create real living and loving circumstances which serve the growth of trust and of solidarity with all creatures?

During the pilgrimage we were confronted over and over again with the question of guilt. Are there guilty ones? Whose guilt is it? This question runs very deep. The soul needs to dwell in quiet and calm in order to be able to look into this at all.

During our pilgrimage and already during our peace camps I noticed that guilt is usually looked for in an entirely wrong plane. And thus the question of guilt, when put wrongly, only rekindles the conflict and leads to new injuries.

Before we are freely able to glance at the question of guilt, we need to develop a high degree of non-identification. Only then, are we free to perceive the processes leading to so called guilt; only then can we recognise it in ourselves and others.

People on either side kept being touched by our play, "We refuse to be enemies." Nevertheless the criticism of: "You are too one sided", kept coming up with intensity from both sides. Sometimes the very same scene was rated as too pro-Palestinian by one side and as too pro-Israeli by the other!

The play lives from a consciously created naivety and from the emphasis given to stereotypes. Little did we know that what we called a stereotype would be met at every turn in everyday life in the Middle East.

We came across them regardless of whether their attitudes leaned to the right or the left. They seemed to reflect something of the basic vibration of the Israeli or Palestinian collective soul.

We too in our leading team had to look at the stereotype of the "typical German." This process did not pass without some tests.

I well remember at Umm el Fahm. We had just finished performing our play. About 200 people were in the audience. Young and old had assembled in the hall, mainly Israeli Arabs, since Israeli Jews seldom dare come to this town. It is said to be the centre of Arab terror within Israel. Others argue that this town is the centre of a potential Arab peace movement.

The play went straight to the hearts of many people. We were given a standing ovation by women, men and children too. We were overwhelmed.

Afterwards when I stood on the stage alone to answer any questions it felt like a test under fire. Despite having been touched and enthused the audience now launched its verbal attack. With glowing eyes they stood in front of me all talking at once. It was as if a barrage had been opened up and all the suppressed surplus anger about the injustices came pouring over me.

"You, the Germans, you are the culprits! You have the whole responsibility. You have brought this fate on us. Because you have shirked your responsibilities we now have to suffer all this. Where is your help? Why is no one doing anything? You have pushed everything away from yourselves. It is you who ought to be in our place."

The full brunt of held-in hate about the international world and especially about the Germans now lashes out against those who have come to try and help to solve the dilemma. For many peace workers this difficulty has turned into a deep practical test. At this point along the road some of them have given up.

Fiercely words are fired at me. Many more taunts followed. I cannot remember all the details. All I can remember is the feeling that I was being attacked in this way by strong men in a theatre brimming full of people. The fear and the identification would have easily led to a temptation to justify myself or to launch a counterattack. Thank God that I did not reach for it. At this moment I experienced quite the opposite. I received the gift of remaining totally calm. I did not identify with what they said. Because of this I was able to listen to them all the more intensively.

Wrong identification, one of the major inner enemies wants to prevent our recognising the issue of guilt. We identify with something and then we begin to fight against this seeming enemy who allegedly has attacked us. Self-defence sets in automatically. It is the sister of identification.

Since I was not identified I was able to listen calmly. I was able to see their anger and was again able to empathise. And then, in front of me, I see the collective body of the German people. And I hear, soberly and without judgement and without identification the core truth in their words.

The Germans as a people have not yet seen or acknowledged their guilt. They run away from their guilt and their bad conscience. For this reason they continue to be part of this perpetually turning wheel of war with its victims and perpetrators. The guilt appears to be so big that one runs away from it. The entire capitalist system is one huge manoeuvre to deflect us from an unbearable guilt.

At times I am able to empathise with how the Jews must feel when they hear nothing but the German language.

Alone its sound triggers deep remembrances of the Holocaust, the entire trauma of their history. Maybe things would change if consciousness could settle down, if we together as the victims and the perpetrators of this massacre would wake up from this hypnosis and begin to recognise the way out of it.

As soon as I identify with the fact that I am a German, I feel unbearable guilt which makes it impossible for me to truly look at it squarely. But from a distance, however, I am able to see the collective guilt of the Germans. I see the guilt which ensues from the mass hypnosis of unconsciousness. At the same time I can also rightly say: I have been born in the post-war era. I have not witnessed the war. I have, as long as I can think, been looking for new ways and perspectives.

Why then this identification? Who or what is it that says "I" to what?

Who forces us to identify with a system and a history which has led us over and over again to the same atrocities, again and again to war, torture, mutilation and psychic and physical illnesses?

Who is it that says "I" to what and why?

I am not the child of a nation. I am the child of a planet.

Neti, neti, this is not you. Slowly we shall recognise that history on this plane has for hundreds of years created its own identifications and its rise and falls. There is no way out. There will come a point when there is nothing left but a very deep choice. To the question of her friend Clara Zetkin "Ought we not resign from the party?" Rosa Luxemburg had responded pointedly: "Ought we not resign from the whole of humanity?"

On a national level there is no solution to the conflict. Israelis and Palestinians can go on discussing who has more guilt for it. It creates for ever new injuries, fears and pains. Only when we recognise that international world supremacy is participating and interested in this war, only when we recognise that German corporations deliver arms and the entire armament industry profits from it, that billions of dollars flow from the US to Israel, only then shall we see the global correlations which stand behind this war. We can then see that a global answer has to be found. We shall then notice that it is absurd to entertain the question whether we are Germans or Palestinians or Israelis and whom it is who is guilty. For a long time as a German I have not been able to identify with the dealings of the German government. Despite it I do love Germany and much of its traditions. Just the same as I could not underwrite what the Israeli government is doing today, even if I were an Israeli. I would have to clearly speak out at the injustice committed on the part of the Israeli government, but would nevertheless cultivate an intimate connection to the traditions and customs of the culture.

*We ourselves are participating in the continuum of violence for as long as we silently partake in a social system based on exploitation. **The war can only end, when we ourselves end the way of existence which is coupled to global violence***", writes Dieter Duhm in his book "Future without War".

This message of another life I meet repeatedly in very many human beings who long ago have silently decided to follow other inner ethics. Often the suffering had to be very deep in order to reach the decision.

A touching example on the Israeli side is the one of Michal, whom we met again shortly before going to Jerusalem in the Jerusalem Forest near the Holocaust Museum. Years ago we had already met her here when we were struck by her youth, her beauty and her purity.

Then, three years ago, she became the victim of a suicide-attacker. We could hardly recognise her again. On the last evening of our pilgrimage we heard her moving story. After the attack she had been so badly disfigured that her own parents did not recognise her.

She had been so seriously injured that no doctor believed that she would survive. Like a miracle she did and in the course of the years has gained back her beauty, although still marked by scars.

The most touching aspect of her message lay in that she did not harbour any anger, no hate and no thoughts of revenge when she woke up out of the coma. She keeps emphasising that she never reacted in fury at the perpetrator. She spoke with pain: "I was 23, but my body was that of a baby. I had to learn everything afresh, to eat, speak, to go to the toilet. Each night I was haunted by nightmares and I still have them. But nevertheless I do not feel any anger. I have visited the refugee camp where the perpetrator came from. If I had grown up there I would probably have done the same as this boy did. It is important to me that you see that there are always two sides to everything."

Her most important message is: "Do not be afraid. Fear breeds one thing only and that is hate. And hate breads violence."

And how do we abandon fear?

Certainly we shall succeed in doing so when we have found an anchor of trust again, when we have woken up to new qualities of consciousness. When we shall be touched again and pervaded by the dimensions of universal life itself, by the Sacred Matrix itself.

While we are still carried away with the identification of our little egos, our countries, our marriages, our educations, our churches and our States, this will not succeed. Only when we learn to draw from the abundance of life and to live without attachment, will the new "human being" be able to begin. We enter into a great new presence. And we enter into the old Indian concept of the Earth belonging to no one, putting all of her light, her power and her abundance at the disposal of all those who are ready to cooperate with her and with all of her creatures.

We may ask, whether those, who have masterminded the great plan of making the so called no-mans-land available for an Israeli State, ever realised the human suffering this would create? Are they guilty? Has it been the Israelis? Or has it been those who wanted to deport them because the "Jewish question" had become inconvenient to them?

"A land without people for a people without a land", was possibly considered a humane device at the time. It was totally overlooked that for many, many generations the Palestinians and Bedouin had been living there, intimately rooted and interwoven with the land and their traditions. Basically, the same thing occurred to the American Indians and it has been acquiesced to and agreed upon by the entire Western civilisation. It is not a question of who is guilty, whether it be the Israelis, who, full of hope, have settled in this land as persecuted Jews, or whether it be the Palestinians, who resort to terrorist actions out of sheer desperation,

The question of guilt is set on an entirely different plane. It is only too obvious that one cannot simply say that Israel is guilty. By doing so, we continue to endlessly prolong the reiterative chain of "victims and perpetrators." It is the global world population which has pushed Israel into this role.

We are dealing with a fundamental correction of the overall global plan, a failed way of thinking and political strategy that has to account for all of these victims on either side.

The question of pardon can only be put forth when the error and its source have been recognised as such and have been corrected. Everyone can then recognise how blindly he has participated in this overall game. We can then partake of the guilt and truly ask for forgiveness so that a new start can really become possible.

The Dangerous Fight against Evil

During this pilgrimage we became a transient community. Its members came from different countries, religions and cultural backgrounds. We had to reach a consensus on what holds us together and connects us.

The first walls which we had to take down were the walls between different views of the world, a world which was now suddenly supposed to be united. Apart from the issue of the conflict between Israelis and Palestinians there was of course our German past that kept resonating. We also repeatedly had hot tempered encounters with regard to American stereotypes.

For the American participants amongst us it was especially surprising to learn of the difference between what they hear about themselves in their own country and what people from other countries think about them. Sometimes, when sitting around the fire at night one heard loud expressions of astonishment: "What, this is what you really think of us?"

The willingness to keep opening up, for ever more and anew, made the changes in the group possible. Without the willingness to change the process of peace can hardly be continued.

Below I will look at some of the current clichés. If we examine the views of the world of the supporters of Bush and his government, we see, that many of them hold the deep belief that the war against Iraq is justified, as in their opinion it is part of the fight of good against evil.

They would say: *For the good cause we have to put up with disagreeable "side effects".* War is necessary. Mass murder of innocent human beings must be accepted as long as it serves peace, the family, honesty and integrity. After all, the world has to be freed of its tyrants.

The history books are full of such examples. Even the books of the major religions reveal this contradiction between humaneness and strategic warfare against evil. Curiously enough the biblical command of "Thou shall not kill" does not seem to hinder God have his people undertake cruel crusades against hostile peoples, against heathens, all in His name. Peculiar ethics! The evil ones are of course always the others. In each criminal story we see the lust of the hero who acts out his desire to kill and his cruelties under the pretext of serving the good cause. This thinking dominates the Christian world, the world of Islam, of Hindus, of the Western world. It shapes all of patriarchal thinking. The picture of male benevolence is imprinted in all of us; the protector, who saves us from evil. This so called "male benevolence" is kept alive by a necessary enemy whom it is imperative to defeat. Also in Adolf Hitler this peculiar mixture of brutality, low self-esteem and delusions of grandeur led to a flush of imperial thinking as never before. Only imagine what might have happened if Hitler had won the war? He would have entered history as a hero – like Napoleon, Caesar and others. This idea is hardly bearable.

There is another side to this "proper world." In Baghdad anger against the attackers after their massive bombings dominates the basic mood up until the present day. Many civilians were and still are being killed and seriously injured. The population is physically and psychically at its end. The misery is indescribable. Even hardcore journalists can often not hold back their tears. They witnessed how and by which type of means the battle in this so called ethical war was fought. They saw cluster bombs being used against the civilian population. Already in the air cluster bombs release a volley of smaller bombs at the time of their explosion. These cluster bombs were used a lot in Kosovo causing great harm to the civil population. After the victory even NATO officers opposed the use of these terrible "shrapnel catapults." It did not help. US President Bush emerged from the reality of this terrible war as the great victor and hero in the eyes of many people. Meanwhile though, even in his own country, he is the most unpopular President of all times. The economic interests behind the war in Iraq have long been

226

uncovered. To save his reputation Bush now plans another war to take place as soon as possible, this time against Iran. A true leader of our times?

The myth of the brave soldier in Iraq added to the whole absurd spectacle. According to the magazine "Spiegel", Mohammed Said al-Sahhaf, the Minister of the Interior under Saddam, announced with an unperturbed expression on his face and with a revolver in his belt, that on that day 43 American and British soldiers had been killed, 13 tanks and 14 armoured cars destroyed, 4 Apache fighting helicopters and 2 unmanned Predator drones shot down What a heroic epic!

Have we forgotten that the so-called terror is but an outcry of the oppressed who are led to it by those who have received money and the necessary training from the Western world?

The possibility that this terror has been initiated through forces in their own government just so as to have a reason to go to war is for most people too horrible to even contemplate. But this possibility has to be mentioned here. After September 11, I studied many papers, articles of background information, and documentaries that it is no longer possible for me to keep silent about it. Even those who cannot fully believe in this should be aware that these sources do exist. And despite the manipulation of the media it is necessary they make an effort to form their own opinions and come to the truth a little closer.

Does it not seem strange that the US government which claims it had no warning and was totally unprepared for the attack on September 11, should afterwards in only a few hours be able to name to the world the perpetrator, namely Bin Laden and his legendary network of terror, Al Qaida? I do not pretend to have the answers to the questions which are no longer discussed in the media. I do though question the concept that shows Bin Laden riding through a sand storm, the apocalyptic rider, the volatile, perfidious and cruel new enemy! The precise planning of the supposed enemy bore no relation to his careless behaviour after the attack, the videos of the attacker forgotten in the escape, the sudden appearance of the attacker's baggage, the passport that was found and much more. One cannot resist the suspicion that a false scent has been deliberately laid.

Until this day every strong social system draws power over our lives by presenting us with a clear-cut enemy. As a small child I had been told the Russians are the evil ones. Today the entire imperialistic world relies on terrorism as the concept of "the enemy", one which is mainly seen as coming from the world of the Islam. The whole Arab world represents a large threat. Parallel to this and like a mirror image there exists on the opposite side the concept of enemy as the "Americans."

Only when we begin to realise that the outer enemy will only exist as long as we resonate with the concept of the inner enemy, only then can the way out of this dead end street be found. Only then will we stop to look for the enemy externally. Many a person will now perhaps say: You are also attacking the Americans now. Or: You side with the Palestinians and stand against "the Israelis." However, there is a difference in declaring "the American", "the German" or "the Israeli" to be the enemy or whether I try to see through the background of the global system of war and therefore disempower it. The structure of all these systems needs to be recognised and left behind.

I remember the words of a landlord. He was one of the richest men in town and whenever he met us women students in the hall way he talked to us: "Watch out," he would say. "Maybe you are in luck. Maybe you too will experience a war. Eight shots in the head and ten shots in the shoulder in one minute, try to match that!"

At the same time he had waited for over 20 years for his son who had fallen in the war. He still hoped that he might come back. Probably his son had to face a hero such as his father had been. I asked him what the luck of experiencing a war might consist of. His answer was simply: "At that time we held together. There was community. There was something at stake."

Earlier in the heroic sagas there were at least two equally strong opponents facing each other. Today though, the murdering is mostly done by pressing a button and by machines. Death and murder have become more anonymous. In Iraq the enemy was first of all disarmed before one was allowed to play at war with him. "It is as if you suggest a race to someone but beforehand break his legs and to boot laugh at him for being unable to walk", says Arundhati Roy pointedly.

If we want to end war then this is the start of a long journey where we begin to recognise and see through our own concepts of who is the enemy. As long as we look for the enemy externally and are not ready to recognise him within ourselves there will be no exit to this dead end street. As long as we are not willing to recognise the human being behind every enemy there will be no peace.

However, at the same time we, too, have to be willing to inform ourselves about the present background of the globalisation of violence. As long as we are not willing to see through the system and to get out of it, self-change will be of no use, since we remain a part of the system.

Evil will exist for as long as we are willing to project our views onto governments and as long as we partake in a system that does not correspond to our true humanity and to our deep longing for true human love.

Recover your humanity and connect with the source of life and love. Stop accusing the systems which have to account for this insanity, but begin with the construction of new human systems which can create a true way out of the endless chain of violence.

In his book "Future without War", Dieter Duhm writes:
Imagine that the World Spirit comes to a group of 200 people and gives them the following task: "You are to find out under which conditions the Earth can be healed. You have at your disposal your mind, your body, your capability to communicate and the collective knowledge of humanity. First of all you have to find out how you can live in a non-violent and healing way among yourselves and together with all the creatures of nature. Begin from scratch and use all of your

229

intelligence, all of your knowledge and abilities, use your full strength of intuitive view and vision building in order to find a common path. The suffering of the world, inclusive of your own, has been caused by human beings themselves and can therefore only be healed by them as soon as they find the path for it. I give you three years for this research project. Until such time you ought to have found the essential paths in the process of healing. Open your "Geist" for my presence and I shall help you whenever you need help. I wish you much courage and joy of discovery in your work.

Do Victims and Perpetrators Exist?

Cry out human being, cry out!

If you read this book for your own inner renewal or self-change, then I suggest to you to permit your attention for a moment to wander to a place where your consciousness normally would never want to go. It is on the dark side of history. Light a candle and allow yourself for one moment to illuminate the human drama without being scared. Look at what is taking place worldwide at this very moment and allow the thought of you being a part of all this and as such also a part of its possible solution.

Dieter Duhm describes this very pointedly:
In many regions of the earth there is such a suffering that can bearly be imagined anymore. Burning, mutilation and torture are the order of the day. The public turns the other way, because it cannot bear the sight of it. In Latin America, villages and fields are being burnt to strengthen multinational corporations by forming Free Trade Zones. In the Tibetan work camps, set up by the Chinese, women and men, who were torn away from their families, starve to death. In Afghanistan children are crying, suffering from the pain of burns from American bombs. In Palestine a wall, eight meters high is being drawn through gardens, school yards and neighbourhoods. In Chechnya grenades were thrown into cellars, where elderly people were hiding, so that a Russian president could win his election. In Germany there was a chancellor who called said president a "flawless democrat." Nobody wants to be a witness; nobody wants to say what is happening. The victims have no public lobby, no advocates, and no protection. They have become numbers in an international roulette about power and profit. Cry out human being, cry out! Cries from the cellars of torture, from the prisons, from the battlefields on earth. (...)
Alas, the cries cannot be heard any longer, there are far too many of them. If all beings who at this moment are tortured could cry out, the

world would be one single cry. And while these lines are being written, hundreds die of hunger, cold and torture. I do not write this because I like to revel in the end of the world, but rather, because I know, that we are capable of ending this inferno. If we are able to recognise the dimensions of suffering, we will be able to estimate the dimensions of the necessary healing."

No false comfort

We should not look for comfort in spiritual truths too quickly since they will reveal their essential core only at a deeper dimension. In the New-Age-Movement it has meanwhile become fashionable to say: Victims do not exist. Or, only too readily, one is apt to quote Krishnamurti, who in his later years of life, presented his central secret to his listeners with the following words: "I have nothing against what is happening."

I expect of all those who have seriously entered peace work and want to end war in themselves and against others to address this issue with great awareness.

One can utilize the greatest spiritual truths to be able to escape the deepest truth. However, only temporarily! The question always is: Do the teachings I represent serve to raise awareness and heal reality or detract from it?

At many esoteric forms these truths are being circulated in a manner that does not portray them correctly. Rather they are used to further deflect from reality. Those in power, planning the greater political strategies, laugh up their sleeves, glad that there is no one there who is able to see through it all to the larger context and be prepared to stand up against the insanity of it. There is hardly any one who enlightens and dares to call things by their proper names. The large revolutionary NO and its strength has almost entirely vanished into thin air. We need them.

This is not the way to deal with the subject of victims and perpetrators! For us, in affluent societies, it is good to witness this process in ourselves, i.e. to see how often we mistakenly believe to be innocent victims of outer circumstances. Within ourselves we can observe how we can stop being a victim by fully accepting whatever is. Right now we have the freedom to study and understand the inner human processes and to provide real help to those who are in distress. But we ought to realise that the many victims on the "other side" of the planet exist because of our unwillingness to recognise and change our side as perpetrators. I expect those who gullibly repeat the words, that agreeing is enough, to go and face the raging human misery out there and to let themselves be touched by the agony of the imprisoned and tortured put away in dark cellars. If they were to know the painful cries of the oppressed, could they still talk like this? Would not the sound of their voice, would not their message change radically in the face of a child hurt by Napalm? Could they still say, without false presumptuousness but with compassion and sympathy, victims do not exist?

And how would they feel, if all of a sudden, they would recognize their own complicity in their own indifference, which has become their second nature, and in the implicitness of closing their eyes in the face of human suffering?

How would they feel, if they were, all of a sudden, to look into the mirror of today's stealthy fascism and have to recognise the hidden reality of their own complicity in it all?

It is much easier for us to identify with the history of the victims than to recognise ourselves as perpetrators. Yes, I am responsible for the suffering on this Earth and I can be a contribution towards ending it. When people are able to do this then they become true spiritual masters and can help.

Then I am able to accept their message and respect it deeply. On the deepest transformational level, where the Sacred Matrix is fully integrated, victims and perpetrators truly do not exist anymore. The more we have recognised and overcome the structures of victims and perpetrators the more we are able to help those afflicted.

The Goddess roars in us

At first we ought to let ourselves be touched by the reality of war. As long as we do not face up to this side of life and keep running away from it we shall sooner or later notice that all we tried to do was to calm down our bad conscious. Something within us is agitated and unconsciously starts to look for solace too early. Spiritual methods do not help in the long run. Life itself and its truth are more powerful and demand full surrender. Sooner or later life itself will illuminate all the meaningless areas of existence where we had not been willing to shed a light on ourselves. Only full recognition will lead us out of the fear. Not running away from our fear, always on the look-out for new views of the world, new teachings, new gurus who are supposed to help us escape from our own emptiness, but looking at it. We ought to recognise that our Western affluent society suffers from overflow and is slowly perishing from this illness. In these structures we keep looking for ever new distractions since we cannot and don't want to look our complicity in the eye. We then may find solace in resorting to the statement: Victims do not exist.

In the insanity of our normality we practice agreement, continually try out new methods, run from one teacher to the next, until exhausted, we have to realise that it does not work.

At some point though, we all have to look into the eyes of truth. Being in agreement can and will only emerge when we accept all of life in its reality. Little does it help to run away from the truth! When I want to wake up, something will force me to look at it. Not to be scared anymore but to see, to recognise, to change. As long as I am not willing to acknowledge that I am part of the massacre and that I too carry the side of the perpetrator inside of me, as much as does the victim, then it will always be the others who have caused the war and are responsible for it. I then remain part of a structure that perpetuates itself over and over again for thousands of years, forever more subtle, more technologically sophisticated and therefore more powerful, cruel, inscrutable and more devastating.

The psychic reality of war which we do not want to see or acknowledge, both in the small as well as in the large, will wield its power over us as long as we repress it. Oh yes, we are responsible for what is happening on the other side of the planet, we are part of the wars and conflicts of this Earth. Only when we recognise and acknowledge our complicity, only when we set forth to develop truly new forms of living, which contain the power of change, will we see eye to eye with a higher level of order at a spiritual dimension where victims and perpetrators no longer exist.

We shall then refrain from spending a lot of money on expensive esoteric beliefs and begin to help ourselves by helping others right there where it is needed. Recognise the structure of war in the smallest! This will make it easier to see through it in the larger sense. First of all begin to look within yourself, then in your close environment and your community! Finally you will see that it is not an individual failure. What are needed are totally new social structures, a new religiousness, a new abode for love and truth and trust, for this insanity to come to an end.

Full joy of existence will blossom in us only when we have found the full power and authority to end the misery on this planet. Everyone, the suffering as well as the victims and perpetrators are part of *one* existence. The compassion of the awakened will not tire until even the last one has been freed of his bonds. Then the celebration of a new Earth can truly begin. True inner transformation is always measured against its outward effect.

It is the Goddess that roars in us:

Wake up, human being! Wake up to new life and love. No longer condemn me to the basements, to the slums and squalor of your culture. Instead let me enter the Holy Land, the palaces of your soul, your gardens of pleasure and of love. Become the guardian of my paradise on Earth. Become the guardian of my truth.

For those who love truth, also love life!

Touching examples of stepping out of being a victim

Hardly anyone has described the steps of ceasing to be a victim more touchingly than Jacques Lusseyran, the French resistance fighter who as an eight year old became blind through an accident. He was one of the few people to survive the concentration camp of Buchenwald. He survived due to his inner guidance which enabled him to see through the structures of victim and perpetrator and thereby was able to elude them.

Incessantly we accuse the circumstances of life. We call them: incidents, accidents, illnesses, duties and afflictions. We would like to force our own conditions on life. This is the point of our essential weakness. We forget that God never creates new circumstances for us, without equipping us in such a way to sustain these circumstances. I am grateful to the blindness for not having let me forget.

Also Etty Hillesum, who on November 30th, 1943 at the age of 29 was murdered at Auschwitz, bears witness to the depth of this experience of total surrender. She did not want to abscond from the fate of the Jews, the "mass fate", although coming from a family of artists she personally would have had the possibility. She did not see how the Jewish proletariat could elude the Holocaust and took it to be her inner duty to participate in their fate so as to not abandon people. In her book "An Interrupted Life" she describes her own development very touchingly:

The sudden breakthrough to something that is to become my own truth. Human kindness for which I have to fight. Not in politics or in a political party but in myself. But still false shame to express it. And God. The girl that would not kneel but came to learn it after all and this, on a rough coconut mat in an untidy bathroom. But these things are almost more intimate that the sexual ones. (...) It is as if, with a jolt, I had returned to my base. A little more independent and autonomous. (…) I wish I could repeat what I murmured half-loud: God, take me by your hand, I will follow obediently, without being too reluctant. I will not elude myself, whatever may come towards me in this life I shall process it as best as I can. But give me sometimes a short moment of rest. I will no longer believe in all simplicity that peace, should it overcome me, will last for ever, I shall also accept the unrest and the fight that are to follow. I like to be in warmth and security but I shall not refuse to go into the cold if only your hand guides me. On your hand I shall go anywhere and I shall try not to be too timid. I shall try to radiate some of the love, the human kindness that is within me, wherever I shall be. But with the word "human kindness" one must not brag. One never knows whether one truly has it. I do not want to be anything special. I only want to try to be the one who is still looking to unfold her self inside of me fully.

Faced with her experience of the concentration camp she continues to write:

The misery is really big, but nevertheless, I often walk late in the evening when the day behind me has sunk away into profundity. I walk with whipping steps along the barbed wire and then it wells up out of my heart again and again – I cannot help it, it is the way it is, it is of an elementary power: Life is something wonderful and big, later we have to build up a whole new world – and each further crime and each further cruelty we have to contrast with a further piece of love and goodness which we have to conquer within ourselves. We are allowed to suffer but we are not allowed to break.

The Battle of the Genders, the Ego Trap and the Ending of War

In Israel/Palestine we encounter the battle in its outer shape - a war over land and survival. At the centre of all the events there was the battle about the elementary issues of life. The human question, the issue of the relationship between man and woman, the issue of the battle of the genders do not so obviously stand in the centre. But still, the battle of the genders weaves its fine net of nerves through almost all of the scenarios on Earth.

Without the battle of the genders coming to an end there can be no peace. Globally, the last battles against the downfall of the patriarchy are taking place. If men and women had managed to respond to their primary longing for each other, if culturally they had been able to build up balanced and loving relationships, and if they had been successful in overcoming the bone hard fronts they have built up over the past thousands of years, would they then still permit their sons and daughters to participate in senseless wars? Would we let governments force us to be inhuman and have them rule over us? Would we succumb to religions dictating forms of life which do not at all correspond with our primary aspirations? Would we practice religions which totally suppress the aspect of the Goddess?

Is there a central cause, an error which repeats itself in the same way everywhere? Is there an inner shift that has to take place leading from damage to wholeness? Might it be correct that what we experience in the outer world is a mere image of our own psychic dramas which keep following the same patterns? Do events that are carried to extremes in areas of conflicts take place microscopically in our interior? Are the macro-cosmos world and the micro-cosmos human being not more identical than we are ever prepared to accept?

On my pilgrimage through Europe, all along, I met with gender conflict. Wherever I went I came across divorces, broken partnerships in which the men and women were not able to speak the truth. Some of them were even unable to speak to each other, so deep were the injuries resulting from the battle.

They are all looking for the causes and the guilt on a personal level. They are all looking for the solution on a level where it cannot be found. And all believe that one of them carries the main guilt.

For years I am a worker on both fronts, working at overcoming the outer wall of war as well as overcoming inner points of fear and anger. And for a long time I have known that this is the traumatic point between the genders which all of us share and has to be healed. The war which we experience in the outer world is mirrored and experienced in our inner world. If we want to end the outer war we must become witnesses of our inner battles. We have to see through our own plays of war and admit to ourselves how we obviously add to it sometimes more, sometimes less. We must indeed end the inner war. And before we can make peace with anyone we have to have made peace with ourselves. We shall end war only when we have seen and learnt something higher, something more comprehensive. What else could be more comprehensive than love? Human beings who have learnt to love, to also sensually love, are no longer governable. They have the power and the knowledge to distance themselves from war.

The ego-trap

On the path many traps await us, mostly set up by the ego since it crouches ready to instigate new wars all the time. It is the ego that continually feels attacked and fights back. It is the ego living and thinking of attack and defence. Its power within us has been traumatised for hundreds of years and has become addicted to the suffering which it nourishes itself. The strategies of war governed by the present cultures and politics worldwide are mirrored in the microcosm of the human being, of each individual. I call it the ego-trap. At some point in the Creation it happened, the human being separated itself from the whole of Creation and with it brought forth the ego. This is a historic process which is connected to the separation of the human being from its divine source and thus has no continuity in itself. Therefore identification with the ego is always connected to fear and pain. The beginning lies principally in the fact that we no longer know our higher self and we therefore cannot truly accept ourselves. We do not have a complete image of ourselves.

A threatened "something" rages within us, something from the past, which we call "I." It keeps itself alive from the glances of others and from the struggle to be acknowledged because it has lost its deepest ground, its shelter and protection in the divine world. You feel that you are not being seen and acknowledged and immediately you begin to fight. You do not feel as if your steps were seen and honoured and you charge others with it.

Whenever something with us thinks: "Too little, not enough, more, not right, unjustly treated", the ego is ready to pounce, hungry for prey especially if it feels threatened. It wants to have forever more and is never satisfied. It takes what it can get. After exuberant happiness, ever hungrier, it reaps misery and suffering all the more; after the amorousness follows the impulse to destroy. It takes whatever it can get, be it matter or "Geist".

The ego disguises itself as the last warrior inside of us. It is the battle of survival and the closer you get to your primal source the more it begins to fight. The return to the source signifies death to the ego. This is the perception of an ego which has not yet recognised that it awaits transformation into a higher gestalt. Just as the caterpillar knows nothing of its metamorphosis into a butterfly, so the ego knows nothing of its birth into a higher, divine self.

The militant ego for all intents and purposes has its good side, too, since lastly it is connected to the hunger for more truth and insight even for more justice. The ego has been necessary for us not to have become a brave, adjusted follower. You had to stand up against patriarchy. It was the ego within you that egged you on to defend yourself against the injustice of this culture. Through a strong ego-consciousness we had the courage to rebel against existing systems and injustices, we dared to leave behind the staid and tried to begin with something new, we dared to struggle, to fight in order to finally understand. To many resistance fighters it gave the revolutionary courage they needed and to many women the strength to get out of patriarchal structures as fast as possible.

However, at some point something within you begins to see more and more: you nourish things you fight against as long as you still fight. Only when you stop fighting will you truly disband old patterns. A long way, a deep way, a necessary way to inner peace! Step by step we climb higher on the ladder to divine source. At some time though the last rung is reached and we shall have to say goodbye to our warrior. Maybe we have taken many courageous steps in the emancipation movement. Maybe we have become a well-known personality. Maybe we have found much acknowledgement in our profession. All this now does not count anymore. Someone within you, a higher consciousness demands that you give all this up. Not by abandoning it but by recognising that this is no longer you. The higher consciousness is an all encompassing consciousness. You no longer have to prove anything to anyone. By stopping to collect points, by stopping to post success and failure to your own account and by stopping to compare yourself to others you begin to have an inkling of a deeper peace within you. You discover that the old pattern of thinking leads you inevitably back to war. Now the air becomes thinner and thinner, and at some point you will be unable to continue with the old methods. Something entirely new has to surface.

A jump is demanded. The jump into a new dimension is the jump to freedom which is to rid the militant ego of its last shackles. You take the step from emancipation out into the world where there are no more enemies. Your strongest enemy will become your best friend since he forces you seek self-knowledge.

This entire insanity has fulfilled its purpose. You see through the ego-delusion of the entire culture. It is good to see it, to recognise it but you no longer fight against it. Meanwhile it has become clear, the greatest insanity is that of identifying with the illness, to believe, that this is oneself. As long as you identify with any of these frequencies you are part of the war. Once you have understood this the ego will become a friendly comrade in a race for higher development. You no longer fight it, since all of this is not you! All of this is the raging body of pain of history which is looking for its victims everywhere, which wants to seduce you to identify with roles everywhere, as soon as unconsciousness pops up. These are the hardened crusts of your tubercle of fear which becomes active as soon as someone comes near it. Sometimes you behave in a way as if someone were to take God away from you.

It is in this false identification that the insanity of our times lies. The same pattern is rampant everywhere, both in the micro and in the macro. The secret of who you truly are will only be lifted when you have left behind all of this more and more. Once you no longer let yourself be scared by the ghosts roused, you will encounter on your search for the true core something very beautiful, something very pure, something very divine.

The last battle

There is a point in the encounter of the genders at which it is decided whether there will be war or peace. I call this point the point of martyr. It is equally deeply anchored in men and in women.

How often have I had to look into its eye in my own person? There exists in us an unconscious bookkeeping which goes as follows: Eve was driven out of paradise. Christ was nailed to the cross. Courageous revolutionaries were burnt. If you follow your true and real path you will be crucified. There is a false identification in our Christian tradition which early in life took hold of our children's hearts. A female deity to whom we can turn has been taken from us. A God to whom we can surrender trustfully, we do not find. We do not find a loving God, but a punishing God. Which child-like heart is able to understand that God agreed for his dearest son to be crucified? How is one to surrender to a God who at the decisive moment forsakes you? "My God, my God, why have you forsaken me?" Jesus calls from the cross. This thought stands at the centre of a culture of abandonment and rather than resurrection. Who wants to become a good human being usually also believes subconsciously that he has to pass through the purgatory of hell. This sits in our souls so deeply that all of sudden one can mistake the film for the reality. The following illuminates this aspect from the viewpoint of a woman. The last and most fatal question the warrior will put to you over and over again: She builds up fear, fear of abandonment. She suggests to you that you must part with everything you once loved. Yes, in the worst case you will have to leave the place you love, leave your loved-ones and all your friends in order to be able to pursue the real path. Almost all love relationships are determined by the fear of abandonment.

The projection is so immense that we are even ready to all of a sudden see the enemy, the overly powerful father, the sovereign or Satan himself in what used to be the lover and friend at whose side after much trying it proved impossible though to pursue the path of freedom. He does not support a free woman at his side. I shall disregard the fact that the man and partner in life probably added his bit of fuel to this fight. He probably was angry or ignorant or unjust. For the inner liberation though this is not the essential thing. Essential is that in such moments we are unable to differentiate between film and reality. Our film is our reality. And we react by attacking. Without noticing we pass on the power and perceive ourselves in the role of the powerless. In this unconscious victim structure we then tyrannise the world.

The film becomes so real that you will no longer understand that the others are not able to see what you can see so clearly. When then the others talk at you trying to appease you, they become the allies of the enemy who is betraying you. Since he is the stronger one who has them under control, no one will dare say the truth. The film will all of a sudden become more than real and we as the party concerned will not recognise it as being a mere projection. At this point the addicted body of pain strikes out, shaped in the course of time as a result of our collective history of pain and hooked on more suffering and for ever larger hopelessness. The unconscious addiction of maintaining the role of the victim prevails. Particularly in us women this body of pain is readily available and is moved as soon as smaller or larger conflicts arise in a relationship. The inquisition of the witches does not lie too far back. A trifle can be enough to mobilise this body of pain. In such moments the entire historic fate of women accumulates in one individual and desperately calls out: *Now you have to fight. If need be even against your best friend. This time you will not emerge from the history as a victim.*

In many cases this film is played to perfection becoming indeed a reality as hard as bones. This is the way we produce the reality of the patriarchy over and over again.

At this point raging desperation sets in. You feel left alone by God and the world. You choose the path of alleged emancipation. You choose the fight to the bitter end, an end often leading to separation. Separation however is not going to be the way to freedom rather it is the last dramatically envisioned horror. He will punish you for saying the truth and he will see to it that you will be cut off from everything you once loved.

Desperately you toss and turn in your bed. But he is my lover after all. Do I have to submit? Do I have to acquiesce? Keep silent? Never! This is the way of subjugation. The ego keeps looking for arguments until it is exhausted.

He all of a sudden is the one hindering you to be free, the one who continually talks about himself, the macho or the "softy", in any case, he is the one to whom you abdicate your power and whom you reject with all your strength. This is the most difficult, the hardest and the most penetrating point, where the ego is fighting for its survival. Here identification is at its deepest: the unresolved issue of women, emancipation or subjugation is the only desperate and continual alternative against a fictitious enemy which has its origin in a dark and unrecognised past. You always need something in the exterior that carries the guilt for your misery, something you can fight against to temporarily pacify the ego. This is the largest and most penetrating trap. At this point the body of pain lunges out and we identify with it over and over again. As long as this film is believed it will repeat itself and become reality and the most beautiful and most truthful love relationships break up in the face of this insanity. Every film will become a reality if only we believe in it strongly enough. As soon as you recognise the film to be a film you will react differently and even if your partner was indeed very much in the wrong. From the calm of perception another authority to act comes to us. You no longer react as a victim of the situation.

The way out

How then do we leave this insanity of history? Our inner attitude in which we react to our experiences is essential. The fight begins only when we are already in the identification with our role of victim.

The only way out is the awakening.

We sense that the path to freedom starts by no longer wasting any thoughts of protest against others.

It truly is not a matter of guilt and judgment. How can one judge something that acts out of the unconscious? Judgment and self-judgment lead to the heaviest revolts and to the most desperate actions of the ego. In truth though, the ego in its desperateness is looking for the way back to its primal source, back to love, back to self-love, back to God. His biggest fear however is in that what it most longs for.

As soon as the first consciousness about these processes start, the circumstances begin to thin out. When we once have recognised the ego within us we are able to quickly recognise and correct our mistakes. Above all we do not linger for such a long time with self-accusation and feelings of guilt. A first awakening takes place. We begin to understand that what is happening cannot be solved at a personal level. We see that those whom we call perpetrators and those whom we recognise as victims are equally victims of this whole drama. We begin to understand that we come in touch with the pain of a primordial trauma that keeps reigniting the battle of the genders. There can only be healing if you embrace love. Shamefaced we begin to see all of what we ourselves have done to the other in the belief to be in the right. But this shame too we let go past us quickly knowing that none of this is us. It was the identification with a collective pain leading us repeatedly in the same dead end street.

At the beginning we are possibly unsettled, becoming clearer as we recognise that on the level we chose to look there is no way out of the dead end street. We therefore put down the arms. Somewhat clumsily but determinedly we begin to recognise the old structures of our thinking and to develop new circumstances under which another way of loving becomes possible. The only chance for these outer structures to manifest themselves on Earth consists in seeing the way into our interior completely and to going to the end of it. We have so far always begun to fight at the point where our fear or our anger would normally set in but the new consciousness now wants to move in. It changes our relationship to the so called enemy on the spot. It is unimportant whether we are in the right or in the wrong. What is important is that we now want to really know all that which before we vehemently disclaimed because of fear. We want to know, we want to heal. We have left behind the fight and the drama. We have to pay the highest attention at this point in order to truly see though this issue within ourselves.

We begin to suspect: No one will close his heart to us if we ourselves do not close it. Love cannot be lost if we stay with it. And true love begins with loving oneself. There is no narcissism in this: Only who has learnt to accept himself fully, can say "yes" full-heartedly to others. In our essence we keep finding this pure and deep beauty. This core is inviolable. This is the Christ nature within us. No one can abandon me, if I do not abandon others. Love paves its own ways when I stay with love. Sometimes this leads to more closeness and sometimes to more distance, sometimes to aloneness but never to abandonment. God cannot leave you. This is the deepest and the latest realisation which fronts all of the martyr-trauma. Deep inside of you, you are nothing less than the mainstay of God. And how could it be possible that God leaves himself? All the desperate attempts at identifying with something other than with the divine source within us stem only from having forgotten that God exists within us. Sooner or later we shall have to return to there. Nothing else will endure within ourselves.

Now the way back to the source begins. You lean back and almost cheerfully you realise: Everything that rages within you is not you!

It is the collective body of pain of your history – the history of women or of your nation or your family or of previous incarnations – which grips you and rages inside of you. In us women it often leads to an almost addictive manner of being the perpetrator while we perceive ourselves as the victim. Our higher consciousness however came through this history completely unharmed. It does not identify with this torture. Patiently it waits for you to return to it. We now know: This was not the path. This is the path we shall leave. The path with God though we cannot leave.

Our way out of the dead end street becomes the way of recognition. We witness the processes within ourselves. This might not only be pleasant since uncomfortable things will come up. Now we have learnt, here too, to stay calm wherever it becomes uncomfortable.

Soberly we notice: "Here we go again, our ego, it wants to fight." When the senses have been awakened you will frequently catch yourself at it. There is no use to get desperate about still being like this. All of mankind is still like this otherwise we would long ago have started to enjoy peace on earth.

Equally it makes no sense to fight against it since the ego is incredibly cunning and undermines even the most spiritual of ways. Even your purest resolutions the ego is able to check and to devour them hungrily. But do not despair now or be ashamed of it, just notice it and become aware of how your ambitions have allowed you to carry you away from true life, from God, to whom you have so often and clearly been so close.

As long as you declare the ego to be your enemy and you continue to fight it, it will always win. Instead, be happy for having penetrated your inside so far that it revealed itself! The walk through the labyrinth of your self now becomes cheerful and calm. You can recognise your truth and begin with the unmasking. Is this not a comprehensive victory? Each discovery of ego structures within you is a step towards awakening. On this path you will make your enemy to be your friend. This is the way out! It will help you in your personal life as well as in your political life. Little by little it will reveal entirely new structures of being. I write this so vehemently, because I have discovered that this is so!

A last and important point: our relationship to thinking. Some negate it others inflate it, the thinking which originally was pure and elementary as is breathing.

On the way to the unmasking you will discover how often the thinking owns you, rather than you owning your thinking and using it like a tool. Originally thinking was a gift of God and a salutary source within you. But instead of being a tool for insight it has become your cage. You all of a sudden notice how your thoughts direct and move you at every turn and determine your actions at a completely unconscious level. It is not you who has a thought it is the thought that has hold of you.

There exist some simple exercises to nourish the change of consciousness within you. If you have an enemy of whom you think embodies evil and you have noticed that something within you continually fights him, then change the role: look for an inner attitude that allows you to discover and see the Christ in him.

You experience the other as the enemy only as long as elements which you hate in him are also present in yourself. These elements seem so powerful to you and invincible in the other because they have not been overcome in yourself.

Look for what you hate in others within yourself. Encounter the opponent as if you are looking for the Messiah in him. You want your enemy to disappear? Your will achieve its disappearance once you recognise and touch this divine point in him, this point which never before has been recognised and touched. This is the deciding point of transformation. As of this moment and when this happens all of the blown-up ego masks will disappear since they do not abide. A cleansed "I" will emerge, a persona, which will accept her responsibility in life being protected and made secure by the divine world.

This is the great transformation sweeping through all of the rows like a heavy thunderstorm carrying away everything that has no permanence - transformation that heals and brings forth the great cosmic life and love and ongoing Creation.

First Analysis: Thirty People can Change the World

My pilgrimage was triggered by the question: What can we do to ward off the imminent war in Iran? Is it within our power to undertake something effective against the globalisation of violence?

Now, after all that I have witnessed and experienced during these past months I believe more deeply than ever before: Yes, it is possible. 30 people can change the world. 30 people who are fully committed to renew their internal course can prevent wars. Certainly this cannot be achieved by turning against the existing situation. Neither can it be achieved by mere grass-root actions nor in a purely spiritual manner. A group of cooperating partners who are able to communicate in full trust have to combine political action, spiritual anchoring and insistent character work. With strict determination such a committed group has to see that social structures and living conditions are created which are able to uncover and terminate latent warlike processes amongst humans. They have to recognize, that a life model in which interpersonal wars no longer exist, including the hidden ones, will have a changing effect on the whole. If this is done fully at a few places on Earth and if this succeeds, it will have a changing and field-building effect for the whole world.

Human beings who have learnt to love and who are not afraid of the truth will no longer participate in any war. More than this, they will be able to demonstrate at any places on this Earth how one is able to live without war. This is my credo. It grows with each new experience. Yes, it is as simple as this and at the same time as profound as this.

But what does this mean to the Palestinian village of Anata, what does it mean to Ramallah, to Bethlehem, to all the places we visited? And these are only a few examples where people are subjugated to live under unworthy conditions. What does this mean with regard to overcoming the wall? What does it mean to the interminable daily suffering all over the world and to which almost all of the people of well-to-do societies turn a blind eye?

Life in Anata carries on. The soldiers will come again. The young people who have experienced the marvel of peace power through our manner of appearance will after all turn back to throwing stones the next day. How could they have understood from only one short such appearance what the secret of peace power is?

The cause for war is to be found in the wrongly channelled longings and life energies of human beings. I repeat once again: Do we seriously believe that the many young soldiers who now stand ready for war would really obey orders if they had another perspective for the channelling of their power, their courage, their longing for adventure and community? It is the unquenched thirst for community, for love and religion which has pushed us into this collective insanity. We have to deal with the task of leaving this madness of our present civilisation behind us and entering on to a new form of life on Earth. A friend who was on the pilgrimage with us wrote to me in a letter:

"We cannot wait until love is freed!"

No, surely we cannot wait. The world is in such a state of absolute emergency that waiting is definitely no answer. The present efforts to stop the wars by the new-age-movement, the alternative league and the spiritual and political forces are in no proportion to the internal and external emergency of all of mankind. It amounts to far too little.

My question is: Given that we recognize this context why do we still wait? Why do we still continue with our smaller or bigger conflicts, with our battles in love, with our smaller or bigger needs? Why do we not undertake everything possible in order to clean out the secret complicity in our own life and actualise the real possibilities of life and love which has been given to us by God? Why do we cling to the habits of the old world, cling to doubts, discussions,

251

lovesickness and compensation? Why do we ignore what we have known all along? Why do we not accept our task?

On our pilgrimage we have experienced many short term marvels where on a deeper level we have recognised the so called enemies as friends. Such marvels must not be allowed to remain purely emotional. First of all we ourselves have to understand the human system of these marvels in order to make them last. Only when we have truly understood the laws which become effective in love can we intervene efficiently and solidly to bring about change.

Do we know the five basic rules of love? Are we aware that the wars we lead in our partnerships are connected to the wars in the world? Are we ready to accept responsibility for this and are we therefore ready to leave the old net of undue ownership, blackmail and demand? In the following I will quote five simple premises of free love for us to measure them up against our daily behaviour. If we adhere to these five guidelines, I am certain, a new matrix will manifest on Earth.

1. God is love and any kind of love has its anchor in God. Those who have learnt to love trust in the love of God.
2. Love begins with self-acceptance. Those who have learned to love themselves and to affirm themselves positively will not be able to use violence against anyone else. Only those who affirm themselves positively are able to love another human being. This simple rule is to be found in the Bible: Love your neighbour as you love yourself.
3. Love is free. You cannot bind any human being to yourself by means of possessing him or of exercising a right over him. You cannot force anyone to be responsible for the satisfaction of your wants and needs. Love and desire are gifts of life, no legal matter. When you begin to demand love and sex you can be sure you have left your track. Return to it as fast as possible.
4. You can only be faithful if you may love others, too. Love knows neither fences nor jealous restrictions. Love knows compassion

and the never ending interest in each other and in the world. True love will lead to faithfulness all on its own.

5. Your love will find duration to the extent of how you are ready to stand by the truth. All of our culture is a bulwark against the truth. Those who truly want to love have to be ready to remove the bulwark within themselves and to risk truth also with regard to small and hidden things.

In order to learn and understand all this we need new centres and communities where this knowledge is taught. An individual, studying to become a peace worker, has to undergo the following process: he has to recognise in himself how much his life has been a bulwark against the truth. He has to be ready to recognise and accept the truth. He has to be willing to break down the inner walls in order to experience compassion in himself for the first time in all its purity and without any disguise. To do this, most people have to visit an area of conflict at some point, witnessing the daily cruelties that are inflicted upon human beings, animals and the Earth in the name of globalisation all over the planet.

Then such a person has to profoundly comprehend the correlation between "outer crisis" and "inner crisis" and to understand it with regard to himself. This person must want to know the truth. When this is so, he or she can go out into the world to a place where the task at hand can be fulfilled the best way possible.

The pilgrimage GRACE must not remain a one-time action. GRACE could be the beginning of a worldwide movement for peace. We can prevent war! A peace movement can stop wars if it acts timely and in an intelligent, strategic, numerous and decisive manner. Let us no longer follow the hypnosis of resignation, helplessness and disappointment! We shall succeed, if only enough decided people will get together worldwide and be prepared to dedicate themselves for one year to do nothing else but to engage themselves unconditionally for peace. The revolution in the external sphere will have to be accompanied by a conscious revolution in the internal sphere otherwise a true victory cannot be achieved.

Today many people know: the Earth can only be saved if human beings undergo a transformation and if they will adopt a new intelligence and a new willingness to practice truth and solidarity. Something has to happen that is deeper reaching and more comprehensive than all previous revolutions have done up till now. A world-revolution which in its essence does not fight against existing systems anymore, but connects with a higher order is already "in the air": the revolution of love – the establishment of living conditions which support a state of being where love becomes self-sustained. Nothing is more powerful than an idea whose time has come.

For the realisation of this big idea I shall continue my pilgrimage for the humanisation of money. I have learnt and experienced that we are quite able to *be* the change we are longing for. I work and pilgrimage for a future without war. The monies that today finance the wars, if invested in adequate peace projects, would be sufficient to keep all of mankind from hunger, poverty and violence. The idea of a world-wide peace movement with the "Plan of the Peace Research Villages" at its centre needs the contact of a larger public. Contacts are needed with industrial experts and specialists in economy, professionals who for a long time have been aware of the necessity for such a comprehensive change of view and are prepared to support it. The peace movement needs to be aware and comprehend the functioning of money without having to bow to its traditional laws. The movement has to overcome old concepts of enmity and support the development of a humane economy. With the cost of one single armoured tank we could powerfully launch the planned peace research villages in the Middle East, in Colombia, India and Portugal.

Imagine: Each person acts wherever he lives aware of "I am the change I want to see in the world."
Imagine: A world-wide net of mental and spiritual connectedness develops, a net of peace projects, futures communities and healing biotopes. They welcome pilgrims, who want to join the

project GRACE and who wish to develop themselves. More and more people take on responsibility for the whole and joyfully accept the necessary work in all its manifold aspects.

The necessary funding is provided by wealthy individuals or groups of individuals. More and more people know and fulfil their professions and tasks in this world-wide net of a powerfully growing peace force.

The participants orientate themselves, also in their personal daily life, on guidelines provided by this world-wide peace movement. All these guidelines originate from the profound understanding of GRACE.

Due to the many existential shocks on the pilgrimage throughout Israel the subject of money moved into the background. A second phase of my pilgrimage will follow and focus on making contacts with people in the financial world. My total trust in reaching the goal of my pilgrimage has grown a lot.

I express my thanks for the many new friendships and for the new partners in cooperation. I have got to know many engaged peace workers who dedicate their lives to peace work. The net of cooperation is growing.

We need a world-wide group of committed human beings who will use their economic, political and journalistic abilities to promote the idea of the peace villages – a global "Syndicate for Peace." It has to be a group who in every situation is very decided and ready to forego personal interests in favour of the common interest. I am travelling to contribute in the development of such a world group.

The international "Syndicate for Peace" shall be responsible for the news to be spread throughout the world and for the setting up of primary training centres where the development of peace villages can be studied. These training centres will be available and serve as hostels and meetings points to the world-wide peace movement and serve as oases of regeneration and cooperation. It is envisaged that the world group could consist of approximately 30 members.

My contribution focuses on the preparation and linking-up of adequate technological, ecological and social pilot models which presently are or have already been developed by various groups all over the world. At the same time I am glad to pass on to others my spiritual knowledge, my experience in community life and gender work.

I ask all engaged spirits for help and support. Please open up contacts to industrial and financial experts who are interested in new future projects. Those who run or know of projects which are prepared to make their centre available as a hostel to peace workers, please contact me.

I am of course ready to inform a larger public about my work.

Whoever wishes to make a donation or has important information to contribute is asked to contact the Institute of Global Peace Work in Tamera. (Address and bank accounts are at the end of the book.)

Heartfelt thanks to all those who have helped to make my pilgrimage possible! I ask for you to continue with your support.

I greet all friends and peace workers on this wonderful planet Earth and wish for us all to become witnesses of a life without war.

Addendum

Glossary of some unfamiliar terms:

Board Computer
A "sixth sense", metaphor for intuitive or unconscious knowledge about correlations and possibilities which can, with appropriate stimulation, be made available to the conscious so as to enable and support decision making.

Checkpoint
Within the West Bank there are hundreds of checkpoints where Israeli soldiers control Palestinian passers-by. The checkpoints are a major instrument of the Israeli occupation. Israel defines them as "a necessary measure for protection against terror." The reality is these control points severely restrict the freedom of movement of the Palestinian people in their own country.

Concrete Utopia
A term coined by Ernst Bloch, denoting a "realistic" Utopia

Cosmogramme
"Cosmic writing". The geomancer and earth-healer, Marko Pogacnik, developed through intuition and artistic work a technique to find a symbolic sign which conveys information to the world of subtle matter. Such a *cosmogramme* is chiselled into a stone pillar and positioned in the landscape to rebalance it energetically.

Field building force
If a critical mass of individuals has internalised new insights, new behavioural patterns or new social values and systems, other individuals will find it easier to learn these steps since they can rely on an existing "field" of competence. The impetus leading to this new information in life is denoted as a field building force.

Field (i.e. morphogenetic field)
A term used by the British biologist, Rupert Sheldrake, to denote a loosely defined biological field (potentially also a social field), which has an effect on the "form-giving causation" for the development of structures.

Frequency carrier
Human feelings and thoughts create a certain atmosphere which can also be denoted by the term frequency. Frequency carriers are those people who are able to, for instance, maintain the frequency of peace and love in challenging situations and thus foster an atmosphere of trust and confidence within a group.

Healing Biotope
Also called "Greenhouses of trust" (incubators of trust). A term coined by Dieter Duhm to describe Peace Research Villages where social, ecological, economic and technical structures create a healing power which enables the inhabitant to live free of violence or fear. The power of healing in such a community is generated through mutual help and support as well as by each person finding his or her own place within the community. In Tamera, Portugal, Healing Biotope I is being developed. If a series of Healing Biotopes were to function worldwide each with about 100 inhabitants, then a global field of healing could be activated.

I Ching
The "Book of Changes" is the oldest of the classical Chinese texts. The I Ching contains the cosmology and philosophy of ancient China. Its basic ideas are the fair balance of opposites and the acceptance of change. The book describes the world in 64 pictures each consisting of continuous and intermittent lines (hexagrammes). In Western culture it is used and understood to be a book of wisdom and prophecy. In China it is being used as an oracle. One specific characteristic: in the sixties it was discovered that the basic mathematical structure of the I Ching complies with the genetic code.

Marian
Of Mary, mother of Jesus. The "marian culture impulse", is a term coined by Sabine Lichtenfels to describe a socially effective force of a feminine, intuitive, sensual, helping or motherly nature which long hidden now wants to be born into society.

Nuestra Señora
Spanish: "Our Lady", the mother of God

Prehistoric Utopia
A concept developed by Sabine Lichtenfels and used in her book "Traumsteine" (Dream Stones). It refers to a timeless utopia of matriarchal communities which might have existed in prehistoric times when people lived together peacefully and in accordance with the laws of nature. From the concept of a Prehistoric Utopia indices can be drawn for a new contemporary peace culture.

Sharing circle
A talking circle where all the participants have the possibility to express their own personal thoughts and feelings.

Shechina
Jewish-kabbalistic variant of Shakti; Inside or feminine soul of God. According to the Kabbalists all evil came about due to God having lost his Shechina. The hexagramme of the Star of David is the symbol for this union. As with its tantric equivalent, Shechina is the origin of all that is animated.

Tat twam asi:
Sanskrit: You are this (Brahman/God). A yogic denotation for the highest form of enlightenment.

Recommended Literature

Sabine Lichtenfels:

Weiche Macht. Perspektiven eines neuen Frauenbewußtseins und eine neue Liebe zu den Männern (1996). **(Gentle Power.** Perspectives for a new female consciousness and a new love towards men)
Traumsteine. Reise in das Zeitalter der sinnlichen Erfüllung (2000). **(Dream Stones.** Journey into the age of sensual fulfillment.)
Sources of Love and Peace. Morning Attunements. (2004)
Ring der Kraft. Perspektiven schaffen für den Frieden (2005). **(Ring of Power.** Creating Perspectives for Peace.)

Dieter Duhm:

Towards a New Culture. (1978)
Politische Texte für eine gewaltfreie Erde. (1991) (Political texts for a non-violent earth.)
Der unerloeste Eros. (1998) (Eros Unredeemed)
The Sacred Matrix. From the Matrix of Violence to the Matrix of Life. (2006)
Future without War. Theory of Global Healing. (2006)

Others:

de Boer, Hans: Gesegnete Unruhe (2000) (Blessed Disturbance)
Geusen, Madjana, Ed.: Man's Holy Grail is Woman. (2006)
Evi Guggenheim-Shbeta, Eyas Shbeta: Oase des Friedens. Wie ein Jüdin und ein Palästinenser in Israel in Liebe leben. (2005) (Oasis of Peace. How a Jewish Woman and a Palestinian Man live together in love in Israel today)

Etty Hillesum, Eva Hoffman: An Interrupted Life - the Diaries 1941-1943 and Letters from Westerbork (1996)

Langer, Felicia: These are My Brothers. Israel and the Occupied Territories. (1979)

Lusseyran, Jacques: And There Was Light. Autobiography. Blind Hero of the French Resistance (1998)

Lusseyran, Jacques: What One Sees Without Eyes (1999)

Moskovitz, Reuven: Der lange Weg zum Frieden. (The Long Way to Peace)

Neudeck, Rupert: Ich will nicht mehr schweigen. Über Recht und Gerechtigkeit in Palästina.(2005) (I do no longer want to stay silent. About right and justice in Palestine)

Pilgrim, Peace: Her Life and Work in her own Words (1992)

Pogacnik, Marco: Healing the Heart of the Earth (1998)

Satprem: On the Way to Supermanhood. (1986)

Thomas, AnShin Claude: At Hell's Gate: A Soldier's Journey from War to Peace (2004)

Tolle, Eckhart: A New Earth. Awakening to your Life's Purpose. (2006)

Ywahoo, Dhyani: Voices of our Ancestors (1988)

Further Information:

The "Plan of the Peace Research Villages", as it is described in this book, is a complex vision based on over 25 years practiced research. An ever growing team of highly committed people are working all over the world to carry it out. What they work on are still prototypes. As with all cutting edge research these models are experiments and need time and resources for their development. Sustainable funding is urgently needed. Whoever is willing to support, please contact the Institute for Global Peacework or donate to

IHC - International Humanities Center
POBox 923, Malibu, CA 90265
Pay to: IHC/IGF
For credit card payments please call IHC:
+1-320-579.2069 (Fax: +1-206-333.1797)

Institute for Global Peacework
Monte Cerro
P-7630 Colos, Portugal
Tel +351-283 635 484
Fax +351-283 635 374
E-mail: igf@tamera.org
www.tamera.org

Breinigsville, PA USA
16 December 2009

229333BV00001B/124/A

9 783927 266254